The Daily Telegraph

SMALL BUSINESS GUIDE TO

COMPUTER NETWORKING

The Daily Telegraph

SMALL BUSINESS GUIDE TO COMPUTER NETWORKING

WHAT YOU NEED TO KNOW ABOUT USING TECHNOLOGY TO IMPROVE YOUR BUSINESS

WENDY M. GROSSMAN

MACMILLAN

First published 2003 by Macmillan
an imprint of Pan Macmillan Ltd
Pan Macmillan, 20 New Wharf Road, London N1 9RR
Basingstoke and Oxford
Associated companies throughout the world
www.panmacmillan.com

ISBN 1 4050 2103 9

1 3 5 7 9 8 6 4 2

A CIP catalogue record for this book is available from the British Library.

Typeset by SX Composing DTP, Rayleigh, Essex
Printed and bound in Great Britain by
Mackays of Chatham plc, Chatham, Kent

To the BOFHs, with thanks

Author's note

Throughout the text technical terms that are explained in the glossary (pp. 237–51) are shown underlined.

Contents

Introduction: The Accidental IT Administrator

This book is for people who never wanted to run an Information Technology (IT) system, but unfortunately find themselves in that position.

When you set up your business, you wanted to exploit your special knowledge or skills: to be a dentist, lawyer, or builder. But increasingly, all small businesses find themselves grappling with the difficulties of running their own IT.

In many ways, this is a good thing. It is now possible for even the smallest business to have facilities that formerly only the largest corporations could have or afford. These include: permanent Internet connections; facilities for off-site staff to connect securely to the company network at high speeds; and the opportunity for staff to work effectively using company resources from anywhere in the world. What small businesses generally still can't afford, however, is sufficient, or often, any, staff dedicated solely to IT support and administration – the rule of thumb is one dedicated support person per fifty employees. Generally businesses with fewer than twenty-five people won't have such a person at all, so it's very common for small businesses to have no one who really understands IT. As more and more apparently non-IT businesses begin to live or die by their IT systems, it is becoming essential to change that situation, preferably at board level.

Most small businesses are on their second or third generation of IT by now. But although that sounds grand, it often simply means that their first-generation Amstrads have been gradually replaced by a motley collection of PCs running Windows 98, with Internet access via dial-up.

Usually, the first benefit most people hope to get out of networking their computers is being able to share files and expensive resources like printers. There are, however, many more advantages. Networking your computers enables you to organize and manage data much better, ensuring that it all gets backed up regularly and that only the most recent version of a file is worked on across the office. In addition, networking enhances your ability to secure your network: using any of the business-oriented flavours of Windows (or other operating systems such as GNU/Linux or the Apple Mac) allows you to control who accesses which data and resources and what they're allowed to do with them. Finally, networking your computers allows everyone in the office to make use of the same Internet connection. Broadband, low-cost, high-speed, permanent connections to the Internet and all its resources that can be accessed by every computer in even the smallest of businesses, is changing the face of small businesses in Britain. The implications for your business is one of the topics covered in this book.

The problem is that none of this is simple in the way operating a toaster or even a VCR is simple. Networking is genuinely complex: it involves many pieces of hardware and software all of which must be working properly and must be correctly configured with great attention to detail. Pieces may interact in unexpected ways that are nonetheless logical when you take the time to understand them. You will have to work out for yourself where to draw the line between situations and technology you understand and can manage yourself, and times when you need to call in expert help. Helping you to figure out where to draw that line is one of the purposes of this book.

It's arguable that the worst disservice the computer industry has done to itself is to advertise constantly how easy its products are to use. In general, they're not, and this is exponentially true for networking, where the problem is to assemble many different pieces into a working system. It would be more accurate for the industry to say, 'It's difficult – but the results are worth it.'

Even so, a surprising amount of networking basics has been automated so that often it is actually possible to plug something in and have it just work. The likelihood of that happening the way it's supposed to, however, is greatly enhanced if you have some basic understanding of networking concepts and how your computer infrastructure works, as well as what's possible and what's easy or difficult.

This book assumes that you have some basic familiarity with computers but not with networking concepts. However, it would be a rare computer user today who has not sent and received email or used the Web, and the book therefore assumes that you also have some basic familiarity with using the Internet, albeit probably only email and the Web. But the Internet can do much more than that for your business. Low-cost broadband means that virtual private networking, once the province of only the best-funded large companies, can allow remote staff to connect to the company network in a secure 'tunnel' across the Internet and use the company resources as if directly connected. A couple of people working out of their houses with a virtual office service to answer phones and provide a mailing address can give their clients an instant response; seven people with a robust network can run a worldwide mail- and Web-order operation that looks and acts like a much larger company. Yes, to make that happen you have to invest in IT. But increasingly, everyone has to invest in IT anyway. The purpose of this book is to help you invest that money as wisely as possible to give you the greatest return.

To support this book there is a page on my Web site: see http://www.pelicancrossing.net/dtnw.htm. The page includes URLs for further information on the major topics included in this book, and will be updated sporadically so that dead URLs are replaced with active ones. The page includes a link to a forum for comments and discussion, and readers are encouraged to direct their questions and comments there.

Wendy M. Grossman
London, December 2002

1 Building a Network

If yours is like most small businesses, you probably have a mix of old machines and older machines, some of which may be networked. As a way of introducing the subject, however, at this point we're going to go through the steps of connecting up a few machines. Partly, this is a practical exercise to help get you started if you're in a hurry to get something set up and working. Partly, it's to give you a feel for what's involved if you haven't tried this sort of thing before. If you're experienced at networking, you'll probably want to skip to Chapter 2. If, on the other hand, you find this chapter too difficult, you may want to skip to Chapter 10 for advice on how to hire a consultant. If that's the case, however, on the way it's strongly recommended that you stop at Chapter 2 and read the sections on choosing suppliers and operating systems (see pp. 23–6). Making the right decisions up front on those points can save you immense amounts of trouble (and avoid lost productivity).

For the purposes of this exercise, I assume you are in the common position of having a couple of PCs running Windows 95 or later. There are, of course, many possible variations on this scenario and it's impossible to cover all of them. You may need to adapt what follows to suit your particular hardware and software.

THE FIRST TWO COMPUTERS

To hook your two machines together, you will need an ethernet network interface card for each machine, a hub, and two lengths of ethernet cable (also known as unshielded twisted pair, usually Cat5). If networking is built into your computer's motherboard, or if it already has a network interface card installed, you can skip the first step, which is installing the network interface card into your machine.

The network interface card (often known as a NIC) must be inserted into a slot in your computer, and it therefore must be the same type as the slot available in the computer. For desktop machines, you will need to open up the case and install the card internally into a slot on the motherboard. Most newer desktop computers use a standard for these slots known as PCI or VESA. You will have to consult your computer's documentation to check what type of slots you have. Laptop computers typically either have networking built in or have a credit card-sized slot in the side known variously as PCMCIA, PC Card, or Cardbus. It may sound complicated but these laptop slots are actually standardized, and you should have no trouble finding a card that will work.

Note what manufacturer and model card you have. Unless the manufacturer's instructions say otherwise, for desktops open up the machine and fit the card into the slot and ensure that it's firmly inserted and screwed in place. If you do not have a free PCI slot, you will have to figure out what cards are in the machine and whether you can dispense with any of them. Turn on the machine. Once Windows has started up, it should recognize that you have new hardware and start the wizard that guides you through installation. For laptops, you do not have to turn the machine off; just insert the PC Card all the way into the slot and the system should recognize the card and proceed.

If Windows can't recognize the card and choose a driver for you, you will be asked what type of network card it is (fortunately, you wrote that down before you closed up the machine). If the manufacturer supplied a disk, insert the disk and direct Windows to it. If the manufacturer didn't supply a disk, look for the manufacturer and model number in Windows' built-in drivers. If that doesn't work and you don't have a disk, skip to Chapter 10 on finding help – you should be able to download a driver from the Internet that will work once you know how to find it. Windows will also ask you for a workgroup name and a machine name. These should be different from each other, and should each be one word (no spaces). You can call the workgroup and computer anything you like, but it's usually better not to pick names of the people who use the machines – it can get confusing, especially if for some reason users swap machines later.

Let Windows complete the installation. If you look in the Control Panel under Networking and Dial-up Connections (Windows XP/2000) you should see that an entry has been added for a Local Area Connection; in Windows 95/98/2000/XP an icon labelled Network Neighborhood (or sometimes My Network Places) will have appeared on your desktop. If you right-click on that icon and choose Properties, you should see that the network card appears in the list as an adaptor with the additional components listed as used by the connection. In 2000/XP these will be: Client for Microsoft Networks, File and Printer Sharing for Microsoft Networks, Internet Protocol (TCP/IP). In Windows 95/98 you will see NetBEUI for Windows networking, and you will have to follow the on-screen directions for adding a protocol and install TCP/IP separately.

If you double-click on the Network Neighborhood icon, you should see an icon for your computer.

Repeat the installation on the other machine. When it is time to enter the workgroup and machine names, the workgroup name should be the same as the one you used for the first machine, but the machine name should be different.

Next, plug one end of each ethernet cable into the hub, and the other end into one of the network cards.

At this point, you have connected the hardware but although Windows (and the Mac operating system and GNU/Linux) has networking built into it, you still need to do some software configuration.

In NT/2000, you can check whether the computers are now able to see each other; double-click on Network Neighborhood on either computer's desktop and check: there should now be an icon for each computer, labelled with its name. (You can reach this same display by opening a copy of Windows Explorer and looking in the directory tree under Network | Computers Near Me or, in XP, by looking in the directory tree Network/Entire Network/Microsoft Windows

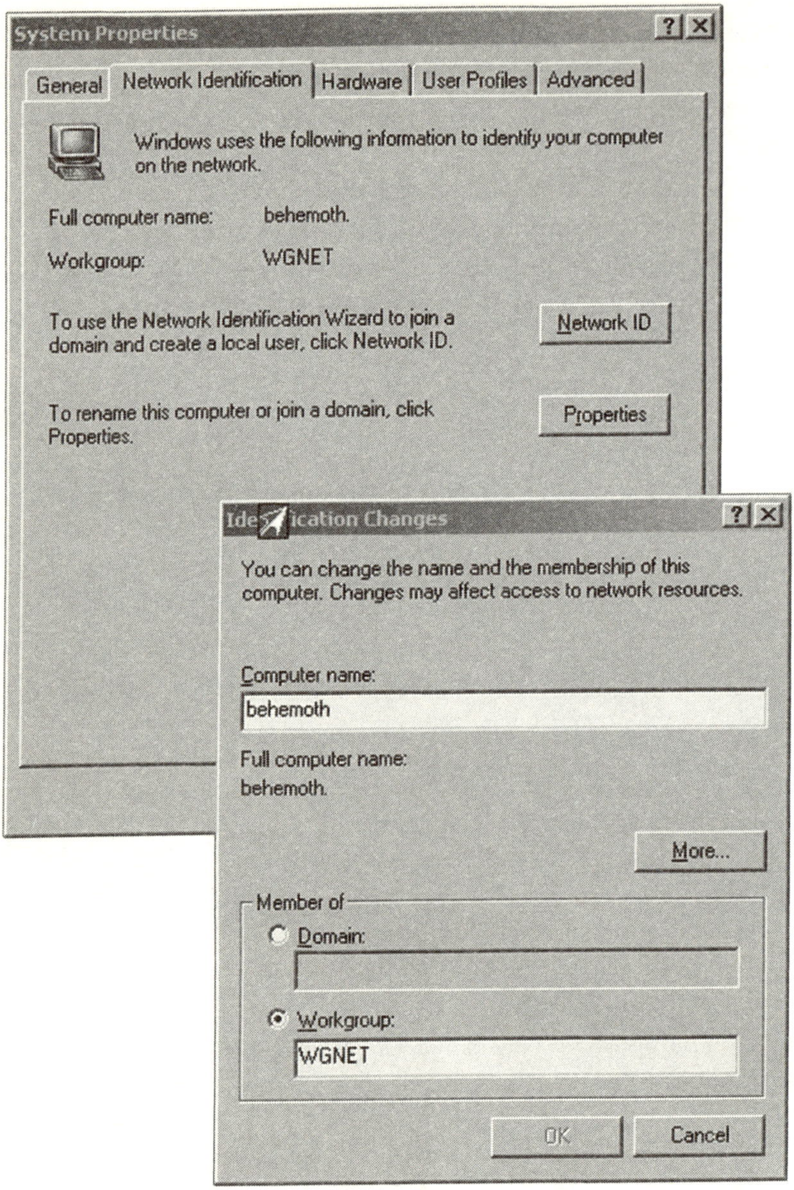

Figure 1

Network and machine IDs in Windows 2000. Note that you can specify that the computer is a member of either a domain or a workgroup (see pp. 73–6 for the difference). Machine names should be unique within your network; the workgroup or domain name should be the same for all the machines in a network segment.

Network/<yourworkgroups>.) If the other computer's icon does not appear, check that the user ID and password you're using to log in are valid on both machines. If the other machine's icon still doesn't appear, check your hardware connections and make sure the two machines are using the same networking protocols. Also check that each machine has been assigned an IP address – this should be automatic. To check, the easiest way to see the full configuration in Windows 98/2000/XP is to open up a command prompt (from the Start menu) and type in 'IPCONFIG/ALL' (in Windows 95 the command is 'WINIPCFG'). You will get back a full list of the computer's settings including its MAC address, DNS addresses, subnet mask, and so on (see Chapter 4 for an explanation); if you type just 'IPCONFIG' you get just the basics, much like Figure 2 below, except that at this stage the top and bottom of the four lines will be blank. The IP address will be one assigned automatically from inside your machine using a utility Microsoft calls APIPA. If the middle lines are blank, you will need to assign your machines IP addresses. Use 192.168.0.2 for one and 192.168.0.3 for the other using the configuration options for TCP/IP.

If, however, you double-click on the icon representing the remote

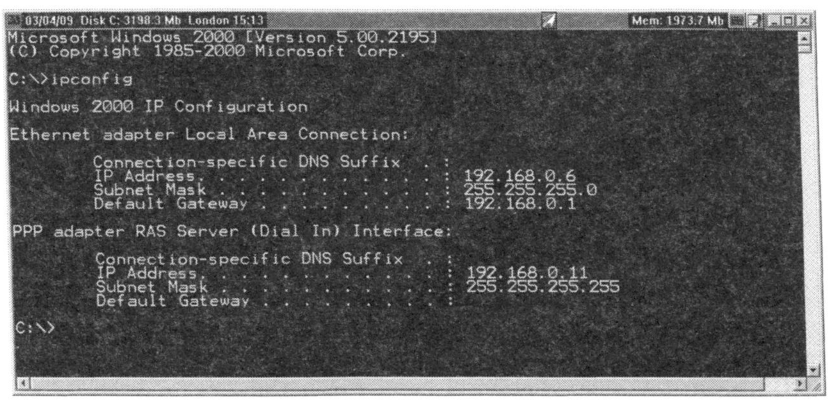

Figure 2

IP configuration settings (seen from a command prompt by typing in IPCONFIG) for a machine on a network with a router running DHCP. The first set is for an ethernet network interface card; the second is for accepting inbound connections (VPN).

machine (from either machine) in NT/2000/XP you probably won't see any directories or files, and in Windows 95/98 you won't see any icon at all. This is because although the computers can actually talk to each other, you still need to give them the right to access each other's resources. When you log in using Windows 95/98, you log in only to the local computer, which does not attempt to validate that user account against anything on a remote computer or server until you try to access a shared resource, and only computers that have shared resources available to you will be visible.

So the next step is to open some resources for sharing. Open a copy of Windows Explorer and pick a directory (or folder) on the machine you're sitting at that you would like the other to be able to access. Right-click on the folder name and choose Properties. Click on the Sharing tab, and then the button labelled 'Share This Folder'. There is a space into which you can type a name for the folder. Typing a name in this window will not change the folder's name on this machine; it just assigns a name by which the folder will be known across the network. Being able to use a different network name is useful if you tend to use the same directory structure on all your machines, as otherwise it can get confusing. At this point, don't worry about the type of share if you're offered options, just accept the defaults. See Chapter 4 for more on granting users access to specific resources.

Now go to the other machine and open a copy of Windows Explorer. At the bottom of the left-hand window you should find Network; look under it for Computers Near Me and under that heading for the first machine's name. Double-click on that. You should see listed the folder for which you just turned on sharing. You should be able to open that folder, view the files in it, and copy one to the machine you're sitting at by dragging it into a local folder. ('Local' in this context means anything attached to or residing on the machine you're directly operating; 'remote' is used to describe anything stored on or attached to any other computer.)

Physically, modern Apple Macs work the same way: they also use ethernet and the same Cat5 cable type, and attaching them to Windows machines is not a problem. Macs using the OS X operating system onwards make it easy to share with and access both other OS

X machines and Windows machines. Windows machines, however, require special software to be able to access Mac file shares. Windows NT and 2000 (Workstation) can share their file systems and printers with Mac clients. Windows 2000 Server can connect to shared printers.

ADDING A PRINTER

Chances are you have a printer hooked to at least one of the two machines. It is possible to set up most modern printers (you may run across some exceptions) so they can be shared by both machines. To use the printer on the second machine (that is, the one it's not directly connected to), sit at the second machine and open Printers from the Control Panel. Double-click on Add a Printer, and tell Windows you're adding a networked printer and follow the wizard's instructions to let Windows browse for networked printers. For this to work, both the remote machine and the printer need to be turned on and you need to have turned on sharing for the printer the way you turned on sharing for the other resources. Windows should find the printer. You may or may not have to install the printer's own software on the second machine – it depends which version of Windows you're running and whether the printer's driver is built into Windows or not. You may be prompted for either the Windows CD or the CD that came with the printer or both.

You can set the networked printer as the default for both machines if you like. But using this method, the machine the printer is directly connected to must be up and running whenever you want to print from the remote machine. More expensive printers now, however, have networking built into them so they are directly connected to the network as devices on their own; these can be used regardless of which machines are turned on or off. But for this exercise we're assuming you have an ordinary printer set up and working with a parallel or USB connection. Wireless routers (see below) sometimes have a parallel port built in and come with print server software so that small/home offices can have full networked functionality with greater convenience and less expense.

SHARING AN INTERNET CONNECTION

Once you have networked the computers, they can share an Internet connection. Windows 98/ME/2000/XP comes with built-in facilities to share Internet connections, called Internet Connection Sharing. It's primarily intended to allow multiple machines to access the Internet through any existing connection (either dial-up or a permanent connection such as ADSL or cable) made on one of them. You enable this function in the computer that's making the Internet connection by right-clicking on the connection in the list and choosing Properties, switching to the Sharing tab, and checking the box to turn it on. You do not need any special software for any of the machines. On the machine seeking to use that connection, assuming that your network connection is already in place and working correctly, you manage the configuration through Properties for your network connection. Select Properties for Internet Protocols (TCP/IP) and ensure that the computer is set to obtain an IP address automatically (more about this in Chapter 3) and, under Advanced, that the entries under WINS, DNS, and IP settings are blank.

One caveat: if the computer has an IP address specified and is *not* set to obtain an IP address automatically, or the WINS, DNS, and IP settings are *not* blank and your network is operating correctly, do not change anything until (1) you've written all the settings down so you can restore them if necessary and (2) you've checked to see whether they're actually needed to make your networked PCs inter-operate by asking the person who set it up. Once you've clicked the various OK buttons, Internet Connection Sharing should be in effect, and if the Internet connection is live both computers should be able to use it. You can test whether it's working by trying to load a Web page.

Internet Connection Sharing is not ideal. For one thing, you are relying on a single machine to stay turned on at all times so users can connect through it. For another, if users are online simultaneously sharing a dial-up connection, even with the fastest modem you'll find browsing the Web painfully slow. In addition, the terms and conditions of your Internet account may not allow you to connect multiple users simultaneously, and you should check this point. In general, for running a business with multiple users, you want broadband and a router.

ADDING A SCANNER

Nope. You cannot network an ordinary scanner. If you want a networked scanner, you will have to buy one that is specifically designed to be networked and follow the instructions to install its software. However, you can set up a scanner attached to a single machine to act as a photocopier anyone can use (as long as that machine is running). This only works with scanners that have a button you can push to start them scanning, and you will need software designed to scan the document in the scanner and send the output straight to the printer (there are inexpensive shareware programs available on the Net that do just this if your scanner software doesn't already include it). Once you've installed such a piece of software, go to Control Panel | Scanners and Cameras | Properties for your device and click on the Events tab, and you will find you can associate a program with the scanner's Start button. Pick the photocopy utility and click the various OK buttons to apply the association. Thereafter as long as the scanner, the printer, and the machines they're hooked to are turned on, you effectively have a photocopier.

ADDING A ROUTER AND BROADBAND

As Chapter 3 explains, you can add to your network by bolting on pieces as you need them. Two machines may be directly connected; eight machines will probably have a hub or router as a central connection point. These days, given the need to share Internet connections and data, if you have only one central connection point it will probably be a router, a connecting box that's 'smart' enough to know which bit of data is destined for which machine. That has the advantage of cutting down on unnecessary network traffic (see

Chapter 4 for an explanation of why) so that the network performs better for everyone.

Adding a hub (as explained above) is a simple matter of plugging the cables into the box's ports. A router is a bit more complicated. For this exercise we'll assume that the router is going in to hook a small network to a cable or ADSL modem, and is going to do NAT, that is, 'network address translation' so that the single IP number assigned to you by your ISP (Internet Service Provider) can be used by the multiple machines on your network. The router will have a function called DHCP built into it to enable it to automatically assign addresses to your machines. But it is also set to *receive* an IP address from the ISP's DHCP server. So, if you look at its configuration – usually these days accessible as a set of Web-style pages organized into understandable chunks of information – you will see that the router actually has two IP addresses. One of these faces outwards to the Internet that is assigned by the ISP (such as 158.152.8.200, for example), and the other faces the internal network and is used by your machines to access the router and through it the rest of the Net (usually 192.168.0.1, a standard private class C address as explained in Chapter 3). That inward-facing address for the router is the gateway address for the LAN (Local Area Network) it connects together, a setting you will come across whenever you look at a computer's TCP/IP configuration.

TIP Label cables where they plug into hubs or multi-way AC outlets so you can tell which is which and don't have to do major 'hunting under the desk' tracing exercises.

To set up the router, follow the instructions to access its configuration. Enable DHCP, by ticking a box in the configuration screen, so the router can pick up an IP address automatically from the ISP. Turn on its DHCP server so it can assign IP addresses to your computers. Set its inward-facing address to 192.168.0.1 (unless the instructions specify something different). Then go to your existing machines and (first writing down any existing configuration in case you have to go back to it) ensure that the TCP/IP configuration is set to get an IP address automatically, deleting any address that's been manually assigned. The gateway address, should you need to fill it in, is the one you've just given the router: 192.168.0.1. Apply the changes by clicking on the various OK buttons and then check the IP configuration again. The machine should have picked up an IP number from the router and be able to see the other machines on the network just as it did before. If the router is correctly connected to the Internet via a cable or ADSL modem, the newly configured machine should also be able to access the Internet.

ADDING A WIRELESS ROUTER (802.11b)

One of the faster growing areas in networking is wireless connections, primarily using Wi-Fi, also known as 802.11b after the number of the standard that underlies it. Wi-Fi was first introduced commercially by Apple in 1999, but in only a few years it has become widespread, and now there are many manufacturers making compatible network cards, hubs (known as access points when they're wireless), and routers for all types of machines. There are other versions of 802.11 in the works – a and g – that are faster, but these are not nearly as common and are currently much more expensive. See Chapter 3 for more details on these.

This – 802.11b – is one standard that really works, and ISPs are partnering with hotel and restaurant chains to exploit it by setting up 'hotspots' for their customers to use to connect to the Internet. Linking up your computers with a wireless LAN (WLAN) is somewhat more expensive than setting up an ordinary ethernet LAN and the speeds are always going to be slower, but in a small or home office the advantage of not having to run cables may outweigh those disadvantages. In addition, if you frequently have outsiders coming in who need to use your network or Internet connection, it's much easier to have them sit wherever they can and use a wireless card than to fuss around ensuring a cable and socket are available in the right location.

Just like wired networking, you will need a wireless card for each computer you want to connect – and an access point or wireless router (see Chapter 2 for a brief buyer's guide).

Assuming you already have a functioning network, adding an access point is actually very easy. You will need to site the access point in a more or less central location in the area you want to cover. The location will need an AC mains outlet and to be within ethernet cable distance of your hub or router. You plug in the access point to the mains power and hub, and turn it on. Install the wireless network card into the computer the same way you installed the networking card (see 'The first two computers' above). The only difference should be that there will be a utility with the wireless card that scans the 802.11b channels for an access point. Once the card has found the access point, everything should just work. Most access points come with a USB port you can use to directly connect a computer if you need to do more complex configuration, such as turning on security (see Chapter 6).

If you don't already have a functioning network, you will probably be buying a wireless router, and setting this up is actually almost as easy. The difficult part comes with configuring each computer to use that router, which works more or less as outlined above, in that you install a network card in each computer, run a cable to the router if needed, and let the router automatically assign IP addresses. Most of these routers are intended for the small business/home user market, and they often come with very good instructions on how to install and configure them. However, bear in mind that they are primarily intended for very small networks. You may find that you need to move the access point around to maximize coverage – 802.11b has a theoretical maximum range of about 300 feet. You might manage that in a field with no obstructions. In practice, in an office or home setting, depending on the number of walls and other barriers in the way, you will probably find the range is fifty feet or less.

Although you can certainly run your network as an entirely wireless one, chances are you won't want to. For one thing, the most popular current version of ethernet runs at 100mbps (megabits per second), which is nearly ten times the speed of 802.11b's theoretical 11mbps, and it is also much cheaper.

REMOTE ACCESS CONNECTIONS

Just like your connection to the Internet, a remote user wishing to access your network may do so via any type of dial-up, whether that be mobile phone, landline/modem, or ISDN. Increasingly, virtual private networks (VPNs) are becoming popular; these involve creating a secure 'tunnel' across the Internet (which is itself an insecure, public network) between the remote user's computer and your network. The ability to accept incoming connections is again something that until relatively recently was only available (or affordable) to large corporates, but now can be set up by even very small companies.

Exactly how you configure a computer to receive an incoming connection varies according to your operating system. In Windows 2000/XP, when you run the wizard to create a new networking connection (look under Control Panel | Networking and Dial-up) you will find that among the list of available connections to configure are an incoming dial-up connection and an incoming VPN. Essentially, the computer the user is going to call must have an incoming connection set up on it, and the computer calling in must have either a dial-up or VPN connection set up with the correct details. In addition, the user must have a valid account and password for the destination machine.

However, although VPN facilities are built into Windows 2000/XP this only works between Microsoft boxes. It's far more common for a business to buy a VPN solution as a service running on firewall hardware, in which case the business is most likely to block the Microsoft VPN application so that incoming users go through the firewall.

For dial-up, the remote computer of course must also have an analog modem (built into many laptops) or, if the line being used is ISDN, an ISDN terminal adaptor. Mobile phone users will need a GSM or GPRS modem. All these pieces of equipment are readily available, but they are all different, so check carefully that you're buying the right thing. Analog modems are the most common, as

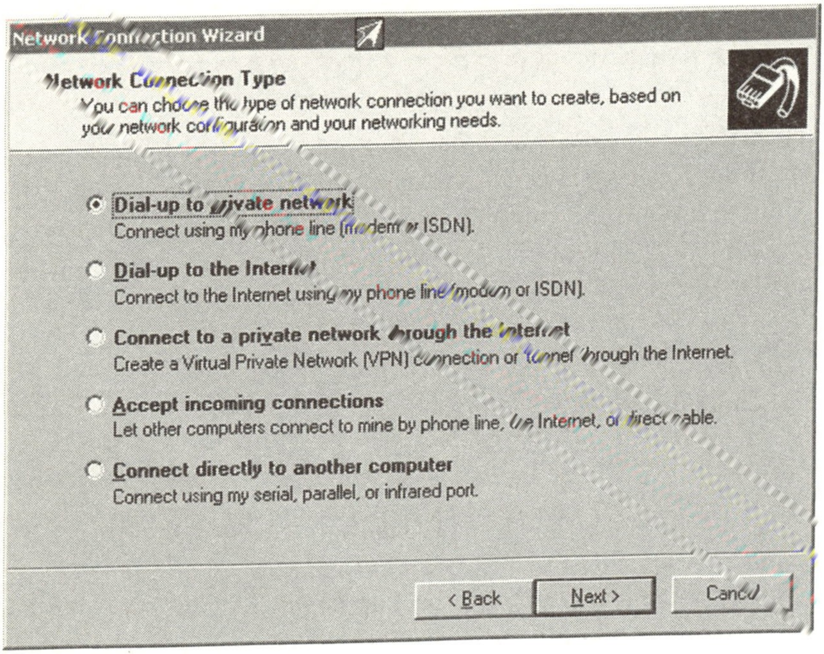

Figure 3

Defining a new network connection in Windows 2000. Note the option to accept a remote incoming connection, which can be used to set up a basic VPN.

these work across any ordinary land telephone line; do not buy anything that runs at less than 56kbps, as slower speeds cost you time and, if you're paying phone bills by the minute, money. ISDN starts at 64kbps, and to use it you will need an ISDN modem at each end of the connection. GSM connections run at a maximum of 9.6kbps (the speed of an ordinary modem in 1992); GPRS at 57kbps (the speed of a current landline modem). To use either, you will need a wireless modem designed for whichever service you have. You can get these as part of combination PC cards for laptops from companies such as TDK and Psion. Alternatively, some companies (such as Ubinetics) make PC cards with slots in them for the memory chip (SIM card) from your mobile phone. To use those, you put the SIM card in the PC card and the PC Card in the laptop and dial. You can even, if you can stand the slow speed and dropouts, use a voice connection over the data connection via one of the VoIP services, relieving you of the need to carry the actual phone.

Over a VPN, remote users should be able to access the network and all its resources exactly as if they were sitting at their desks using their machines over a direct connection (albeit a good bit slower). If you want to use a VPN, you will probably need a non-NAT service with fixed IP at the host end. Telewest is making an effort to work out a way to offer small businesses VPN facilities over dynamic IP, and this is a field that's likely to see rapid progress, as after the ability to host their own email servers, VPN facilities are the second most desired functionality broadband business users typically want.

BACKUPS (MEDIA, SERVERS)

Having a file server or a live backup device that could update itself in 'real time' was until recently out of the financial or technical grasp of small businesses. File servers tended to be general-purpose computers that had to be set up and configured by someone who understood network operating systems. The upshot is that when it comes to backups most people still think in terms of tape using software that's run at night: for a long time tape was by far the cheapest option. Tape is still probably the most commonly used backup medium, as it's still the most convenient and easily automated method for backing up large amounts of data for off-site storage. Even so, it has many problems. The medium is not entirely stable: tape can stretch, decay, or suffer from tracking errors that render a given tape unreadable on any but the drive that recorded it. In a crisis, you may not even be able to find the right *model* of drive. Check that your tapes restore correctly as part of a regular security and disaster recovery review (see Chapters 7 and 8).

For smaller amounts of data, you may be better off with writable CD-ROM (650Mb), which should be readable on just about any PC, since all modern machines are equipped with such drives (CD-R, not CD-RW). As DVD standards settle down, the same should become true with the much higher capacity writable DVD (4.7Gb). The long-term survival of digital archives is, however, a problem with any medium, not just tape. If you have archived CD-Rs, for example, ideally you should make fresh copies every couple of years to give you the chance to move the data to whatever medium is current.

Backup servers have now become affordable enough for even small businesses to consider having them for storing copies of shared databases and documents. They are valuable if what's important is keeping downtime to a minimum. In general, the more of a delay you can tolerate while the backup server is brought live the more choice of products you have and the less expensive the solution is likely to be. Cluster servers distribute tasks over multiple machines so that the system keeps running even if there's a single failure in one server, but these are the most expensive.

More simply, reasonably affordable file server devices whose installation and use is streamlined now exist. These include Quantum's SnapServer, a weird-looking affair the size of a shoebox you configure from a Web browser. Setting up a SnapServer, with capacities of 20Gb and up (unfortunately, the units are not upgradeable), is not difficult. First you plug it into an ethernet hub with a standard cable. If you have DHCP turned on, the SnapServer will pick up an IP address by itself, or you can enter one using software loaded from the accompanying CD. The software will prompt you for a machine name for the SnapServer, an administrator name and password, and the current date and time. From there on, the SnapServer should appear as another networked computer in your workgroup. You can, if you like, store all your data on it so all the other machines can use it as a filestore. Or, alternatively, you can use software such as the shareware program SecondCopy to copy all the network data onto it regularly throughout the day. With all the data collected in one place, it's easy to use backup software to make a copy that can be taken off-site for safekeeping.

A less flexible option, but one that may be worth considering for data storage, is to have external hard drives; as of late 2002 you can get external drives using the high-speed FireWire interface for as little as a couple of hundred pounds for 120Gb. To be used as a central data store the machine it is attached to needs to be kept on all the time and to be equipped with a FireWire port. But FireWire cards and adaptors can be had for as little as £50, and the drives are easy to install, simply appearing as another hard drive on the attached machine. To use them across the network, you will have to turn on sharing as you did for files and folders above. They are also much faster than tape drives, although not nearly as portable as an individual tape.

The new generation of MP3 players being made with capacities of 20Gb and above can also be used for data storage, as can smaller devices made to do nothing else, such as the keychain-sized Pendrive and its many clones, Compact Flash cards and postage stamp-sized Smart Media/Secure Digital cards, although these last don't handle more than a gigabyte of data. Any of these last options, however, are extremely portable ways to take data offsite.

More complex drive systems known as RAID (Redundant Array of Inexpensive Disks) are designed to ensure that in case of a disk failure there is a mirror (exact) copy to take its place. Configuring these is generally a job for an expert.

Finally, there are online services that will store up to a specified amount of data, giving you the ultimate in a readily accessible off-site backup.

Whatever you do, make sure that you plan your backup strategy carefully. Being able to store data safely is one of the major benefits of having a network in the first place, and the more backups you have and the more disparate places they're stored in, the better your chances of resuming business with minimal interruption if there is a catastrophe (see Chapter 8). Backups should be the first thing you think about every time you add anything to your network, and they are always important. Without backups, you are a flake of metal oxide away from losing your data and, with it, potentially your entire business.

TIP Colour-code special types of network cables – for example, yellow for a crossover cable and grey for ordinary ones – so you can tell at a glance that you've got the right type. If you have phone cables in the same patch panel, use different colours for those, too (ISDN use the same Cat5 cable as ethernet, but it carries 50 volts, and if you plug one into a network card it will cease to function).

THE THIRD COMPUTER

It's arguable that adding the third computer is where a lot of the complexity starts. Technically, of course, adding the third computer is the same process as hooking together the first two: first you make the physical connection, then you configure the computer's network identity and ensure that it connects to the two others, and finally you turn on sharing for whatever resources you like. The one bit of difficulty is in making the physical connection. If you're following the basic steps outlined above, you will have to either add a hub or add a second NIC to one of the machines in order to allow three computers to interconnect via ethernet. A few years ago, people commonly opted for a different type of cabling and topology (see pp. 47–9) because you could connect more than two machines without buying a hub, switch, or router (see also pp. 9–11), even though this style of network connection is less reliable. These days, the necessary connecting equipment has become so cheap that it makes no economic sense to cut these corners. You will have to buy a router in any case if you're going to network a broadband connection across the office.

At a more abstract level, complexity increases exponentially with each new machine you add. When you have two computers, they can function successfully as a peer-to-peer network. If they have sufficient capacity, the two can act as backups for each other, so that if one goes down the other can fulfil all the first one's functions temporarily if necessary, and all the data can be mirrored on both machines. In addition, if you're looking for a particular piece of data, there are only two places to look.

This happy situation starts to change with the third computer. This is the point where the need to keep control of your data begins to dictate that you install a server to centralize administrative functions and data storage and, in some cases, centralized applications that use a client/server architecture.

You are probably more familiar with these architectures than you think. Client/server architecture essentially means that an application is made up of two complementary halves. Probably the most everyday example of a client/server application is the World Wide Web. The browser on your machine is the client; the software on the distant computer sending you Web pages for your browser to render and display is the server. Client/server architecture pervades the Internet. Your ISP stores your email on its server, from which your client email software retrieves it. If you watch a video clip across the Net, the player on your machine is the client, and the remote computer sending you the video is the server. And so on. In the example of Internet Connection Sharing above, the machine with the Internet connection is effectively the server and the machine accessing that machine to use its connection is the client. Within a small business, however, true client/server applications are relatively rare; examples include accounting programs or database applications where queries are partially processed before being sent to the server for completed processing. Even so, as soon as you have more than two or three machines, it rapidly becomes preferable to abandon pure peer-to-peer networking where all machines are equally likely to have their own data and applications in favour of installing a server from which all machines retrieve the data they work on.

Within your own office, with a network that's still small, a server needn't mean anything so elaborate. But designing your network so that data all resides in one place – a server – means it's much easier to ensure that routine backups include all the data that needs to be backed up. Storing data centrally also helps with version control, ensuring that whoever is working on, say, a report in progress isn't wasting his time with an old version that's already been superseded, ultimately making more work for someone to consolidate the various versions.

As your network grows you will find that more and more functions become too complicated to manage on a peer-to-peer basis. Fortunately, many network tools and standards have been developed to take care of common problems such as assigning addresses, managing users and access rights, supporting remote users, sharing scheduling, and centrally managing and archiving email. For those reasons, programs designed to enable collaborative work across a network such as Lotus Notes and Microsoft's Small Business Server are all client/server applications.

EXPANDING YOUR NETWORK

As the continued growth of the Internet – the network that interconnects other networks – shows, there is no upper limit on the size of a network.

As you add machines and other devices – networked versions of electronic gadgets such as stereo system components, personal video recorders, and other audio/visual systems are beginning to appear on the market – you will inevitably have to add infrastructure to cope with them. Throughout you should keep in mind the need for balance between current costs and allowing room for future growth.

Many components can be bolted on as your needs increase. You can, for example, add another hub (or switch or router) when your existing one runs out of ethernet ports. You can increase the bandwidth of your broadband connection as you add more users who make demands on it. You can add more machines, and more server capacity.

Even so, at times you will hit upper limits where further expansion involves a new level of expense or expertise. As you add users you will reach a point where tasks such as sharing out files, storing email, and managing administration will require a dedicated server that does not double as a user's machine.

For example, Microsoft's Small Business Server is designed to work on only one site for a maximum of fifty users; if you add a second site and want it networked to your first one and you want both sites to have the same functions, you will have to migrate to Back Office. As you add to your network – especially if you have professional help in the form of consultants – it's worth ensuring you know where those limits are.

In the next chapter we will look at some of the kinds of decisions you will have to make as you set up your network and in Chapter 3 we discuss basic networking concepts.

TIP You do not have to solve your whole IT problem at once. Take small steps – but don't lose sight of the big picture.

2 Decisions, Decisions

One of the problems with networking is that systems can grow haphazardly because every decision is made at a moment of crisis and no one ever stops to examine the big picture. One of the results is frequently a fragile network that is difficult to update or upgrade without breaking something. For this reason, it's important to keep a strategic eye on how your network develops, and to remember that your network is an implementation of your business strategy, not the other way around. The more crucial IT becomes to your business the more necessary it is to have someone at board level who understands its importance. Similarly, if you hire a consultant, request that he sign a non-disclosure agreement if you have to, but do not conceal from him important strategy decisions such as mergers, acquisitions, splits within the company, and other major upheavals. If you do, the consultant's recommendations may be seriously off-target for the business strategy you've adopted, and you may find too late that the consultant would have suggested moving in a different direction if he had known the real situation.

This chapter can't take the place of someone who knows your business situation and makes specific recommendations accordingly. However, there are some issues that are common to most small businesses. Chief among these is the choice of operating system, which we look at first. As noted in Chapter 1, many of the issues that used to be important decisions – which protocol, which physical networking type – have now been effectively resolved as everyone has more or less standardized on one or two common choices.

This chapter also looks at issues of wired versus wireless, which types of wireless connections are appropriate for which types of uses, choices of backup media, and the importance of planning ahead as you update elements of your network. The important matter of what type of Internet access to choose – dial-up or broadband, and which type – is left for Chapter 4.

If you read nothing else in this chapter, do look at the section on operating systems, as small business consultants say that one of the best productivity improvements they are currently able to make is switching their customers from consumer versions of Windows to business-oriented operating systems. In other words: your machines do not have to crash every day.

Besides these desktop versions, there are two server versions of Windows, Windows 2000 Server, and its successor, Windows Server 2003. Windows 2000 Professional (or Workstation) will only accept ten incoming connections.

DECISIONS YOU MAKE

You will inevitably have already made some decisions that affect how you're going to set up your network. For example, you probably already have older machines you want to incorporate into your network, along with the operating system software running on those machines. You also probably have existing email services, office software, and perhaps even specialized software for your particular line of work. However, as part of networking your system you may want to rethink some of these decisions, and some you may want to rethink even if you decide not to go ahead with your networking project. For example, many small businesses cut corners when they buy machines by choosing cheaper machines that are really intended for home users. The operating systems that come with these machines are often not designed for the level of reliability that businesses need.

One of the best favours you can do yourself and your business is to think how much time gets wasted in recovering from computer crashes, waiting for things to process or print, or in other avoidable bottlenecks. If that time is significant, then the first thing on your to-do list should be to eliminate those problems. That doesn't always mean buying expensive equipment; it may mean investing in training for key staff (in anything from specific software use to touch typing), or revamping and streamlining how you organize your data or schedule your backups.

In addition, bear in mind that if the box you buy takes an extra hour to set up and configure over the one the supplier recommended, a saving of £100 can be eaten up very quickly.

CHOOSING A SUPPLIER

One of those key decisions is choosing a supplier. People are used to thinking of computers as commodity items and yet are still so confused by them; small vendors report they commonly get lengthy, hour-long calls in which they're asked everything from computer prices to software advice – only to have the caller then go and buy the equipment on the Web because it seems to be cheaper. Quite apart from the fact that this behaviour penalizes another small business just like yours for being helpful, quite often cheaper products from a box-shifting mass-market supplier do not actually come with the same service and backup as you'd get from that small vendor. Yes, it's true that there are small system suppliers who overcharge and give expensive advice; equally, it's possible to make huge mistakes with mass-market suppliers who offer no assistance. A good supplier is worth paying for.

TIP Never change more than one thing at a time. Do the change, make sure everything's working, then make the next change.

The reason – as anyone with a modicum of computer experience has noticed – is that despite the cheerleading coverage in many magazines, computers do not always work as advertised. You'd think people would know this after two decades of frustration, but nonetheless hope springs eternal with every new purchase. So the first question to ask yourself when choosing a supplier is: when this equipment does not work as expected, is this supplier going to help me, and under what circumstances? A big direct hardware seller is obviously going to help if a machine is dead on arrival or if the monitor supplied with a computer fails to display properly. That company is almost certainly not going to be of assistance, however, in setting up a network or troubleshooting a software installation.

Whatever you buy, particularly if you're planning a network, it's safest to assume nothing is going to go 100 per cent according to plan. Maybe the salesman says the machines you're buying will network out of the box but forgets to mention you'll need a network card for each machine (and cabling, hubs, and so on).

It's also safest to assume that the solution is not going to be getting a friend's teenager who 'knows about computers' to come in and make it work. That person may know about computers; but he or she is unlikely to know about configuring and running a business system with the necessary detail and robustness, particularly when it comes to setting up servers, accounting software, and backup systems.

Therefore when you compare packages from different suppliers make sure you're comparing like with like. Is the warranty the same length and type (return-to-base versus on-site)? Is one a business machine running Windows XP Professional and the other a consumer machine running XP Home? Does one include a network card and the other not? Go through the entire specification, comparing video card, memory, hard drive capacity, processor speed. There are bound to be some differences; it helps if you're ready with a list of what features you're looking for in order of priority. Packages from a small supplier who takes the time to listen and make recommendations based on your business needs may prove cheaper in the long run. Maintenance, technical support, and staff time trying to make things work are all costs to your business that you must take into account along with the raw purchase price. While you may not realize it, when you choose your supplier you are also making a decision about who is going to provide your technical support when things go wrong (see Chapter 9). The quality and availability of that help is more important than getting the absolutely cheapest possible deal.

However, that does not mean you need to buy all your hardware and services from the same supplier; shopping around can save you money, as always. Just make sure that you understand the specification that's been recommended to you, and before you cut corners, check whether cutting those corners will actually cost you more in the end.

OPERATING SYSTEMS: WHICH?

What follows applies to the computers on people's desks, not to servers or machines for specialized applications, where of necessity you have fewer choices and where your choice of operating system is governed by the software that's going to run on it.

Most people who buy computers take whatever operating system that comes with them. In 90 per cent of cases, that means Windows. There are exceptions: people who buy bare boxes and install all the software personally from the ground up, and people who like a particular operating system – usually Apple or Linux – who buy that, merely specifying the box it runs on. But in the mainstream Windows world, most people do not understand the difference between one version of Windows and another, and they buy on price. This has led to a mythology that, like many mythologies, was once true but is no longer: namely, that Windows inevitably crashes. It depends which Windows.

Microsoft divides its versions of Windows into two strands: home and business. The home strand includes Windows 95, 98, ME, and XP Home. The business strand is Windows NT, 2000, and XP Professional. And they are not the same. The home versions of Windows in general offer better support for games, but most (95/98/ME) are far less stable. Many games won't run on the business versions, but starting with NT4 these versions of Windows tend to be extremely stable, to the point where if an individual program does crash it rarely takes the whole machine down with it. Even an IT journalist's main Windows 2000 machine acting as a server for a small network and doubling as a review machine with software being installed and removed all the time may have continuous uptimes measured in months.

If you are running a business on your computer, whether you are doing it at home or in an office setting, you should be running a business version of Windows. This is doubly true if that computer is the central computer on a network and a crash could disrupt the entire business. Saving money by buying a cheaper machine with a home version of Windows and a shorter warranty and less entitlement to technical support (as many of these machines have) is false economy for a business. If your machine is at home and your kid wants to play games, get a play machine that you do not use for critical applications. The extra costs will be more than made up for by the hours you now will not lose in recovering after crashes, redoing work that's been lost, and general frustration.

For similar reasons, while the pricing for second-hand equipment can be tempting, in most situations you're better off with the warranty and technical support you will get with new machines, especially if you also have to buy system software for the second-hand machine. If you are tempted to buy a second-hand machine and the seller offers to include the software installed on it, make sure that valid licences to use that software are included; otherwise, you get to choose between deleting the software and violating copyright law (see pp. 31–4).

Finally, as your network grows and administration becomes more centralized and security more of an issue, you will find the limitations of the home strands of Windows really start to bite. Home versions of Windows cannot log onto a domain, the centralized database of user accounts provided by Windows 2000 Server, only onto a local workgroup. That restriction is a serious limitation.

THE TROUBLE WITH LINUX

A lot has been written in the last few years about Linux as an alternative to Windows. It has a number of advantages: the software itself is free, it is very stable, it can be well secured, it requires lower hardware overheads, and there are fewer viruses out there to attack it. If you are planning to use Linux to run a server – Web, file, print, email – these are all assets, as is the number of Internet-related things that Linux does very well. For this reason, Linux is always an option to consider for those applications, especially when they're going to be managed by someone who is technically skilled.

When it comes to the desktop, however, there are some significant disadvantages. The most noticeable on a day-to-day basis is the problem of finding staff familiar with how it works. As Microsoft Office has come to dominate the market, it's become easier and easier to find staff who are familiar with its applications. The same is not true of the various office suites that run on Linux: if you decide to standardize on, say, Open Office or Star Office, you must expect to train your staff on the software and to have to train any new staff you take on. This problem will be even more noticeable on the occasions when you need to hire temporary staff, as the chances that the local agency will be able to supply someone familiar with the software will be remote. So when you make your cost/benefit assessment you will need to take the ongoing cost of staff training into account.

TIP Small Business Server has an upper limit of fifty users, after which you must instead install Back Office, an expensive change. So: if you're growing and you have thirty-five users and want this kind of package, buy Back Office. If you're laying people off and have seventy-five users, buy Small Business Server. If you're fairly stable and have twenty-five users, buy Small Business Server.

This is just one subset of a larger problem, namely that if you need to hire someone to maintain your network for you, it may be more difficult to find the right set of skills in the Linux world. This is particularly true because there's a much greater variety of available options on the Linux world. In the Windows world, if you're running an email server, it's almost certainly one of two or three versions of Exchange Server, over one or two possible versions of Windows. In the Linux world, you may have one of any number of Linux variants as the operating system, and one of four or five different mail servers. There are, therefore, many more possible configurations, and being sure that any given consultant has the right set of skills is much more difficult. Worse, the consultant who specifies that set of software may, for all you know, be the only person in your area who thoroughly understands it, with all the risks that entails (see Chapter 9 for more on this issue).

On the other hand, Linux is used in a number of small businesses to run mail servers and file servers, not just because it's cheap to buy but because as the number of users grows Linux typically doesn't escalate as suddenly in cost as does its Windows counterparts.

Even so, Linux has come a long way, and there are now few applications areas where there isn't at least one available choice. Linux devotees will tell you that current implementations of Linux such as Red Hat or Suse make it as easy to install as Windows; this is largely true, though the terminology facing users is less friendly. They will also boast that Linux is not prone to viruses in the way Microsoft products are; this is true, too, though less due to superiority of technical design than to the fact that Linux, like Apple, is a small enough part of the market for most virus writers not to bother. The larger the installed base of Linux software becomes, the more it will be considered a worthwhile target for the sort of person who thinks disrupting the world's computers with viruses is a fun thing to do.

However, those caveats apply only to the desktop. You will find an increasing number of 'network appliances' that run behind the scenes on Linux not only because it's inexpensive but because manufacturers can modify the code as needed. Linux has without question an important role in running mail servers and file servers, and as the operating system embedded in other such behind-the-scenes machines, where it can help save on overheads and be very reliable. In 'black-box appliances', such as the Snap Server mentioned on page 16, it doesn't matter what the operating system is as long as the device is reliable.

APPLE VERSUS PC

Like it or not, Microsoft has done a lot to close the usability gap between its machines and Apple Macs. Even in Apple's strongest niche, publishing, there are now Windows versions of all the major applications that are nearly indistinguishable from their Mac counterparts. It's still arguable that Macs are better for design, graphics, video production, and music, but the gap has narrowed considerably. This means that to all intents and purposes user preference can dictate the choice of Windows or Mac. Even the physical cabling, as noted in Chapter 1, is now the same, since recent Macs come with ethernet built in, the usual connection type for Windows. Less powerful Macs, such as iMacs, Powerbooks, and iBooks, generally have ethernet 10/100 (mbps). The most powerful Macs, such as the Powerbook G4, the LCD iMac, and desktop PowerMac units, come with ethernet 10/100/1000.

The big sticking point with Macs used to be the all-important need for good backups. Even now, there is far more backup software available for Windows than for Macs. However, there are now some products that do handle both Mac and PC backups from either platform, so even this problem has diminished. This means that you can use either Mac or Windows for the server (whether it's Windows 2000 Server or Small Business Server). Users who need or want them can have Apple workstations while users of business process software such as accounting systems and the like can use PCs. In either case, data is stored on the server and backed up from there.

Apple's OS X's networking compatibility makes sense when you realize that underneath it's really UNIX, the operating system invented at AT&T and made available to academics for free in 1984. There are a number of UNIX variants out there (including the free operating system known as FreeBSD), and Linux is more or less a clone of UNIX. Many of the most important computers on the Internet still use UNIX (which was the dominant operating system in the Net's early days). What OS X does is to put an Applishly friendly face on top of UNIX, which has been described even by users who love it as 'as user-friendly as a cornered rat'. There are some significant differences between Windows and Macs in terms of access rights and security defaults, but overall the Apple implementation is much simpler than Windows has managed.

As you'd expect, configuring a machine or user involves going through a series of panels. You need to know the same information

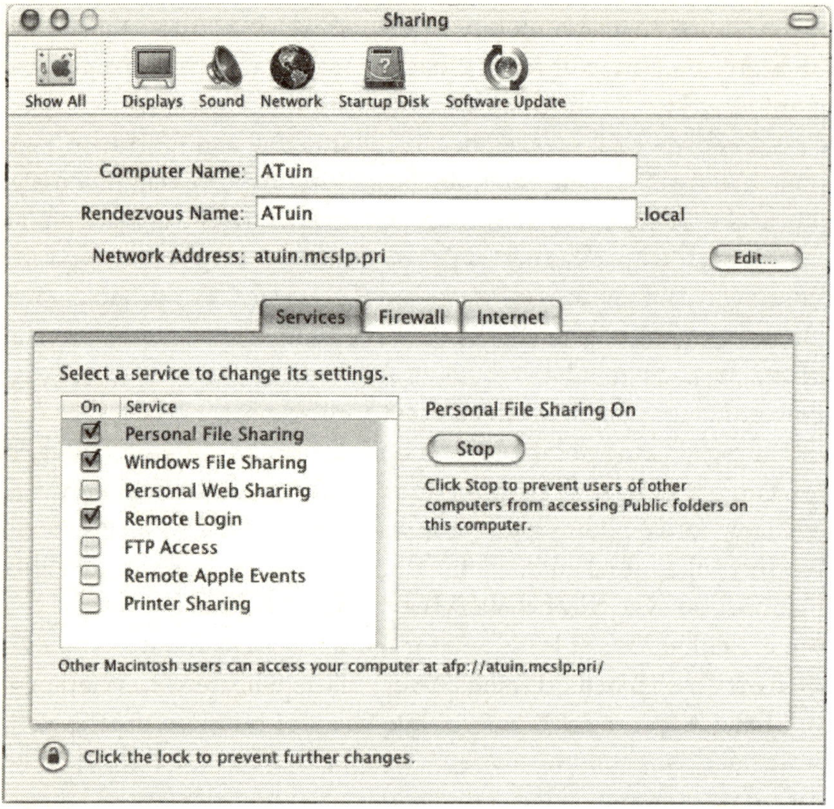

Figure 4

Configuring shares on an Apple Mac running OS X.

you would for a Windows machine – IP address, subnet mask, and so on – but Apple has done a good job of pulling all the configuration together into a logical sequence using understandable terms.

For example, where in Windows you can go through systematically and choose whether each folder on any given machine is to be shared and who may have access, in OS X you share only one folder, the Public folder. Anything you want to make accessible, you place in that folder. Everything else is private. While that's a less flexible system, it's also less likely to be subject to user errors. Like Windows XP, OS X has a firewall built in to protect the single machine it's installed on. With both, to protect a whole network you will need to install a separate firewall, though versions of these are available to run on OS X and OS X Server.

A few other differences in how Mac OS X handles security are worth noting. The system is similar to Windows, but slightly easier, since any given object (file, folder) can only have one owner and one group assigned to it, where Windows allows any combination. This means that the complex and confusing interactions that can be difficult even for very experienced technicians to track accurately in Windows are greatly simplified with Macs. Windows also offers more choices for what permissions a given user may have over an object; on the Mac there are only three choices – read, write, or execute.

SOFTWARE LICENCES

Software isn't like most things. You don't actually buy it, even though it seems like you do. What you buy is a licence to use it. The terms of the end-user licence (often called EULA, for end-user licence agreement) which you usually click on without reading at installation dictate the conditions under which you are allowed to use the software: how many users, how many machines, and sometimes what you may use it for.

The intellectual property laws governing the sale, copying, and use of intangible goods such as software are under much debate at the moment. The arrival of file-sharing services such as Napster, Gnutella, and others has frightened the entertainment industry into demanding both tougher laws and more protective technology. It may be that the laws that are eventually settled on will render the standard terms of software end-user licences invalid. That should not, however, matter to you, who are doing business and would prefer not to go through the upheaval of having your software audited and the embarrassment of being publicly named and shamed if your system is not compliant.

One of the difficulties that arises with a network is keeping track of the software you have installed and ensuring it's all correctly licensed. It is very tempting for a small business faced with shelling out thousands of pounds for multiple licences, especially when it's already paid for one copy, to cut corners by installing the software on every machine and to assume that no one will ever know. And you may in fact be right that no one will ever know. However, if that's your strategy, you'd better be very nice to all your employees and consultants, if any; a significant way that the organizations that enforce software licences find out about businesses that don't have them is when someone snitches. You may also find that any consultant you've decided to bring in to work on your system may refuse to take you on as a client. Many consultants believe that a business that skimps on paying for its software will baulk at paying the consultant's invoice as well, and walk away rather than risk spending valuable time and effort on a potential non-payer. Finally, you may have real trouble getting any kind of technical support.

TIP Last time you added a machine or a disk drive, did you remember to change the backup routine to include the new machine/drive?

That is not to say that you must have a licence for every user for all software, or that the same user with a laptop and a desktop must have two licences. It depends on the terms. Most software manufacturers recognize that the same person can't in general use the same package in two locations at the same time, and that the fact that one user on a network does, say, computer-aided design doesn't mean all the users do. The problem is that very often you cannot read the terms of the end-user licence agreement until after you've bought and begun to install the software, at which point you generally cannot get a refund. The notable exception is software you can download first in trial versions from the Net.

For larger networks, manufacturers also make available networked installations that allow you to avoid the trouble of going to each machine separately to install an upgrade. Many of these start with as few as five seats.

Manufacturers have gone to greater and greater lengths to prevent copying, including lengthy keys the user must type in (write them down and don't lose the original jewel case the CD came in). In 2000, Microsoft began a scheme known as product activation, which allows users either fifty runs of the software (Office XP) or thirty days (Windows XP), and then shuts the software down if it hasn't been activated using the wizard supplied. This applies to Windows XP and Office XP, and doubtless many more products in the future.

TIP Is the software you rely on still supported by its manufacturer?

In practice, this doesn't affect users all that much. Open versions of these products are available for businesses as small as five seats; for consumers, vendors pre-activate the software already installed on the machines they sell. The people affected by product activation, therefore, are primarily home users and small businesses who upgrade to these products. Product activation, which merely involves validating the product key, is separate from registering the software and, according to the company, is intended to prevent piracy by ensuring that a particular piece of software is not installed on multiple machines unless it's been paid for. After 120 days, however, the product key is wiped from the database, and installing the software on another machine is no longer blocked.

Certain types of software, such as anti-virus and content filtering, require annual subscriptions, but this is not for the licence to use the software itself but to pay for the updates the vendor must issue in order to keep the software current with emerging trends. This is a different situation from the large companies that hope to turn software from something you buy a permanent licence for to something you subscribe to as a service. So far, the subscription model has not made much inroads into mass-market software. If it does, the benefit will be not locking yourself into ageing technology. The downside will be that you are not allowed to use the software when the licence expires. Microsoft's Licensing 6.0, which applies to products from Windows 2000's service pack 3 and beyond, follows this type of model, in that you buy a two-year running contract for a server platform that will cover whatever Microsoft is shipping. The good side is that you can move when you want to, without worrying about whether an upgrade is pending.

One other note about software licences: keep an eye on the date at which the software you rely on goes off the list of products the original manufacturer will support. Microsoft has promised to fully support all business products for five years from the point of release. This means that, for example, NT goes off the list in the summer of 2004. Windows 2000, which was released in March 2000, will be supported until July 2005. XP was released on the desktop in 2001; the replacement for Windows 2000 Server, Windows Server 2003, was released in April 2003.

You must pay attention to these product life cycles. Most businesses need to be on currently licensed software. This is particularly true if yours is one of the minority of small businesses that has computerized accounts. An accountant may be unwilling to sign off on your annual accounts if you are running on unsupported software, since accounts software by its nature must be updated every year. If you have one of those businesses, by the way, you had better make sure you have absolutely rock-solid procedures for backup and disaster recovery: if you lose nine months' worth of invoices your business will be dead.

WIRED VERSUS WIRELESS

Wi-Fi, also known as 802.11b, is a standard for local area networking that replaces cabled ethernet connections with wireless ones. The number 802.11b refers to the working group of the Institute for Electrical and Electronic Engineering (IEEE) which sets a number of technical standards (you will sometimes see Firewire referred to as IEEE 1394 for that reason). There are other versions of 802.11 in the works, and 802.11a equipment is already available, although within the UK 802.11a is not yet licensed for use (with a few exceptions for schools). Unfortunately, 802.11a and 802.11b are not compatible, as they use different radio frequencies (2.4GHz for 802.11b and 5GHz for 802.11a). So as the equipment becomes available and licensed, you will have to choose one or the other. 802.11a is up to five times as fast as 802.11b – but the equipment is accordingly about twice as expensive. In public locations such as hotels, restaurants, conferences, and airports, where it's becoming common to find public 802.11b Internet access (either free in the case of conference settings or for a daily, monthly, or annual subscription in the others), it's unlikely that 802.11a will be substituted for such access for some time. The next version, however, 802.11g, the standard that was agreed at the end of 2002, will be faster than 802.11a (54mbps) but use the same band (2.4GHz) as 802.11b; it will be backwards compatible so that 802.11b and 802.11g network interface cards and access points will interoperate. However, 802.11g will probably have a shorter range than 802.11b.

It seems to be axiomatic that at any given time the available wireless options are going to be slower – many times slower – than the competing wireline connections. Ethernet, for example, is beginning the transition from 100mbps to 1gbps at the same time as 802.11b, which runs at a theoretical maximum of 11mbps, is becoming widespread. 802.11a quintuples 802.11b's speed, but it's still many times slower than the wireline standard of 1gbps it will emerge alongside. Bluetooth, the second emerging wireless standard of 2002 and 2003, is an order of magnitude slower than even 802.11b, but it's intended for different purposes (see the next section).

For small networks, particularly in a home office setting, even though it's slower, wireless is very tempting nonetheless. Not having to run wires everywhere is a big bonus, since most small offices aren't designed for them, and the distances are usually going to be short enough for everyone to be within networking distance of the wireless access point or router. The availability of relatively inexpensive (£200 or thereabouts), simple all-in-one wireless router packages, including networked parallel printer port, firewall software, and three or four ethernet ports on top of the wireless connections, is also a plus, since these are designed for non-technical users.

However, you do need to pay much greater attention to security with wireless connections than with their wireline counterparts. Anyone within broadcast range will be able to piggyback on your Internet connection or, if they are sufficiently technically clever, use a packet sniffer (see Chapter 6) to capture the data you send back and forth. That could include the text of email, passwords sent in the clear (that is, without encryption to secure them against prying eyes), and unprotected files of projects in progress. It is much easier to control access to a physical network, since anyone wanting to connect must be seated at the end of a cable and is therefore easily spotted. With wireless, which can penetrate at least some walls, it is perfectly possible for someone to intercept your connection from a nearby home or office, or even from the street, without your ever realizing it. As more and more people install wireless connections, it will become more and more like it is already in Silicon Valley, where it's perfectly possible to sit in the office of a secured wireless LAN and surf the Internet using the connection next door without realizing you're using the wrong one. As 802.11b (and the forthcoming 802.11g) shares its frequency band with microwave ovens, cordless phones, TV/video senders, some burglar alarm systems, Bluetooth, and a host of other unlicensed applications, that portion of the spectrum will become increasingly crowded. However, the two networking standards are extremely robust, and it's usually not that hard to manage devices to minimize interference.

WIRELESS: BLUETOOTH AND 802.11b

In general, you are unlikely to have to choose between Bluetooth and Wi-Fi, also known as 802.11b, but it's worth understanding the different ways they're used. Both use the 2.4GHz unlicensed radio frequency band, which is also used by microwave ovens and video senders. Bluetooth is a low-power connection running at speeds of up to 1mpbs that is used to connect many types of devices over short distances – that is, less than thirty feet. Backed by a massive consortium including companies like Nokia, Microsoft, and the networking company 3Com, Bluetooth is being built into all kinds of devices from mobile phones to headsets, PDAs, laptops, and digital cameras. The idea is to end the necessity of carrying half a dozen cables to enable all your devices to connect while also doing away with the line-of-sight requirement of infrared. Unlike infrared, Bluetooth can maintain its connection from inside a pocket or briefcase – line of sight is not needed. If you have a really fancy phone or PDA (Personal Digital Assistant), you may feel more secure keeping it out of sight while you talk over a headset. Drivers also find Bluetooth to connect a phone and headset more flexible (if it's legal to use the phone at all while driving).

TIP Beware the technical adviser who disparages technologies simply because they themselves are not expert on that subject. If you are talking about new purchases the adviser has to support, then it makes sense to accommodate that person's strengths, but if you're being advised to rip out working machines users are happy with (for example, to replace working Macs with PCs) and that have other business advantages (for example, being able to recruit permanent and temporary design staff who are more comfortable with Macs), question the value of the advice.

Wi-Fi, on the other hand, is intended for wireless networking, and replaces ethernet cabling (albeit at slower speeds) in circumstances where cabling is awkward. But it draws more power than Bluetooth, although arguably prices have dropped so much due to increasing volumes that it's actually currently cheaper to install than Bluetooth. As millions of Bluetooth-enabled devices hit the market, that will change, however.

Adding Bluetooth to older machines is a matter of adding a Bluetooth adaptor. For computers, these come in either the form of a USB device or a PC Card. Adaptors for printers plug into the printer's existing parallel port. There are even Bluetooth print servers that will let you integrate your printer into your existing network while also accepting Bluetooth connections. Also on the market are tiny Bluetooth cards that plug into PDAs, headsets, mice/presenters/joysticks, Bluetooth battery packs for certain models of mobile phones, and access points that allow mobile phone users to connect to a local network or the Internet. In the pipeline are Bluetooth pens that will let you write notes, convert them to ordinary text, and transmit them via Bluetooth to a PC, PDA, or mobile phone. Increasingly, any mobile phone you buy will have Bluetooth in it at little or no extra cost.

When it is powered up, your Bluetooth-enabled device scans for other available Bluetooth devices, and gives you a list in a 'connection manager' so you can choose. You might, for example, want to transfer the photos from a digital camera onto a computer or to a mobile phone, set up a new printer for several desktops to use, or move files as needed from your computer to a visiting machine that isn't networked to yours.

Built-in security lets you make a device either invisible or available to other Bluetooth devices. You might, for example, want to ensure that no one can find your mobile phone and use its connectivity without your knowledge but make your printer discoverable by anyone. You can also password-protect devices whose use you want to control.

Once you have located a device, you must pair it and your device before they can communicate. This is not difficult in general, although some of the terminology is confusing for non-technical users. Essentially, when you connect via Bluetooth you are using virtual connections named after those familiar from the physical world: serial port, for example. Instructions should be included with the devices themselves. But the industry needs to improve these interfaces substantially. By comparison, setting up an 802.11b connection is easy.

ADDING WIRELESS: ROUTERS AND ACCESS POINTS

If you already have a router running your network, especially if it's doing NAT, you probably want an access point. A wireless router that's also doing NAT will work in the sense of letting your wirelessly connected computers see each other and the Internet, but your wired computers and your wireless computers won't be able to talk to each other. However, if you don't already have a router, a number of companies, such as SMC, make relatively inexpensive (£200) wireless routers that include three or four ethernet ports as well as, often, a parallel printer port and serial port. The printer port allows you to network an ordinary printer so that any machine on the network can run it independently. Often these routers even come with basic firewall software. Purists tend to prefer each of these components to be a separate box, but these routers do provide a relatively simple all-in-one package, although they are intended really only for small networks. If you know in advance that your network is likely to expand beyond three or four wired computers, don't buy one of these routers. Instead, for greater flexibility, buy a bigger wired router and use one of its ports to hook up a wireless access point.

The most common wireless standard for use in LANs at the moment is 802.11b, which has a maximum speed of 11mbps. A single router or access point can handle multiple simultaneous users, usually thirty to fifty. Later standards such as 802.11a are faster, but the equipment is much more expensive and much less readily available and the range is shorter. If you want to be able to take advantage of restaurant and hotel 'hotspots' and have a good chance of being able to accommodate visiting users (or use other people's networks when you're visiting them), 802.11b is the safest choice. Equipment made for 802.11a is not backwards compatible with 802.11b, because they use a different radio frequency band. Equipment made for 802.11g is backwards compatible with 802.11b.

You should also check that the wireless access point or router you plan to buy supports the protocols you intend to use. Generally, this isn't a problem as long as you're sticking to common protocols such as Windows file and printer sharing and TCP/IP. If you need to accommodate AppleTalk, NetBEUI, or other protocols, check that the gateway supports these. Some of the wireless routers (such as Apple's AirPort) include a modem to allow you to share a dial-up connection among your wirelessly linked computers.

Wireless network interface cards typically are PC Cards; the ones intended for desktops come with a PCI adaptor. You might as well have as versatile a system as possible, so if you wind up buying a desktop model, make sure the PC Card style NICs that come with the PCI board can also function as standalone cards that you can plug into a laptop – not all of them can. (You will not be able to use the PCI board to plug other PC Cards into the desktop.)

TIP If you're having troubles with your current technology, don't assume that new, untried technology is the answer. It could be that you just don't know what its problems are yet.

When you install your wireless access point or router, you should remember that any wireless card within range can connect to the access point unless you turn on the security provided. Worse, they can do so without your being aware of it, since they only need to be within range of the access point, not physically present at the end of a known cable. Someone unscrupulous could certainly install a packet sniffer and eavesdrop on your wireless network traffic, picking up email, passwords, and patterns of communication. It's much more common, however, for people to piggyback on your network connection simply to gain free Internet access for themselves. (In fact, there's a whole culture of sharing 802.11b connections, and a system of chalked marks on the pavement known as 'warchalking' which indicates where there are open wireless networks whose bandwidth people can borrow.) Turning on Wireless Encryption Protocol (WEP) should deal with the first situation; requiring authentication (a cryptographic challenge that requires the connecting card to answer with the correct string) should deal with the second. Some routers come with additional security that can be configured to effectively hide your network from anyone who doesn't know it's there. There has been a much publicized crack for WEP, and software to break into it is available on the Net, but WEP does provide protection against all but the most determined and prepared crackers.

3 Networking Basics and Infrastructure

This chapter is intended to explain the concepts behind the simple exercise in hooking things together we went through in Chapter 1. Some of this chapter may include more networking theory than you feel you really want to know, but there are two reasons why it might nonetheless be useful. The first is that when something goes wrong with your network understanding some theory may help you figure out approaches to fixing it. Networking is made up of many pieces, and it's easy to overlook some of them. The second is that, at the very least, it will show you how much of this technology you're going to be able to deal with yourself; with any luck, this chapter, coupled with Chapters 9 on finding help and 10 on working with consultants and technical staff, should tell you whether and when you need a consultant or other expert advice. If you do hire a consultant, understanding a little bit of the theory may help you understand that person's advice better – and anything that cuts down on the amount of a consultant's time you use will save you money.

There is of course a third reason, which is that it always helps to understand a little bit of what's going on behind the scenes with any tool you use. We often say that the car industry has been far more successful at accommodating non-technical users than the computer industry because you don't have to understand how a combustion engine works in order to drive one. That's true, but nonetheless you can use the gears more intelligently and make better decisions about how to steer a car in a skid if you understand how the gearbox works and how the steering mechanism relates to the wheelbase (to say nothing of understanding why it can be dangerous and expensive not to add oil when the light comes on). The difference with cars is that you can understand how the gears work by observing the same basic design on a bicycle, whereas the internal workings of computers and networks are of necessity hidden and therefore more difficult to understand (unless you're a programmer).

NETWORKING CONCEPTS: LAYERS

Understanding networking is easier if you approach the subject the way computer scientists and professionals do: in layers. The idea of networking layers came originally from a 1970s International Standards Organization initiative to create a worldwide networking standard known as Open Systems Interconnect (OSI). The OSI standard itself was never implemented because in the meantime everyone began using the Internet standard, TCP/IP. However, layers are still very useful conceptually.

Internetworking is usually divided into four layers: network, Internet, transport, application. (OSI had seven – eight if you count politics.) The network layer covers the actual physical connection: networking cards, cabling, and the way data is divided up and transmitted. The Internet layer deals with addressing, and how data is routed, compressed, and divided into packets and reassembled. The transport layer deals with error correction and enables connection-oriented communications (as, for example, when you log into a server and establish an open session); it also translates data into a form usable by the application layer. The application layer allows applications (such as, for example, a Web browser or email) to use the network. The application layer is all most users see or care about. These layers tend to be differently divided up depending on who you talk to, so the terms you come across may vary, or they may sound the same but not mean the same as the terms used here.

If we apply this structure to the simple connections we made in Chapter 2, the network layer covers the work we did in installing network cards, plugging in cables and hubs, and so on. At that level, what a network interface card (NIC) does is transform the data on your computer into electronic signals that can be sent across the network; it also has the job of receiving the signals and turning them back into data your computer can read and store. The configuration we did with granting users access rights is the top layer, the application layer. The layers in between are largely invisible to users, as they have to do with the mechanics of how data is formatted, sent, and received. The political layer you will have to supply yourself.

TIP Have spares of standard inexpensive items: ethernet cables, power leads, USB cables, keyboard, mouse, phone cable. If one of these standard parts fails, insert the spare and replace the spare instead of having to panic and rush out to find a replacement at short notice. Also, being able to swap leads helps identify the causes of system failures.

As you make the decisions necessary to set up your network, remembering this concept of layers may help. Several topics, such as addressing and protocols, will turn up within more than one layer. This is because data starts at the top layer on the sending computer, moves down through to the physical layer, is received by the receiving computer on the physical layer, and moves back up again to the top layer for the application to deal with it. (The full set of layers is often referred to as a 'stack'.)

PHYSICAL LAYER: EQUIPMENT

At this point, it seems logical to run down the types of equipment you will encounter in networking. Each has its place. You are unlikely to use all of these items, but it helps to know what they are when you're asked to make decisions about your network's physical design.

As noted in Chapter 1, each computer in your network must have a network interface card (NIC) installed. A network card takes the data stored inside your computer and converts it to electrical signals that can be transmitted to other computers; it also receives electrical signals from other computers and converts them back into data. Each network card needs to be connected via a cable either directly to another computer or to a central point such as a hub, switch, or router, which in turn is connected to other computers. There are also wireless NICs which communicate by radio; these don't require cables and they can talk to each other directly, but they do require a wireless access point in order to connect to a wired computer or to a broadband modem for access to the Internet.

Many new machines have networking built into the motherboard. On desktops that don't, a network card fits into a slot inside the machine. Usually these days the slots conform to the PCI standard.

Laptops also often have ethernet connections built in, but for those that don't networking is usually added via a PC card, a device slightly larger and thicker than a credit card that fits into a slot in the side of the computer and installs like any other network card. These vary in how they handle the ethernet connection: they may have a standard RJ45 socket recessed into them, or they may have an adaptor that trails the necessary socket on a short cord. If the latter, you will have to be careful not to lose or damage the adaptor, as without it the laptop won't be able to connect (either buy a different type of PC card, or buy a spare adaptor just in case).

Within a network segment all the network cards and connecting equipment (hubs, switches, routers) must use the same type of connection, usually these days ethernet over Cat5, with a plastic plug on either end known as an RJ45 (for Registered Jack, a series of standards for plugs). If you have a network spread over several floors, you may need to consider a backbone for your network with higher capacity. This is usually done with fibre optic cable. Fibre optic cable is not normally used within small network segments, since it's expensive and requires a great deal of skill to install correctly.

Older small networks may use coaxial cable (coax), but there are good reasons not to do this any more. Computers hooked together using coaxial cable are connected in a chain with a terminator at each end. The section on network topology (see pp. 47–9) explains why this is inherently a more fragile design than using ethernet cables and a hub. In the days when hubs and other connecting equipment were expensive, coax was a reasonable choice as a low-cost alternative. Now, it's simply false economy, since using this type of design makes it much harder to locate points of failure. In addition, modern

100mbps ethernet cards can't use coax – and the savings surely aren't enough to be worth keeping yourself stuck with data rates of one-tenth the speed.

CONNECTION POINTS

Once you have your computers set up with NICs and cables, you must connect them together with one of a number of types of connecting box. We will go through these in order of increasing intelligence.

A hub has multiple network ports that make physical connections (in a star topology) between pieces of the network, such as several computers or several clusters of computers. Hubs have no internal 'intelligence' to tell them which computer gets which bit of data. They simply broadcast the lot and the NICs select the packets of data intended for the computer they're attached to.

Repeaters, which are built into hubs but may be purchased as 'standalone' devices, receive signals and retransmit them at their original strength, essentially extending the effective length of a cable. They are necessary because as the electrical signals travel they weaken in strength, just as the further you are from a light source the weaker the illumination. Repeaters do not filter or translate signals, so the network segments on either side must be of the same type – that is, ethernet, token ring, and so on. In practice, this is unlikely to be a problem since most small networks now are ethernet. A hub is essentially a multiport repeater.

A bridge is a device with some intelligence that stores the MAC addresses belonging to the sending computers, building up a table mapping machines to MAC addresses in its memory. When a packet with a known address as its destination is received, the bridge forwards it to that specific machine, cutting down on unnecessary network traffic and making the whole more efficient. A bridge can also interconnect different cabling types (such as twisted pair and coaxial) although the attached segments need to use the same protocols.

A switch is similar to a bridge, in that it can route data packets to a specific machine, but different in the sense that it works out what MAC address it's intended for and, if it knows what port that MAC address is on, it sends the data only to that port. It learns the MAC addresses by reading the source addresses of packets as they go through. It is a multi-port bridge. Switches can improve the security of a network by making it harder to gather information such as passwords sent without the protection of encryption without having physical access to the switch – if you put a packet sniffer on one of the ports it will only pick up traffic destined for that segment. Switches can also significantly reduce conflicts between incoming and outgoing data (collisions).

Routers are the most intelligent of all these devices. A router acts like a bridge or switch in the way it is able to identify the destination of data packets. However, routers use software-configurable network addresses and can also determine the best and most efficient path for the data to take because they hold an internal map of the network (known as a routing table). If the best path fails, the router is capable of resending the data via an alternative route if one exists. In the case of the Internet, routers therefore not only increase the efficiency of the network but make it fault-tolerant as well because there are many alternative paths. Routers can also translate between different types of network architecture. The term 'fully routed network' means that each computer on the network has its own permanent unique IP address – that is, the routers are not doing NAT and each machine is directly accessible from the wider Internet via an IP address that is not one of the addresses set aside for private use.

The difficulty is that a lot of boxes with multiple capabilities are now called routers. Routers are small computers in their own right, and many include user-configurable filtering (to allow you to block certain types of undesirable traffic), firewalls (see Chapter 6), assigning IP addresses, and other functions. Wireless routers using the 802.11b standard often include several ethernet ports in addition to functioning as an access point for wireless users, and may also include a printer port and print server software, as well as firewall software; they are intended to offer a small, home-based network a complete broadband-ready network in a box.

Gateway is sometimes used to be synonymous with a router, and you will see it used that way when you configure a Windows workstation to access the Internet. You will be asked for the 'default gateway', which means the router between that machine and the Internet. The term also pops up in relation to email servers, which may need to translate between one set of protocols and another.

Of these many devices, the ones a small network owner is most likely to use or think about are hubs and routers. You may have the functionality of one or more of the other devices, but they will usually be built into one of those two (or in some cases, your broadband modem).

Finally, a network segment is an independent section of a network; it may be set off by a router, bridge, or switch.

PHYSICAL CONNECTIONS: NETWORK TOPOLOGY

Network topology refers to the way the physical connections between the various computers are organized, which is where all those different types of boxes come in. Networking textbooks talk about many choices, but most of these are dying away. In most cases, your network will be connected with ethernet, and use what's known as a star topology or, if it's large enough, a tree topology (essentially a backbone with stars hanging off it).

The choices you will see talked about are: star, ring, mesh, bus, tree, and fully connected. In a ring network, for example, each computer is connected to two others. In a star topology, each computer is connected to a central point (such as a hub, bridge, switch, or router), through which all transmissions to other nodes must pass. A tree topology looks like multiple star networks connected together. In a bus or linear network, all nodes are connected together with a single backbone cable with a terminator at each end. A fully connected network is one in which all nodes can communicate directly with all other nodes. In a mesh network, at least two nodes have multiple paths connecting them. A hybrid topology mixes together two or more of these designs.

Most of these options are unlikely to apply to you, and the only ones you're likely to run across are star and linear. A small business may well, for example, have a linear network with all the machines connected with BNC coaxial cable. If you do, read on, as the way your network is laid out can have consequences for the amount and severity of downtime you can expect to have. In a ring network, for example, if one node goes out it will take down the entire network by breaking the chain of communications. In addition, it's a design that's really only suitable for small networks (or small network segments) because of the network lag that can build up as a chunk of data destined for one machine traverses a large number of others to get to its destination. In a star network, if the central node goes down, all the stations are disconnected from each other, too – but you can add to the network by adding more central nodes and connecting them (into a tree), and that allows your network to remain flexible and resilient as it grows. Mesh networks are even more resilient, since if one path goes down there is a second to use, but they are the most expensive to set up and complicated to support, and you are unlikely to see them in a small business. They are primarily used to connect sites on a wide-area network; for example, if your business had five sites, each with its server running a LAN, you might mesh the five servers in the interests of redundancy and fault tolerance.

Linear topologies were popular for a while – they're cheaper to install because the lengths of cable are less than they would be in a star network, and you don't need connecting boxes such as a hub. But a linear network, like a ring network, is inherently more fragile because if a single node on the network goes down the entire network stops working. In a star topology, where many nodes are connected to a single point, if the central point goes down you lose the entire network, but if a single node goes down it's an isolated failure. A second benefit of that design is that failures are relatively easy to locate, whereas on a bus network it may be very difficult to tell which node is causing the problem. Plus, you can add or remove devices from the network without taking the network down, a significant benefit for a small business.

In general, therefore, if you have a series of machines connected with the older BNC coaxial cable (coax) design, you would do well to consider replacing the system with a hub and modern unshielded twisted pair cables. The necessary cables (usually specified as Cat5) are cheap, as are network cards (sometimes as little as £10), and hubs (under £50). You will end up with a much more robust and much faster network. These days, ethernet via Cat5 goes at a speed of 100mbps (and even 1gpbs), while BNC coax lags behind at a 10mbps maximum. If your staff must regularly ship data around between the networked machines, you will be amazed at the difference.

As your network grows larger, you may need to divide it into segments. A network segment may be a chunk made up of a single router with a set of computers and possibly hubs hanging off it. That is, it can be a functioning network in its own right, and can be connected to other segments into a single network (like the Internet) by making connections between the router and other routers. A computer in one network segment cannot 'see' – that is, talk directly to – a computer in another segment. However, data can be sent between them in a variety of ways, taking advantage of the intelligence built into the routers. This is where numbered addresses such as IP addresses (see pp. 61–4) are so valuable: they can be organized into hierarchies so that the necessary routing tables can be as efficient and memory saving as possible. Like any computer, without such organization, routers could run out of memory space.

PORTS: HOW APPLICATIONS TALK

In network applications, a 'port' is a logical channel for communication, just as the parallel connection on your computer is a physical port. That is, it's not a physical plug like the serial or parallel port on your computer, but a doorway defined by software. The protocols TCP/IP used on the Internet and by many local area networks running ethernet use a standard set of numbers to distinguish these logical channels on a single networked computer. These standard port assignments are managed by the Internet Assigned Numbers Authority; software publishers register their applications and the ports they use. Lists of these assignments are published in RFCs 793 and 768, which are available on the Internet (http://www.iana.org/assignments/port-numbers or http://www.portdb.org, for example). There are literally thousands of these standard port numbers, as each Internet application is assigned one of its own. So, for example, 80 and 8080 are assigned to HTTP, the Web protocol, 115 is file transfer protocol (FTP), and 25 is the SMTP protocol used for sending email.

TIP Don't plug your laser printer into the uninterruptable power supply. The way it draws power will overheat the UPS and shut it down. Then you won't have any emergency backup power.

The fact that each application uses a separate port makes the problem of controlling what type of traffic to allow to reach a particular computer or through a firewall relatively simple: you block or open the specific port as needed. One of the problems with the security built into certain types of broadband service (see Chapter 4) is that such decisions cannot be implemented by the end user, so that even if you want to open up certain ports for specific services, you can't.

When security experts talk about 'back doors' into your system being left open by or for hackers, this is one of the possibilities they mean: an open port that can be exploited by someone with the right software. Bear in mind that badly written legitimate software, or software that has been altered to carry a type of malicious software known as a 'Trojan' (after the Trojan Horse), can open ports in your system without your knowledge. A 'listening' port is an open port that is ready for the application that uses that port to connect to it. The technology that blocks this from happening is a firewall.

In general, it's wiser not to leave ports open unless you're actively using them, as they can provide entries into your system for malicious attackers as well as harmless software. There are a number of security-related Internet sites (such as http://www.grc.com) you can visit on the Web that will probe your computer and check your system for open holes. The usefulness of this is obvious: once you know what holes are there you can close them. But don't rely on them too much: the best way to know your system is protected is to install a firewall and close everything down by default, opening only the ports that are necessary. See Chapter 7 for more on firewalls.

THE PHYSICAL LAYER: CONNECTING

It's not enough to physically connect computers together. They must use the same rules for exchanging data so that the computers on each end of the connection can use it correctly. To make a human analogy, if you phone someone in France it's not enough for them to pick up the phone; to establish communication you both must agree to speak the same language. If you can't, you will need a translator (or, in computer terms, a gateway). At this physical level, the standards for exchanging data have nothing to do with the operating system you run (or, loosely, the type of computer you have). Operating systems (such as Windows or the Mac operating system, or even network operating systems such as Novell NetWare) are at the top level, the application layer (see pp. 54–7).

In this section, we are going to talk primarily about ethernet, as it is the most commonly found standard. Apple computers used to use a standard of their own known as AppleTalk, and some IBM computers used to use token ring, but in practice you are unlikely to encounter these or to want to use them. In general, networking is standardized on ethernet for wired networks and 802.11b for wireless (although this may be replaced in a few years by 802.11g).

Since everything in networking is in layers, there are a couple of different levels of rules for how networks connect. At the physical level, the rules that make up the standard govern how data is transmitted.

What makes all this additionally confusing is that the same names may pop up at different levels, and they don't necessarily mean the same thing. For example, 'ethernet' is both a type of cable (also known as Cat5 or unshielded twisted pair) and a set of standards that govern how data is communicated across the cable. Originally, 'ethernet' meant coaxial cable (coax); today it usually means Cat5. The connection over the BNC coax you see running from one computer to another in older, small networks organized in a linear topology is also ethernet. If you have a small cluster of machines successfully working over coax and you want to add new machines but don't want to rewire (on the 'if it ain't broke, don't fix it' principle), you can use Cat5 to connect the new machines and plug them into a hub that has a BNC terminal as well as ethernet ports. This type of hybrid hub is inexpensive and easily obtainable. However, as noted earlier, most experts will tell you to dump the coax in favour of more robust and fixable Cat5 cables and a hub.

Ethernet was invented in 1973 at Xerox by a researcher named Robert Metcalfe, who later founded the company 3Com to exploit the technology commercially. The standard has been improved upon and extended since, so that its effective range has been increased from a hundred metres to tens of kilometres, and the speed has increased from 10mbps to 100mbps and soon 1gbps.

The basic idea is that there is a single common medium that creates a path along which electrical signals can travel between devices connected to that medium. Each such device (which may be a computer or other machine such as a PDA (Personal Digital Assistant)) is known as a node.

Data to be transmitted across the cable is sent as variable-length messages known as frames, which are formatted according to the ethernet standard. Each frame has a header that includes a source and destination address that uniquely identify the sending and receiving nodes, as well as other fields that can be used to specify the length of the message, how long it 'lives' before it is discarded as undeliverable, and a number of other technical specifications. Each node on the network must have a unique IP address (see pp. 61–4). A signal that is broadcast across the network segment is received by every node; each node examines the destination address, and discards unexamined any frame that is not addressed to it. A broadcast address allows data to be sent to every node on the network and be processed by all of them.

Ethernet includes mechanisms to ensure that data does not collide – that is, that two competing streams are not being sent across one cable at the same time, interfering with each other. Essentially, the node listens before beginning to transmit data, and only proceeds if the coast is clear. Nodes listen and broadcast simultaneously, so that if two nodes begin to transmit at the same time, they receive back garbled versions of their data, which alerts them to the fact that there has been a collision. Each then waits a random amount of time before retrying.

One consequence of this design, however, is that there's a limit to how many devices you can connect to a single segment before the number of collisions increases to the point where it becomes difficult to get data moving. When the network has grown so much that performance degrades substantially, the solution is typically to subdivide it into smaller segments. This means that the nodes in each segment will only send and receive traffic to the other nodes in the same segment. This is where devices such as bridges, switches, and routers come in; they make the network more efficient by enabling communication between segments while ensuring that traffic intended for nodes in one segment is not (wastefully) sent onwards to others.

To cover briefly other types of networking: token ring was developed by IBM, and works similarly to the type of group therapy in which everyone sits in a circle and passes a stick around, with only the person holding the stick allowed to speak. Token ring networks use a circular topology (as the name suggests), and a special frame known as a token moves around the circle until it reaches a node that has data to transmit. That node then holds onto the token, sends the data, and also circulates a data frame to replace the token. When that data frame returns to the sending node, it removes the frame, creates a new token, and sends that on to the next node. Each station therefore gets an equal chance to transmit data. However, like linear network topologies using coaxial cable, the difficulty with token ring can be locating the point of failure. In addition, the speeds – between 4mbps and 16mbps – are much slower than modern ethernet.

Token ring techniques are, however, used in FDDI (Fibre-

Distributed Data Interface), which used a pair of fibre optic rings to connect smaller networks at a speed of 100mbps. With ethernet now surpassing that speed, FDDI is less often used.

Apple computers historically had their own networking standard known as LocalTalk, which was built into the machines and allowed them to connect using ordinary serial cables. Macs could also connect to PCs using ethernet cards and a special type of Cat5 cable known as a crossover cable (so-called because the wiring inside the cable is crossed over). Modern Macs using OS X and later have ethernet ports built in and support ethernet up to gigabit speeds. OS X also includes the legacy AppleTalk standard and, from 10.2 onwards, supports Rendezvous (Apple software intended to simplify finding and connecting to network devices over TCP/IP networks).

Linux and free but less famous versions of UNIX such as FreeBSD all support ethernet as long as you install an ethernet card in the computer and can find a compatible driver to allow the operating system to communicate with the card. Instructions for configuring ethernet under Linux are readily available on the Web.

Finally, ATM (Asynchronous Transfer Mode), which was developed in the UK in Cambridge, is a high-speed networking technique intended for video and audio traffic as well as data, and is used to connect remote local area network segments into wide area networks. Many UK ADSL providers use it.

THE APPLICATION LAYER: PROTOCOLS AND NETWORK OPERATING SYSTEM

Generally speaking, if you are setting up a new small network you will use the native network operating system in Windows, Apple, or Linux (in order of likelihood), and you will use the TCP/IP protocols. This section explains some historical context and what protocols are; the inner workings of TCP/IP have their own section on pp. 68–9.

Just as a computer has an operating system, networks also have operating systems. The purpose of a computer's operating system is to provide a standard way for the computer to access and use its resources, so that developers writing individual applications do not have to write the same subroutines to tell the computer how to communicate with resources such as memory, hard disk, and printers. A network operating system provides a standard way for networked computers to enable applications to communicate with one another so the data that is being transmitted can be used. It also provides basic services such as sharing files, printers, and other resources, provides centralized security administration, and co-ordinates communications among devices on the network.

It's easy to lose sight of the network operating system now, because these functions have been subsumed into most current 'standalone' computer operating systems. Apple included networking (AppleTalk) as a standard from very early in its history (as did the BBC Acorn), and Linux is more or less based on UNIX, which is the operating system most commonly used on the academic computers that were the first to connect to the Internet. PCs were the exceptions and formerly PC users would buy a network operating system separately and install it on each machine in order to get them to talk to each other. Microsoft began incorporating networking in Windows 3.11, and by now Windows' networking capabilities are strong enough so that the separately bought network operating systems of earlier days are slowly vanishing.

TIP For links to additional resources visit http://www.pelicancrossing.net/dtnw.

The best-known network operating system was Novell NetWare, which dominated the market in the mid-1990s with a 75 per cent share. There were many other contenders that are now so obscure you're unlikely to encounter them. For new installations of small networks you are unlikely to consider anything other than Windows' own networking capabilities. If you have a legacy network running Novell, you will have to assess your own situation to see if it's worth keeping it or changing. By now, in most situations, certainly those involving small networks, there is little difference in functionality.

Novell has lost a lot of ground, even in large enterprises, partly through aggressive marketing by Microsoft and partly because for most people it is much simpler to have a single operating system supplier. In addition, as has been the pattern with many other markets, Microsoft has gradually whittled away at the gap between its offering and Novell's technical superiority. Novell's market share is now down to under 20 per cent.

Bear in mind that it is certainly possible to connect network segments that use different operating systems. The Internet, for example, is the marvel it is because the protocols on which it runs, TCP/IP, made it possible for any type of computer to exchange data with any other as long as both used those protocols. It's as if everyone in the world decided the benefits of mutual understanding made it worth putting in the effort to learn Esperanto and to use the same alphabet. This is why a single network can have multiple Windows machines, a few Macs, and a Linux email server all communicating successfully.

Just as most choices of system architecture come down to one type of network topology, most come down to one or two networking protocols, that is, the set of rules computers follow in order for programs to be able to use the data that is sent back and forth. TCP/IP (for Transport Control Protocol/Internet Protocol) is the set of protocols the Internet uses, and as the Internet has become widespread TCP/IP has increasingly become the protocol that LANs use to communicate internally as well. On an average Windows machine, you will install TCP/IP, Client for Microsoft Networks, and File and Printer Sharing for Microsoft Networks and have little choice about them.

However, there are several other sets of protocols you will see listed if you go to the configuration options in older versions of Windows, for example when you're adding a networking card. In new installations you are unlikely to need anything other than TCP/IP and Microsoft file and printer sharing. Other options, such as NetBEUI (the default protocol in Windows 95) and IPX/SPX (NetWare) are unlikely to apply to you unless you have an older network already running on them. These days, because everyone wants TCP/IP to connect to the Internet anyway, few new installations bother installing a second set of protocols. In Windows XP, TCP/IP is the preferred protocol; it can't be uninstalled and is the default protocol used for all networking functions. XP also provides IPX/SPX and NetBEUI, but other, older, more exotic protocols such as Banyan Vines are gone. NetBEUI is unsupported in Windows XP so you can't get any help on using it from Microsoft, but if you have network functions that need it or IPX/SPX you can use them.

MULTILAYER CONCEPTS: ADDRESSING

It's confusing but it has to be faced: there are addresses of different types at all of the different network layers. At the physical layer, each network interface card, whatever the device and however well hidden the NIC, has what's known as a Media Access Control (MAC) address. This address looks something like 00-03-47-2B-63-91, and is meant to be unique. Recently, however, routers, both wired and wireless, have been supplied with the ability to 'clone', or copy and apply to themselves, the MAC address of a device attached to them. The usefulness of this is that many cable broadband suppliers around the world (including in the UK) require users to register the MAC addresses of devices that will be attached to the cable connection with the company. The claim is that this is part of the security arrangements, but since the cable companies also typically want to limit how many users can be connected to, say, consumer services (which are not designed for multiple users), part of the point is to block such use. You may find your ISP limits the number of MAC addresses you can register – typically to something like six. That is at least enough to let you use the connection with a desktop and a laptop. The router's ability to clone the existing address simply makes it easier and quicker to get it all working without having to go back and register another device.

MAC addresses, however, are not what humans want to use when they're sending data around the network. At the application layer, the top layer, humans typically use names they like and find easy to remember and type. You assign these names when you set up the network, and the usual drill is to pick a family of names that will give you room for expansion, for example characters from *The Lord of the Rings*, or colours, or even names that describe the machines' functions or their users.

The words that make sense to humans, however, are meaningless to computers, and in between the bottom and top networking layers translation takes place. If your network is small and not connected to the Internet, you could – and in some cases may – have the MAC addresses directly mapped to the names, so that if you type in the name, the network knows to send the data to the machine with the NIC that has that particular MAC address. However, today even a very small network that's connected to the Internet, even if only via dial-up, will typically use IP addresses as an intermediate layer – the network layer.

The wider Internet works the same way, in that human-friendly names such as *pelicancrossing.net* or *telegraph.co.uk* make it easy for you to remember and type in email and Web addresses. Behind the scenes, though, all computers on any TCP/IP network, whether it's your small company network or the Internet itself, are assigned IP addresses. These look like four dotted clumps of up to three numbers each. On your network, when you type in a machine name, behind the scenes the router translates that name into the corresponding IP address and sends the data to the appropriate machine. On the Internet, the number of machines to be named means that the names themselves must be more complex but the basic design is similar. A name like *pelicancrossing.net* is known as a domain name, and special servers known as DNS servers (for 'domain name system') hold copies of a centrally updated database that matches domain names to IP addresses. When you send an email message or request a Web page, the first thing that happens is that your ISP's computer sends a request to a DNS server to convert the domain name into an IP address so it knows where to route the request. When, as happens occasionally, you see an error message that tells you of a 'failed DNS lookup' or that the system is 'unable to resolve host name' it means the domain name cannot be found in the DNS database (or that your computer has been unable to reach the DNS server). As part of doing business on the Internet, you will probably want to register your own domain name. This is easily done (see pp. 88–91).

IP addresses are four dotted clumps of up to three numbers between 0 and 255 each – such as 158.152.8.200 – and are used throughout the Internet and on any network that uses the Internet protocols as its transport system. (See pp. 61–4 for more on IP addresses and how they work.) In a very small network, it's easy enough to manually assign a permanent IP address to each machine when you add its LAN connection. If you do, that IP address will be used for routing data, and it will be permanently assigned to the machine's name and also to the machine's network card's MAC address. That all seems very straightforward and possibly sort of pointless. Why have three addresses for the same machine?

The answer to that question becomes obvious when your network grows, and it becomes difficult to remember which IP address is assigned to which machine, and impossible to remember MAC addresses at all. Network cards get swapped around and replaced. Locations change and machines are assigned to different workgroups, or decommissioned entirely. Further, given that there is overall a limited number of IP addresses available (at least until IPv6, the next version of the Internet protocols, which includes enough addresses for every electron on the planet, rolls out fully), being able to use an automated server to assign and reassign IP addresses dynamically as machines are added and removed from the network vastly simplifies administration.

Accordingly, routers and servers these days typically have an internal server known as DHCP – Dynamic Host Configuration Protocol – built in. DHCP servers contain a database of IP addresses they can assign to computers attached to them (even if that connection is wireless). On the client computer, DHCP makes configuration simple – you just check the box that says 'Obtain IP address automatically' and the computer and the DHCP server do the rest. Essentially, when you turn the computer on the network card sends out an announcement that it's looking for a DHCP server, which responds and assigns an IP address. If a computer goes offline for a period of time, the DHCP server knows it and reassigns the address as needed.

On a small network connected to the Internet via a service using a dynamic IP address (whether broadband or dial-up), you will find this pattern repeated more than once. The ISP's DHCP server assigns your machine or router an IP address on the fly (dynamically) out of its pool of available addresses, and that address is the one by which your router or machine is identified to the rest of the Internet. But your router or directly connected machine also has an IP address by which it's known to the machines on your internal network; this is often 192.168.0.1. Either may also have a DHCP server inside it, and that server assigns your machines dynamic addresses from the range reserved for private networks, usually 192.168.0.2, 192.168.0.3, and so on for as many addresses as the router is designed to handle or as your network needs. This design is known as NAT, for network address translation, and it was devised as a way of conserving IP addresses (see pp. 96–9 on NAT and non-NAT for a further explanation).

While this all sounds confusing at first, in fact it makes configuring your network very flexible. If you change the network card in a given machine, you don't have to change the machine's name (so other users can still recognize it). If you swap in a new machine, it can immediately be assigned an IP address and join the network, with no confusion, even if you reuse the old machine's network card. And so on. One exception: if you run a mail or other server you should assign it a fixed address to ensure continuity of access.

TIP Whenever you need to buy a new machine, give it to the user in your company with the greatest need for computing power (usually someone who does CAD, image/audio/video processing, heavyweight database or spreadsheet crunching, or DTP). Create a hierarchy of users according to need for power and bump the old machines down the hierarchy. That way, the power users always have the fastest machines. Roaming profiles (built into, for example, Windows 2000 Server), which let users sit down at any machine on the network and retrieve their familiar desktops and settings, make this easy.

Finally, there is a fourth layer of identification, which is user names/IDs. These are not network addresses, but it's important to remember, particularly when you're setting up users and access rights, that a user and his or her machine are not the same network entity, even if that user never touches any other machine. Do not assign the same names to machines and users – a novice mistake. The reason is that it's simply too easy to get confused about which one you're configuring. Two machines, for example, may be set up to fully 'trust' each other so that they can act as complete mirror backups for each other. But the user who sits at one of those two machines may be given access rights to act on both machines as the system administrator, while the user who sits at the second machine is only given limited access rights on both machines – enough to be able to accomplish the work assigned, but not enough to make substantial changes to the system or access confidential data. These types of distinctions become increasingly important as your network and the number of users grow. (See Chapter 4 on managing users and access rights and Chapter 7 on security.)

IP ADDRESSING AND SUBNETTING

In order to communicate using TCP/IP, each computer needs an IP address which, as we've seen, is made up of four clumps of numbers separated by dots. Each IP packet transmitted or received carries both the source and destination IP addresses. If you've configured a network or followed the connection exercise in Chapter 1, you will have already seen that each computer is assigned an IP address plus a subnet mask. This section explains what these are and how they work. IP addresses are the fundamental glue that make an IP network communicate successfully, just as writing an address and postcode on an envelope is necessary to enable the Post Office to deliver a letter to the correct recipient.

It's easier to understand IP addressing if you remember that the numbers we see are decimal representations of binary bits, which in turn are our way of representing electrical signals inside a computer, which can only be either on or off. Each IP address is a 32-bit computer 'word' broken up into four 'octets'. For example, 11000000.00000000.00000010.11001000 translates to 192.0.2.200. Note that since each octet is eight bits long, the decimal value for each must fall between 0 and 255 (because 256 is the number of possible permutations of 1s and 0s in eight bits).

IP addressing is designed to ensure that no matter how big the number of interconnected networks becomes the vast majority of IP traffic is local, travelling only between computers on the same network. The connections between networks are provided by gateways or routers, as discussed above. These are specialized computers whose primary function is to manage the passage of traffic between different networks. To do this, each computer must have an address that differentiates it from the other computers on the same network and that indicates which network it's on. The way this is done in an IP network is to snip the 32-bit IP address into two parts: the first part represents the network address and the second part the specific computer ('host') on that network.

Exactly where that cut is placed varies, allowing maximum flexibility in network design. The longer the portion of the address that identifies the network, the smaller the number of hosts, and vice versa. This system is needed to give addresses sufficient flexibility to cover the entire world – otherwise there would be considerable wastage of addresses. Therefore, for any given IP address, there is an accompanying network mask that tells you how much of that address specifies the network.

The network mask, sometimes called netmask or subnet mask, is also a 32-bit binary word that looks like an IP address. This is where binary representation is helpful. A typical netmask, in fact probably the one you'll encounter most often, is 255.255.255.0. In binary this is 11111111.11111111.11111111.00000000. Looking at the binary version, it's very easy to see where the netmask ends: the host portion of the address is all the 0s. Therefore, with this netmask the first 24 bits of the IP address refer to the network and the last eight bits are the host address. With the same example IP address as before, the subnet mask is 255.255.255.0, the network address is 192.0.2.0, the host address is 200, and the broadcast address is 192.0.2.255.

In practice, if an example computer at, say, 192.0.2.200, wants to talk to a second one at 192.0.2.225, the computer uses the netmask to calculate how much of both its address and that of the remote computer is the network address. In both cases, the network address is 192.0.2.0. From this, the computer knows that it and the destination computer are both on the local network and can talk directly. If, on the other hand, the computer is trying to contact 192.0.3.125, it will extract the destination network address as 192.0.3.0. It will see that this is clearly not the same as the local network, will contact a local gateway and hand off the packet, trusting the gateway to know how to deliver it to the correct network, which of course will have its own gateway that knows how to deliver the packet to the destination host.

A lot of the time, the netmasks you'll see are set at an octet boundary, that is, at one of the dots in the decimal representation; it's just easier for humans. Those are generally the only netmasks you'll see in use in a private network, which is defined as either a network that never connects to the wider Internet or that does so via a gateway that does network address translation (NAT) so that traffic intended for a specific machine on that network can be directed to it even though the network as a whole uses only one IP address on the wider Internet. The netmasks in use for the public Internet are often, however, more complex.

A small business or home user may encounter the netmask 255.255.255.252, which defines the smallest possible network above a single address, which would be represented with a netmask of 255.255.255.255. With the mask ending in 252, only the last two bits of the IP address represent hosts. Those two binary bits allow only four possible host addresses, 00, 01, 10, and 11. In any IP network the first host address (00) is reserved to indicate the network itself, and the last host address (11) is used as a broadcast address (so that there is a way to send all traffic to all machines on the network), so only two addresses are left for host computers.

To make it simpler for humans to read these addresses – the full address of a computer in the last example would be 192.0.2.201 255.255.255.252 – shorthand is used to specify the number of network bits: 192.0.2.201/30.

In general, you will not have to do much in the way of choosing IP addresses. On the wider Internet, you will be assigned IP numbers by your ISP, and these will generally change if you change ISP (to keep routing simpler). Within your own private network, you must use numbers from the ranges reserved for private network use. These are 192.168.0.0/16, 10.0.0.0/8, and 172.16.0.0/12. Most people use the first of these, although Apple machines default to the second. In addition, Microsoft has registered a portion of the address range for use by Windows machines to assign themselves IP addresses in situations where no DHCP server is available (see APIPA). The last type is rarely used as it's trickier because of its non-octet-boundary mask; the full range available is 172.16.0.0 to 172.31.255.255. Within your network, how you use any given range is up to you. You may find it convenient to subdivide your network using the same techniques as the wider Internet (known as subnetting) to speed up routing and make the flow of data more efficient.

If you do, watch out for the two biggest traps: assigning either the network or broadcast address to a host, or creating overlapping networks by miscalculating the bounds of the subnets. Both of these tend to result from incorrect binary arithmetic; use one of the many subnet calculators available on the Net to get this right.

HOW EMAIL WORKS

Most people probably don't think too much about how an email message gets from one place to another. But it's a good example of how all these different pieces work together.

To the information you type into an email message – the subject line, the message itself, plus the address it's going to – your email software adds some standard information that you or your system administrator entered when the software was first set up. This includes the source address (From), the address for replies (Reply-to), a date and time stamp, a message ID number designed to be unique, and any of a number of other fields specifying, for example, the type of content (Content-type), the character set (charset), and the email software in use.

In terms of the networking layers talked about above, the email software passes your message to the lower layers that make up your network connection. There the message is divided up into chunks known as packets, which are put into data 'envelopes', effectively another set of headers that contain directions for putting the chunks back together into the original email. The data is also converted into an electrical signal that can travel across the physical network. If you're using a dial-up connection, the modem you use to connect with converts the digital data into analog signals that can be transmitted across phone lines; if you're using ISDN, cable, or ADSL, the data is transmitted and received in its digital form.

At the application layer, the email message is handed from your email software to the SMTP (Simple Mail Transfer Protocol) server at your ISP (using your port 25) or to your own SMTP server if you have one internally. If the message is destined for another user of the same ISP, the message is handed to the ISP's POP3 server for delivery to the appropriate user. Otherwise, the SMTP server looks up the domain name for which the message is destined on a DNS server. Once it knows the numbered IP address for that domain name, the SMTP server uses a program known as Sendmail to hand the message to the SMTP server for that domain, and that server hands it to that domain's POP3 server, which puts the message in the recipient's mailbox. (If the mailbox is not valid, the POP3 server hands it back to the SMTP server with some added headers indicating that the mailbox is not valid, and the message bounces back to you as undeliverable.)

If your ISP's SMTP server can't connect to the remote SMTP server, it puts the message in a queue, and will keep trying at intervals until the message gets through. If it still hasn't been sent successfully after four hours, it will send you a message alerting you to the problem. After five days, Sendmail usually gives up and sends you back the message as undeliverable. The POP3 server itself maintains your mailbox as a plain text file, and simply adds each new incoming message to the bottom. Your email software, when it picks up the text file, uses the headers to parse the messages into the organized display you see on your computer. If you examine the headers on messages you receive, you will see that the machines they've passed through en route to you have been added to the headers so you can trace its path. This part of the headers is used by experts to help determine the true source of junk email whose sender has falsified ('spoofed') the return address in an effort to avoid being sent barrages of complaints.

All of the steps in this process are really very simple, and a human can read the commands these programs send each other and the steps they take and readily understand them. Exactly how these things work is specified in RFCs 822 and 1123.

One reason these things can all be so simple in operation is that the Internet is designed only to carry text messages; that is, messages must be made up of characters from the standard 7-bit ASCII character set (basically, the upper and lower case Latin alphabet, the digits from 0 to 9, and some basic English punctuation marks and identifiers (including $ but not £)). The extended ASCII character set that includes non-American English characters and punctuation (such as å, é, or ¥) is known as 8-bit. This terminology refers to the fact that characters are expressed to a computer as a set of binary bits – that is, electrical signals that can only be on or off. So 7-bit means that the number of characters is equal to the seventh power of 2, since that is how many possible permutations there are of seven slots which each may contain a 1 or a 0. That would be 128 characters that can be represented; but of course 0000000 is unusable (since the signal is simply completely off), so the final number is 127. Eight-bit just about doubles that (the eighth power of 2 minus 1) to 255.

What you know as word-processed documents are not plain text – they are what's known as binary files. If you open one of those files in a text editor such as Windows Notepad, you will see all sorts of gibberish characters. Other types of files, such as spreadsheets, audio, pictures, video, and programs are also all binary files. These files are sent across the Internet every day, but to do so involves an extra step that your email software probably hides from you.

To send these types of non-text files across the Internet, they must be converted into plain, that is, 7-bit ASCII, text. The software to do this encoding, known as MIME (or the older UUEncode) is built into your email software, and when you attach a file to an email message what you are really doing is instructing the email software to encode the binary file and append it in its encoded form to the bottom of your message. If you set your email software so that it does not automatically decode these attached files back into their binary form, you will see what looks like acres of gibberish at the bottom of the part of the message you can read as ordinary text. The readable portion of the message will be topped with a note that the message is MIME-encoded, the type of file that's been attached, and the name of the file. Underneath the readable portion will be a tail identifying the start of the encoded portion. This tells your software which part of the message to decode, what type of file it should be, and what to name it.

When someone asks you, therefore, to send a message as plain text, what they mean is to copy the text out of the word-processed file and paste it into the body of the email message you're sending. Then it will go through as ordinary readable text.

Because programs can carry viruses and email software that seamlessly handles attached files is now so widespread, email-borne viruses have become a serious threat over the last few years. Before that, viruses were usually transmitted via infected floppy disks or CD-ROMs. The problem of emailed viruses began when Microsoft Word became dominant and email software made it easy to attach files, because individual files may bring with them the little macro programs you can create to automate commonly performed tasks. Macros can be embedded in the template you use to open a particular document, and so a malicious macro can infect your system if you open a Word document in which one is a hidden stowaway. Current anti-virus software detects and eliminates such viruses.

More recent email-borne viruses are cleverer and more dangerous. These rely on disguise, their writers secure in the knowledge that commonly used email software hides the headers described above from users and may even be set to automatically decode and run attached files on arrival. (If your software is set to do this, change the settings so it isn't.) State-of-the-art viruses disguise themselves to look as though they've come from a colleague (examining the headers will usually reveal the true source), use subject lines that sound like they're responses to ordinary messages, and may even throw in a bit of an ordinary email so they look genuine. Anti-virus software (see Chapter 7) should detect and eliminate these viruses, but because new viruses are released all the time you must keep it constantly updated.

For more information on dealing with problem email – high volumes, junk, servers – see Chapters 5 and 6.

TCP/IP PRIMER

TCP/IP stands for Transport Control Protocol/Internet Protocol, the protocols on which the Internet runs. Developed by a US Department of Defense research project into advanced networking, TCP/IP was successful because it delivered the basic services everyone needed across a wide variety of computing platforms. Like all communications protocols, TCP/IP is designed in layers. IP is at the Internet layer; TCP at the transport layer. IP handles the exchange of data between host computers; TCP manages the exchange of data between applications. Two other protocols complete the suite: UDP, which is a more lightweight and less reliable protocol than TCP but also manages the movement of data between applications, and ICMP, which transmits error messages and network statistics.

IP is the single most important protocol, as almost all data uses it to get to its destination. IP is responsible for defining datagrams, the basic unit of transmission for the Internet; defining Internet addressing (the dotted clumps of numbers); routing datagrams to remote hosts; and splitting a stream of data into datagrams and reassembling the stream at the other end. IP is what is known as a 'connectionless' protocol, in that it does not assume or try to create an ongoing connection with a particular host before sending data. Built into IP is ICMP (Internet Control Message Protocol), a protocol that lets hosts and gateways report errors if a datagram can't reach its destination or the gateway for some reason can't forward it (or can use a shorter route than that specified). Because IP is not designed to be reliable, ICMP provides important feedback about problems. The network utility Ping (see below) runs on ICMP.

TCP, on the other hand, requires a connection to be established before two computers can exchange data, and it includes error correction. The two machines go through a handshaking exercise similar to the negotiation when two modems begin a connection: the first machine sends a request known as a SYN (for synchronize sequence numbers) packet; the second replies with an ACK (acknowledgement) if the packet is received successfully and it's willing to accept the connection. When the stream of data has been sent, an ending handshake takes place so that both systems can terminate the connection.

The package of subroutines that provide access to TCP/IP on most systems is known as 'Sockets'.

NETWORK UTILITIES

The utilities that follow are generally run from a command line. On a Windows machine, all of these should be available if you open up a command prompt. The advent of graphical interfaces makes it easy to forget that underneath the Internet is an entirely text-driven system. Knowing about these utilities actually has a practical application. Ping and Traceroute are important network debugging utilities, for example.

TIP Don't let the cleaner unplug the server.

Ping

This is a text command that lets you test whether a particular machine is connected and responding correctly as part of debugging a network. Within a local network, typing 'ping <machinename>' at a Windows or UNIX command line sends four little packets of data to the named machine and measures the length of time it takes for each one to be acknowledged. The result is an on-screen printout that shows each attempt and a summary. Across the Internet, some Web sites have disabled Ping (see p. 163 for why), but if you can't get to a particular Web site it can be worth pinging it to get clues as to why.

Traceroute

This is also a text command that literally traces the route between you and the target system. Traceroute is also a debugging tool, as it lets you see where the blockages are if a connection between you and the target machine is fouling up. The syntax is similar to Ping. Type 'tracert <domainname>' at the command prompt. The system will send back an acknowledgement from each router that directs the request onwards along with the length of time each hop took. A computer in London might take twenty-two hops to get to one in California, for example.

ARP

Standing for address resolution protocol, this shows and allows you to modify the tables of MAC address/IP address assignments. Typing 'arp -a <IP number>' will give you back a table of the relevant assignments.

FTP

Meaning file transfer protocol, this is a utility (originally UNIX) for downloading and uploading files from/to remote machines. For downloads, FTP is included among the functions of your Web browser. FTP uploads are used by some ISPs as a way of uploading a Web site for public viewing. FTP is built into Windows as a command-line (text-based) application, but there are a number of graphical versions available as shareware or freeware that can make it much easier to use. (See especially FTP Voyager, which lets you drag and drop updated files onto your Web site directory much like an Explorer window would.)

Telnet

This program allows you to operate a remote computer as though you were directly attached to it. Telnet as a command-line program turns up most often with certain types of older online systems and ongoing text-based games known as MUDs. But because Telnet is a versatile type of Internet connection, it's often hidden inside software that logs onto remote systems in order to accomplish specific tasks, such as retrieve email. If you have occasion to use it directly, you will find there are many Telnet clients available on the Net; choose one that supports SSH, which is a secured version of Telnet, so that anyone trying to eavesdrop can't read your traffic.

4 The Trouble with Computers: Users

Installing a network automatically raises the question of access rights: who is allowed to use which resources? You don't, for example, want the company's payroll files to be accessible to all employees; equally, you want to ensure that the library of product information is accessible to everyone inside the company. The network itself you want to protect from unauthorized access by outsiders.

These rights are managed via user accounts. If you've ever typed a name and password into a Windows machine at startup, you've seen a user account in action. On the Web, many ecommerce sites store the personal information their customers provide with their first transaction so that subsequent transactions can be put through more quickly and easily. This information is also typically protected by a user name and password, and is another example of a user account on a computer system. The fact that normally you can only see your account and not those of other customers shows how finely these things can be controlled.

In general, try to keep the rules you use to assign rights and permissions simple. The more complex they are, the harder they are to administer and the easier it is to make errors in configuring them.

USER ACCOUNTS

On any network, users must log on and verify their identities in order to gain access. Usually, this verification is done by means of typing in a password the user must remember (see Chapter 7 on the importance of keeping these secret). Some recent computer designs are beginning to include fingerprint scanners or smart card readers for authentication. In some cases, removing the smart card puts the computer on standby for added security, but these are generally used only in large businesses or ones demanding an extraordinarily high level of security.

✎ **TIP** If you have the bandwidth, mirror your data drive across a wide area network so your off-site backup is remote and up to date.

Users may be 'local' or 'global'. A local user is an account defined on a specific machine that's intended to give the user access to that machine. The same ID and password won't be valid to gain access to another machine on the same network. A 'global' (or, in Windows 2000 and above, 'domain') user is one that is defined on a central server and can access resources anywhere on the network. Local user accounts work adequately in very small environments, where setting up accounts and rights on each machine is not overly time-consuming and the number of resources those accounts need to access is reasonably small. As the network grows, however, it becomes simpler and more streamlined to manage users from a central server. In the Windows world, that means changing from a workgroup to a domain.

WORKGROUPS VERSUS DOMAINS

A workgroup is a peer-to-peer network made up of two or more computers. All the computers are more or less equal and each holds its own information about which resources are shared and which users have access. Even in a workgroup, some machines may act as servers for specific applications, of course: for example, the workgroup printer may be attached to one machine, making that machine a print server for the rest, or the machine with the biggest hard drive may store copies of the data on the other machines, which then all gets copied to a backup medium. A new machine joining a Windows workgroup is configured in the way shown in Chapter 1:

all you need to do is give it a network identity consisting of the machine's name and the workgroup's name for it to join the workgroup.

Users of those machines still need accounts, of course, and even in a workgroup it's possible to control which users can access a particular resource and what they may do with it. But each computer maintains its own security database, and there is no overall authentication. It is very easy to lose track of who can do what as your network grows to include a larger number of machines and other resources.

Domains offer a way of centralizing control of user accounts and access rights. In this context, the word 'domain' means simply a group of computers and devices that are administered as a unit. In a domain, a single computer maintains a single security database, and it acts as a server for the other machines. In a Windows 2000 network, this computer is known as the 'primary domain controller'. Because this machine is a single point of failure – if the primary domain controller goes down, no one can access anything on the network – the design of a domain always includes at least one backup domain controller. This means, even if the domain controller is out, any user with a local account on a given machine can use the resources on that machine.

This is another area where the difference between the home and business versions of Windows is significant (see p. 25). XP Home, for example, cannot log onto a domain, only a workgroup (95/98 can log onto a domain but they don't fully interoperate with Active Directory). The domain controllers themselves must be running on NT or Windows 2000 Server or Server 2003 (not Workstation or Professional). This means that adding a domain adds some cost in terms of operating system software. But there are certain kinds of networked applications you can't run without a domain. These include commonly used products such as Exchange Server.

There are several reasons why running a domain helps the quality of the security on your network. For one thing, in a workgroup, depending on how the administrator has configured the system, some users may have blank, i.e. empty, passwords. This is not allowed in a domain: all users must have passwords. In addition, every user's logon must be authenticated by the domain controller. For users, a domain can be somewhat more convenient, because a single logon gives them access to all the network's resources.

However, a domain requires somewhat more work and attention to detail to maintain. If you do not need the higher level of security, don't want to run server products that require domains, and don't need the network to grow to the point where administering each machine's list of users separately is too time-consuming, you're probably best off sticking with a workgroup configuration.

Setting up a domain by itself isn't difficult, although the added security it imposes may represent a significant cultural change in a small company where security has previously been somewhat loose. In Windows 2000 server, for example, you run a wizard to configure the server and check the box to make the server a domain controller. On the other machines, the user logs in with the user name, password, and domain name, and the domain controller authenticates the user.

TIP Do not let your kids play on the work machine. Get a separate machine for them.

Within Windows, computers designated as domain controllers have a utility called Active Directory Users and Computers that administrators use to set up and manage user accounts. The administrator must be logged onto the domain, not just the local machine. The equivalent in Novell is NDS (Novell Directory Service). You can nest domains, so that each individual department has its own and all fit under a single umbrella domain across the whole company.

One big advantage of having a centralized administrator for users is that you can create what are known as 'roaming profiles'. The usefulness of these is that they store the user's desktop and configuration settings – with the result that any user can sit down at any machine on the network, log in, and find his or her own familiar desktop and data. So if a computer goes down unexpectedly or gets stolen the user can be back at work in minutes on a spare machine because the user account is all on the server (as long as the server itself doesn't get stolen).

Roaming profiles (which are built into a number of networking systems) also let you streamline the process of updating machines and allow you to target the fastest most powerful machine at the user who most needs it. Identify the person who has the biggest need for power, usually the one who does the computer-aided design (CAD) or multimedia processing, and make a rough hierarchy of users according to their need for computing power and allocate the computers you have on that basis. When someone needs a new machine, buy the best machine you can for the power user and move the remaining machines down the hierarchy. With roaming profiles, this is completely straightforward. Otherwise, it's easy to wind up with situations where the machine that's used four hours a week by the temp typist blows up and is replaced by a shiny new machine that's faster than anything else in the office but is barely touched, while the power users seethe with frustration as they wait around for their machines to finish processing.

TIP Define user access rights by the user's task and role in the company, not the specific person, and use hierarchies to organize groups of users. Keep it simple.

USER ACCOUNTS: GROUPS

Because it would get very complicated and time-consuming to reconfigure, say, every user in a given department every time a resource changes, both workgroups and domains allow you to manage users in groups. Grouping users and applying rights is an old technique; UNIX systems (including the UNIX-like Linux) work this way, as do Novell and Apple OS X. What is important in setting up any of these systems is to be aware what default groups exist and what rights they have. Otherwise you may have more security holes than you imagine.

In Windows, several groups come built in: administrators, who can do everything; power users, who can do most things; backup operators, which have rights limited to what's needed to do backups; replicators, which can do only what's needed to replicate certain types of files; ordinary users, who are restricted to specified applications; and guests, the most restricted of all. It is up to the system administrator to configure these groups for a given network's particular setup.

You can, of course, set up your own groups with specified rights. This is useful if, say, you want to give the entire sales department the same access to weekly sales figures and a contacts database, but want to keep them out of the accounting files, while giving the accounts department access to both.

In the Windows world, groups exist for both workgroup computers and on domain controllers. On a workgroup computer, adding a user to a group gives that user the local rights assigned to that profile. For example, the administrators group has full access to everything on the machine; adding a user to the administrators group gives that user the same rights. On a domain controller, you create groups in Active Directory, and the users you add to those groups can be anyone throughout the entire domain or across multiple domains.

When you set up your network, carefully read the documentation that explains what default groups are provided and what default rights members have, as these vary between operating systems and versions of Windows. You will find that the interaction of rights between, for example, two domains that are set up in different ways can be quite complicated. In some systems, if there's a difference between, say, the rights a user has locally versus the rights granted across the network, that user will get the greater of the two sets of rights. In other systems, the user will get the lesser of the two sets of rights. Across a network with multiple domains and many types of machines these variations can combine to produce unexpected results. Keep the rights you assign and the variety of groups you set up as simple as possible. Any time you upgrade a server or reconfigure the network, the more complicated your user setup is and the more likely it is that someone will make an error in updating the configuration.

If you frequently have temporary staff who need limited access to a specific set of resources, you can set up a group for that purpose as well. You should, however, remember to delete the temporary staff member's account or change its password once that person's work period is over. You can keep the group and its rights intact even if that group has no users in it. But it's a security risk to keep accounts active when the people who used them no longer work for you; former staff are a significant source of security troubles. The same is true of permanent staff: when they leave the company their accounts should be deleted or the passwords changed, just as you would ask them to return their keys or the security ID that lets them into the building.

DEFAULT ACCOUNTS AND GROUPS

On any Windows NT/2000/XP Professional box, you will have two default accounts: administrator and guest. The administrator account is the ultimate god in this situation, as it has full rights over all the computer's resources. You will need an administrator account to install or remove software, set up users, and turn on sharing for resources. As soon as the computer has been set up, you should copy the administrator account to a second such account. Ideally, you should then rename the original administrator account and assign it a difficult-to-guess password (see rules for choosing passwords, p. 80). You should ensure that the administrator account's name and password are stored somewhere safe – for example, on a piece of paper, in a sealed envelope, in a fireproof safe – and ensure that no one uses that account unless it's absolutely necessary. You should do all the day-to-day administration using the copy account.

You should also ideally disable (or rename or remove) the guest account. It doesn't represent the kind of risk the administrator account does, in that you will still be able to manage the system if it gets corrupted (the default guest account can't do that much). But because it's a default account and people often forget to set a

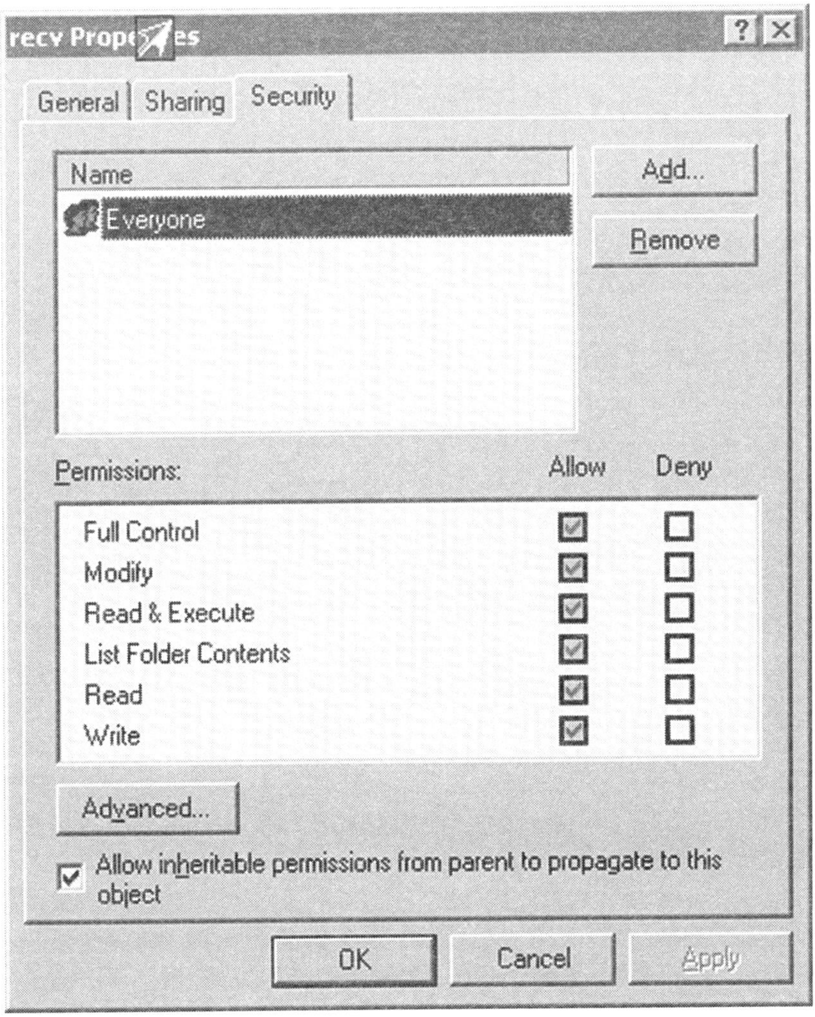

Figure 5

Security settings for a file folder/directory called 'recv' in Windows 2000 (with NTFS file system it is accessed by right-clicking on the directory's name in Explorer). It shows one of the common loopholes, the Everyone group. Remove this group from the list authorized to access the resource and add instead the appropriate group of authenticated users.

password for it, it represents a security hole. Someone who knows Windows, is curious about your business, and has the opportunity, either because they're working for you as temporary staff or because they've found a way to get into your system over the Internet, can take advantage of the guest account to have a look around.

One more killer: in Windows 2000 when you turn on sharing for a particular resource, if you look at the Security tab for that resource you will see a list of who is allowed to use it and what they may do with it. On each such resource, the default list includes a group called 'Everyone', and members of that group are allowed to do anything they like with that resource – 'Full Control'. Most people, if they notice these settings at all, assume that 'Everyone' refers to authenticated users. It doesn't. It means *everyone* who connects to the network. This means that if you have, for example, set up a wireless network with no security enabled, anyone may be able to use your network resources. It also means that you may think you have limited access to, say, the directory in which your accounts data resides, so that only accounting personnel can access it, when in reality that directory is open to any member of your staff.

You cannot delete the Everyone group globally in versions of Windows through XP. You can, however, remove it from the list that can use each individual resource and add instead a group of authenticated users so that only those users have access to that resource.

CHOOSING AND MANAGING PASSWORDS

Most people these days find they have a lot of passwords to remember and manage, starting with network accounts and passwords at work and continuing on to online banking and retail Web sites as well as those news sites that require registration.

Picking good passwords is a perennial problem, in part because a typical user eventually needs so many. The obvious strategy is to use one password for everything. Don't. The problem with doing that is that if someone learns your password to one site, they can get into all of your accounts. Remember, the risk is not just that they may see your information but that they can actually impersonate you, moving your money around (if it's a bank account), buying goods (if it's a retailer account), or sending out email as if they were you (if it's an email account). A better strategy, therefore, is to use individual, carefully chosen passwords for the relatively few really important accounts, such as those with your network account and online bank or stockbroker, and use a different, single password or family of passwords for sites where you do not store personal data of any consequence and where you and/or your reputation cannot be damaged if someone impersonates you.

On the office network, user passwords should be part of the security policy you develop. You should decide in advance, for example, whether users are allowed to have blank passwords, and whether and how often they will be forced to change them. Bear in mind that although changing passwords regularly is better security in the sense that someone learning them one year for temporary use won't be able to use them the next, it adds difficulties for your users, who may have trouble thinking up a good password just once, let alone one a month. Still, in situations where temporary staff are coming and going all the time, it's valuable to have a reminder to force you to change the passwords on those particular accounts. In a membership organization where a password-protected PC is a shared resource, it may make more sense to have one account that all the members use and whose password is changed on the date that subscriptions are renewed every year.

TIP Do not give users administrator rights.

Also bear in mind that staff who are used to a rather casual way of working, where everyone knows everyone else's passwords, may resist the change in culture towards more stringent security. This kind of change is significant enough that it can't be imposed overnight. Staff will need to be educated as to the reasons for the change and its importance as your company grows. It is one thing to have casual security in an office of three people who all know each other very well, quite another to have the same approach in an office of fifty where strangers are coming and going regularly.

The best passwords are easy to remember (so you don't have to write them down somewhere that a thief might see them) but difficult to guess. It's considered risky to pick ordinary words that can be found in a dictionary for a mainstream language. You're probably safe with words in, say, Basque or Scots Gaelic, since these dictionaries aren't easily found online, but with more commonly known languages there are password-cracking programs that can run through an entire dictionary looking for valid passwords in a matter of seconds. Also avoid using easily associated passwords that would be easy to guess by anyone who knows you: for instance your spouse's, children's, pets', or mother's maiden names, your birth date, or your or the company's address. Instead, pick something like the name of a restaurant with personal associations, a fictional character, or childhood memory, and add a non-alphabetical character or two. On systems that use case-sensitive passwords (meaning that the system distinguishes between upper and lower case letters), you can make the password even more difficult to guess by capitalizing one or two of the letters.

Some larger security-conscious companies like to ensure their employees pick good passwords by assigning complex strings of letters and numbers. The problem with that strategy is that the passwords, lacking any personal association, can be very difficult to remember, leading staff to write them down on Post-It notes and stick them on the monitor where they'll be handy when it comes time to log in. This is a very bad idea, as anyone visiting the company can make a note of the passwords for later use.

5 Internet Enablement

Almost every business these days uses email, though not always effectively. Increasingly email is as vital to a business as the telephone. This is not, of course, universally true. A couple who manage a twelve-barrister personal injury practice from their basement network of three networked Windows NT machines, for example, say that their most important means of communication is the Hays DX private courier service. That gets the huge bundles of handwritten applications, photographs, and other evidence back and forth across the country overnight, whereas scanning all those documents would be prohibitively time-consuming. But even they use email (over ISDN) within the practice for electronically created documents and administration, and have a rock-solid three-machine NT network on which the practice is run.

Britain's small businesses are undergoing a massive change as facilities that formerly cost as much as £12,000 a year and were therefore out of reach have become affordable at prices nearer £1,200 a year. Flaky, slow dial-up connections on metered telephone lines that limited small businesses to retrieving email a few times a day and severely restricted Web use (partly because of the cost and partly because of the slow speeds) are giving way to broadband, which is fast, flat-rate, and permanent. The result is nothing less than a revolution. Small businesses with tiny staffs can look and act as though they are much larger companies; and their reach is global.

Adjusting to this new way of life is not always easy. But increasingly small businesses will have to invest in the technology and make the adjustment or die. If you don't, you can be sure your competitors will make the investment. As the chairman of the chip company Intel, Andy Grove, said as long ago as 1999, 'In five years' time there won't be any "Internet companies". They'll all be Internet companies. This is not an option.'

This chapter looks at the issues inherent in switching to broadband and integrating the Internet into your business, along with email management. Setting up a company Web site and enabling it for ecommerce will be covered in the next chapter; using the Web for research is covered in Chapter 9, on getting technical help.

CHOOSING AN ISP

What follows applies to the connection you choose for your business as a whole. Individual users who need remote access to the network or email will most commonly do so over an ordinary dial-up connection, and the choice of ISP for that purpose will largely depend on whether they need access while travelling outside the UK. If they don't, almost any UK-based ISP will do; if they do, they will need to sign up with an international ISP such as CompuServe or AOL, or a UK ISP with international roaming agreements as many now have.

As businesses derive a more and more significant portion of their revenues and supplies from electronic commerce and must compete on the basis of the quality and immediacy of customer service, the reliability and quality of their Internet connections are vital. And yet, because Internet access is such a recently arrived necessity the choice of service provider is often haphazard; in fact the choice is often based on who has the most widespread and recently seen ads. The one big problem with choosing an ISP for your broadband connection is that you can't tell how reliable the service is going to be until after you've bought the service. Nonetheless, there are some steps you can take, depending on how many choices you have. These are dictated by where you live.

TIP Keep a log of system settings and changes including new software installed, hardware updates, and changes to important parts of the configuration, so that you can identify the last change when something stops working and undo it.

There are a few areas in the UK, mostly in and around Greater London, where people can choose between cable and ADSL. In the majority of areas, however, you will find only one of these is available. Just about all the cable companies offer broadband, so if cable TV is available in your area you should be able to get a cable modem to access the Internet. There will, however, be only one supplier and you will have to take or leave the cable company's terms. Cable Internet access will not generally enable you to host Web or other types of servers.

The availability of ADSL is patchy, in part because several conditions have to be right for it to be a possibility for you. Generally, you need to be within 5.5km of the exchange. You must have an ordinary BT phone line; Home Highway and ISDN lines cannot be converted for ADSL. In addition, the exchange itself has to have been updated for ADSL. In areas where this has not been done, BT is collecting signatures from those interested in getting the service. When the list is long enough, BT will undertake to convert the exchange.

Before you can get ADSL your line will be tested to ensure that it can handle the data. A newer version of ADSL, known as RADSL (Rate-Adaptive DSL), works over slightly greater distances.

If you can get past all these hurdles, however, you will probably be able to choose among a number of suppliers, as BT is required by law to sell ADSL wholesale to other ISPs who want to sell it retail to their customers. One of the suppliers you can buy from will almost certainly be BT Openworld, and a lot of people think that because BT is the biggest and best known it's the most logical choice. Resist this temptation, and do some research on what other options you have available. You probably won't save much on the basic price, since everyone's charging roughly the same, but you may find that different facilities are included in the price which may (or may not) add up quite differently in the long run.

There are a number of reasons why you might want to buy your service from a smaller ISP. For one thing, dealing with a company that itself is a small business may mean you get more personalized service. While ideally what you want from broadband is to never have to think about it at all, as your network grows and your needs change you may want advice or additional services or increased bandwidth. When you get to that situation, you want an ISP big enough to be able to offer those services – but small enough that the staff know you and your business. This is especially true for technical support; when you need help, it's less frustrating if the person at the other end of the phone line knows you well enough to have some idea of your technical competence and can pitch the help accordingly. ISPs that have been around a long time, even if they're now large, may have enough experience to manage that delicate balance. They are also likely to make a distinction between business users and consumers, providing a different level of service and, especially, technical support for the two tiers of customers. As this has been a problem, particularly with BT Openworld, check this point before signing up.

However, bear in mind that as of the beginning of 2003 all ISPs offering ADSL except Easynet are reselling BT's service. The upshot is that when there are problems with your connection – and these should be infrequent, but unfortunately they do occur – you may have to deal with both your own ISP and BT to get them resolved. With cable, the entire connection is owned by the cable company and resolving disconnection problems is much simpler. However, there are no 'small' cable companies offering broadband; the suppliers are all large companies such as Telewest or ntl. Some of them nonetheless do offer separate technical support for their business users and priority to business customers when the system goes down.

COSTS

Basic prices for broadband start at as little as £25 a month, with setup costs in some cases as little as £50 or less.

Keep some perspective on costs. Don't assume that if you buy the most expensive package from the biggest ISP that it has to be right. Similarly, although it is possible to cobble together lots of free bits and pieces into a very low-cost service, remember to factor in the time it takes to build and maintain such a kludge, and that the cheapest ISP may be selling the connection below cost, which long term is not a viable business plan. In a sense, the internal economics of the industry need not concern you, but there are some things you may find it useful to know if you're considering signing up with a small ISP and are concerned about the company's viability.

At the beginning of 2003, BT's wholesale ADSL price to a retailer ISP was £14.75 per connection. If the ISP is charging £25, out of that £10.25 margin the ISP has to cover its costs for providing services such as mailboxes, proxy servers, and its own infrastructure, including call centre staff. In addition, the ISP must pay for the bandwidth you use, and as its user numbers go up it has to finance adding additional bandwidth to accommodate these increased demands. A 34-megabit pipe to BT from the ISP at the beginning of 2003 cost £20,000 a year, plus £15,000 to install, according to industry figures. The ISP has to include those costs as well within its fee.

Therefore if the ISP you're considering charges less than £20 a month, expect no frills – technical support may not be free or may be on a line charged at premium rate, for example. For that reason, before signing up you should also look at the costs of any extras you may be likely to need later, such as added Web space, extra mailboxes, domain name hosting, forwarding, and/or transfer, fixed IP, and so on.

It is of course possible to set up a system at extremely low cost. For example: you could build your own router (rather than buying one) with an old PC, a copy of Linux or FreeBSD, a couple of network cards, and shareware such as Zebra, and use a hub (£50) instead of the ports built into most routers. You could use a free email service such as Hotmail or Yahoo!; the free Web space bundled with free dial-up accounts, and so on. However, unless your main business is teaching people how to live for free or very cheaply, it is counterproductive to do this. For one thing, if you have a business case for Internet connectivity at all, the savings by trying to do everything ultra-cheap are surely not enough to justify the trouble. If you don't have a business case, then the time and effort aren't justified anyway. In practice, it's almost impossible to find an ADSL modem that isn't packaged in a router in the UK.

For another thing, having a Geocities Web site and Hotmail makes you look like an amateur and makes your email more difficult to manage (see email management, pp. 102–4). Quite apart from the image of teenagers and spam that those addresses have, they are intended for consumers, and have limitations that are deliberately set in place to make those accounts inappropriate for businesses.

Finally, the absolute key issue for a business online is constant availability and rock-solid reliability. If you deal with customers and/or suppliers, you can make them feel you're sitting in the next office if you reply promptly to the email they send you. If you sell or provide information via a Web site, you want that site to be reliable. You do not want it shut off temporarily because you're getting too much traffic and haven't paid for a commercial site.

So treat Internet services like any other professional service you'd expect to pay for. Bear in mind that the cost of connectivity has dropped by 90 per cent in only a few years. In that context, £100 either way is not significant. However . . . don't go overboard. Compare carefully the costs of items beyond just the basic service. For example, facilities such as fixed IP, retaining a block of addresses for use on a fully routed network (that is, one on which each machine has a fixed IP address that is accessible from the outside) may incur monthly charges from one ISP but only a modest one-time set-up cost from another.

DOMAIN NAMES

One important decision you will have to make is whether you want to register a unique name, known as a domain name, by which your company will be known on the Internet. Since it's now quite possible – and cheap – to get a hosting service to hold a Web site and register a domain name for you, there's generally no reason not to do this, and many reasons why you should.

For one thing, having a Web address that's hosted on Freeserve and a series of staff email addresses that are all over the map looks unprofessional. For another, if you have a domain name, even if the email all goes into just one user name and you have to sort it manually, at least you have control of the email. If staff use their own addresses, if they leave your employ any email they get sent is out of your control. In addition, Web-based email services may not always make it easy for you to archive and back up messages stored on their servers.

Usually you can get the ISP that's going to host your Web site and handle your email to register a domain name for you, and this can be extremely cheap. The one thing to make sure of is that the ISP will readily transfer the name if you choose to move to a different service. The process itself is not complicated. To transfer *.uk* addresses, you will need to find out a bit of information known as the 'IPS tag' from the new host and give it to the old host. The old host company should then transfer your domain to the new tag, after which all administration will be done by the new company. Other addresses are handled more simply; just follow the instructions from your ISP.

People get very wound up about their domain names, but the truth is it doesn't matter that much exactly what the name is. It's nice if customers can guess it – but if they can't there are search engines to help them find you. It's nice if the name is easy to remember – that is, ordinary spellings without a lot of confusing hyphens. Ideally you want to pick a domain name that reflects your company's name, your best-known product, or something abstract around which you can build meaning. But essentially, whatever domain name you choose, once you start putting it on all your stationery, brochures, and publications, and it starts being indexed by the search engines, people will get to know it.

The name you register is the inner part of an entire address. For example, in *pelicancrossing.net* the name you would register is *pelicancrossing*. The *.net* part of that address is known as the top-level domain, and because that one does not specify a country it's known as a global top-level domain. The other best-known global top-level domains are *.org* and of course *.com*. New ones that became available for purchase in 2001 include *.biz*, *.info*, and *.web*, but they aren't in common use. The other general class of top-level domains that you might consider are the country codes, especially *.uk*. Most British companies that do not do business internationally should usually register under *.co.uk*; charities, non-profit organizations, associations, and clubs are probably better off under *.org.uk*. Nominet, the organization that administers domain names within the UK, restricts *.plc.uk* to public limited companies (and *.ltd.uk* to limited companies) registered with the name they've chosen at Companies House. It has also created *.me.uk* for individuals. Ordinary individuals and companies can join Nominet and register names that way, but usually for a small business with only one or two domain names to administer it will be simpler and more economical to register your domain name via a third-party service such as NetBenefit.

All domain names must follow the rules set down in RFC 1034. These specify that the entire name, including the top-level suffix, may be no more than sixty-three characters in length. The only allowable characters are lower-case letters, digits, and the hyphen character, which may not begin or end the string. So: *pelican-crossing* is acceptable but *-pelican&crossing* is not (fails on the leading hyphen and the middle ampersand). These rules may change somewhat, in that the attempt is being made to internationalize the domain name system so that those in non-English-speaking countries can register names that work in their own languages using their own character sets. However, internationalization will be only a veneer; there will be a translation mechanism and underneath the names will still be alpha-numeric strings punctuated only by the occasional hyphen, albeit these strings will be ones you would never register in English because they'll look like gibberish.

If the domain name you want is taken by a squatter – someone who grabs the name and wants to sell it to you for a high price – you should probably resist the temptation to pay it. The simplest and cheapest response is to think of something else and register that. If you think the owner of the domain name is passing his business off as yours, then you may be able to bring a case on that basis, as there are laws against that. If you think the owner is deliberately squatting in order to extort money from you for the domain name, you may be able to use the Uniform Dispute Resolution procedures administered by organizations such as the World Intellectual Property Organization on behalf of the Internet Corporation for Assigned

Names and Numbers (ICANN) to overturn the squatter's ownership of the name. However, it will always be cheaper and faster to register something else, and pursuing these types of cases can give you a bad rap on the Net if it looks like you are attacking an individual who has built up a legitimate site over a substantial period of time. The bigger you are, the worse the impact of this kind of action will be on your Net reputation.

Conversely, you may want to check whether the domain name you have in mind could potentially be regarded as an infringement of the trademark rights of a bigger organization with more funding for lawyers. While it is unfair for such an organization to demand that you relinquish a name just because it says so, you will find life easier if you choose a name that avoids such potential conflicts in the first place. The last thing you want is to spend years building up an Internet business only to have the domain name challenged and perhaps suspended while the dispute is resolved.

CHOOSING A WEB/EMAIL/ DOMAIN NAME HOST

Except for your own convenience in choice of payment methods, it matters not at all where your Web site is hosted. You may want to buy all these services from your ISP. Or you may not: the choice is yours. The one thing you should definitely avoid is the scenario common to many cost-conscious small businesses where you cobble together a kludge of free services like the one outlined earlier. It's simply false economy; Web, email, and domain hosting is now so cheap (under £200 a year in some cases for first-class service) that it's absurd for a business to go down that route.

The advantage of buying the whole package from one ISP that gives you good service and is reliable is that you're dealing with one company that, especially if it's a smaller company, will get to know you, your business, and your needs, and be able to offer you appropriate advice when you need it. The disadvantage is that if that company has technical troubles it will affect all parts of your online presence. If for some reason you want to change ISP at short notice, it's much easier to do so if all that company is supplying is your raw connection.

TIP Keep a list of important user names and passwords (such as the ones you need to log into your Internet connection and email, or the administrator passwords for your Windows 2000 boxes), along with CD-keys for commercial software, registration numbers for shareware, and store them in a safe place off-site. Remember to update the list whenever you add new software or change the passwords.

Domain names within *.uk* may cost as little as £3 a year, with names within *.com* starting at about £9. Typically, the company that registers your domain name will also either host or forward both Web and email. If the company hosts your Web site, that means that your Web site lives on that company's servers, and to update it you must log into their machines and upload the necessary files. If the company forwards Web traffic, that means that the Web site itself is hosted elsewhere (either on your own server or on another service). Getting Web requests to your site then becomes a two-step process in which the domain name system routes requests for your Web site to the company that registered your name and that company in turn forwards the requests to the actual Web site, wherever it actually is. The same applies to email associated with the domain. Exactly how you pick up your email, wherever it's collected, depends on your configuration. Most hosting companies that offer this type of service include a set number (usually one to five) of mailboxes with the package you buy, and give you the option to pay extra for further mailboxes. Usually you will need a mailbox per user, plus perhaps a few extras such as a single address for customer enquiries from the Web. You should also have, in line with Internet standards, a mailbox for 'postmaster' and 'webmaster' that are more or less continuously monitored by humans, so that someone wishing to report attacks apparently emanating from your domain or a defaced Web page can do so easily. In many cases, you can get email to any address at your domain forwarded to your system so you can do your own sorting.

When you're first using email, the most likely scenario is that individual users will collect it from your ISP using POP3 client software such as Outlook or Eudora. However, over time backing up can become a problem if each user winds up with his or her own email archive on a separate machine. As the volume of email and number of users grows, this will become difficult to manage. At that point, the most common solution is to install a mail gateway using the IMAP protocol that will maintain a central store of email that the users can access with a POP3 client, just the way you currently access your waiting email at your ISP now. The difference is that you are the one that manages the central store, which gives you a much better chance to ensure that proper backups are made and the archives are accessible to users as needed.

BROADBAND PRIMER

Generally speaking, when people talk about broadband they mean either high-speed cable or ADSL. These services first became available in the UK in about 1999. There are, however, other types, such as satellite down-link, fixed wireless broadband, two-way satellite, and SDSL. Over time, the choices should grow. As of the beginning of 2003, however, in most areas there is only one choice; if you have two options to choose from, you're fortunate.

ADSL, which stands for 'asymmetric digital subscriber line', is a method of using an ordinary telephone line to send data at high speeds. As noted previously, you must be within 5.5km of your nearest exchange and have a digital exchange in order to have ADSL installed. At installation, your existing BT phone line is converted and a microfilter installed. The microfilter separates the channels: data travels over the line at different, higher frequencies than voice does. The upshot is that you can make and receive phone calls over your converted line while using the Internet connection. You pay a flat fee for the ADSL connection and normal rates for the telephone calls.

Your cable Internet access is a separate connection from your cable phone or TV, and can be installed separately or on its own. Potentially, cable can be offered at speeds of up to 30mbps (megabits per second). Far greater capacity will be available for Internet access on the cable network once analog TV switches off.

Both ADSL and cable offer higher speeds for downloads (you receiving files) than uploads (you sending files), on the theory that most people and businesses are net consumers of data rather than content providers themselves, a theory fiercely resisted by Net pioneers. When you see a speed rating such as 512/128, what it means is that the download speed is 512 kilobits per second (kbps) and the upload speed is 128kbps. The difference in speed is the reason for the 'asymmetric' in ADSL. BT ran trials of SDSL ('symmetric digital subscriber line') at the end of 2002, and this service offers the same speeds, between 128kbps and 2.32mbps, for uploads and downloads. VDSL (very high bit rate DSL) can manage speeds of up to 25mbps at up to fifty metres, and is useful primarily on campuses. Easynet began offering SDSL in 2002.

There are essentially four types of ADSL on offer in the UK. The consumer service is 512K/256K with a contention ratio of 50:1 (see p. 45), and the business services are 512K/256K, 1M/256K, and 2M/256K, with a contention ratio of 20:1. These may come as a full package including all the equipment you need, or 'wires-only' connections, where you supply the ADSL modem and any router (usually sold as one box) you want to use. Most businesses will buy 'wires-only' connections. The connection to your system can be either USB or ethernet; USB is billed as easier for connecting to a single PC, but a small business is better off with ethernet, as it can be networked throughout the office. The USB version installs like a modem connection in Dial-Up Networking in Windows, and can be shared via the built-in facilities for Internet Connection Sharing (originally intended for ordinary dial-up connections so two computers could share a single phone line). A business should buy the business service, if only for its better contention ratio, rather than try to scrimp by on the home service. If you want to run your own Web and email servers, or virtual private networks (VPNs), and other inbound services, you will need to ensure the service you buy comes with a fixed IP address.

What those contention ratios refer to is the fact that the bandwidth from the exchange to your ISP is shared with other users, up to forty-nine for the consumer service and up to nineteen for the business service. As the number of subscribers in your area increases, BT undertakes to add bandwidth as necessary to ensure that the group of users fighting – contending – for a slice of that bandwidth does not exceed the numbers specified. When you're the first person in your area to subscribe to the service, you will get lightning speeds. As subscribers increase, at busy times of the day – such as late afternoon and early evening, when kids are home from school and playing online games – you will notice a significant slowdown in your line speed. This is especially true with cable because of the way that neighbourhoods share bandwidth. As broadband penetration increases, contention ratios will become more of an issue.

With the wires-only version, once your line has been converted you will need to buy (usually from your ISP, for about £10) a microfilter to plug into the phone socket. You can buy and choose any ADSL modem and router you like, rather than being required to use the one that BT supplies. Within the UK, there is a sole wholesale supplier of ADSL (and other DSLs): BT. This situation is set to change as local loop unbundling proceeds, a scheme whereby other telephone companies (telcos) are allowed to install their own equipment in BT's exchanges as part of ending BT's monopoly on telecommunications. So far, this is proceeding very slowly. This situation means that when you order ADSL it will be supplied by a combination of engineers from your ISP and from BT, and you will have to install a BT phone line if you don't already have one. If you buy the full-service package, you must specify whether you want NAT installed by BT, as BT will configure the router for you; in most cases you should specify non-NAT and do your own configuration.

In rural areas, where it's common to be too far from a BT exchange and cable doesn't run, satellite may be the only option. One-way satellite services are also asymmetric: only the downloads come from the satellite link. You must dial up to initiate connections and send email or Web page requests. However, once the connection is established and the file you want is downloading (or, in the case of live video or audio, streaming), you can disconnect and the data will continue to arrive. To use these services, you will need a satellite dish pointed at the correct satellite. Suppliers include Eutelsat Open Sky and BT.

In major urban areas, fixed wireless connections are available from Liberty Broadband (formerly Tele2), although by September 2002 only 3,000 users nationwide (out of nearly 900,000 broadband customers overall) had this type of service. Other services are springing up to offer broadband packages including a wireless, rather than wired, router, and the next few years should see many innovative possibilities.

SPECIFYING BROADBAND

People often talk about ADSL as NAT or non-NAT, but NAT is implemented in your router. NAT, which stands for 'Network Address Translation', has two functions: it helps secure your network against attacks and it helps the network as a whole make the most efficient use of the limited number of IP addresses available (although when IPv6 eventually rolls out, this should no longer be necessary as it will allow enough addresses for every electron on the planet).

Simply, NAT maps multiple machines on a network to a single IP address. For ISPs, this means simpler administration and routing. When you sign up for broadband, you're allocated a single IP address for your entire network by your ISP; the router attached to your ADSL or cable modem ensures that incoming data is sent to the correct machine. As noted in Chapter 3, the IP address ranges 10.x.x.x and 192.168.x.x are reserved for private use, and if your network is set up to automatically configure itself you will see addresses in those ranges being assigned to your machines. Broadband providers generally supply consumer and basic business service with NAT turned on and a dynamically assigned IP address for security reasons. ADSL providers also offer businesses a non-NAT service with one or more fixed IP addresses. There again is another advantage of using NAT: if you change ISP you only have to renumber the router while the rest of the network continues to function exactly as it did before.

Cable broadband is not available with a fixed (or 'static') IP address and a non-NAT version, although some of the cable companies are beginning to offer partial alternatives to give small businesses the facilities they want (knowing that otherwise business customers will desert cable in favour of ADSL). Telewest, for example, offers hosted Exchange Server at a cost of £10 per user per month on the grounds that running an email server is the primary reason why businesses want non-NAT. The company is also working on the second most commonly named such reason, a hosted VPN service that will allow customers across the country, whether or not they subscribe to Telewest's cable service, to securely access their own networks. This service rolled out in 2003.

One-way satellite connections that involve dialling out, like dial-up itself, are less of a risk because those connections are not kept permanently open. With other types of Internet connections, such as UWB (ultra wideband, a type of fixed wireless connection), you should check not only what type of security is (or is not) supplied for your Internet connection, but also what type of security is applied to the data in transit. Usually, the new fixed wireless technologies use a technique called 'frequency hopping' which means that the communications system keeps changing the radio frequencies used in transmission. An outsider seeking to eavesdrop on a connection won't know which frequency will carry the next bit of data.

The advantage of fixed IP and doing your own NAT is added flexibility: you may want to host your own email and Web servers, allow virtual private network connections for remote staff, or run an IRC server to enable inexpensive company-wide conferencing including remote users. The downside, however, is increased technical complexity: you must install a correctly configured firewall and review your security periodically. Of course, you should be doing that anyway.

There are two reasons to buy a non-NAT service. The first is the general principle that the best security is security you control. To ensure you have the least risk possible, you are better off installing a firewall that does its job correctly and whose configuration you can customize rather than relying on the all-purpose security configured by an ISP. With or without NAT, you can configure your router to do port forwarding so you can still be able to run an email server or a specific piece of, say, file-sharing or other interactive software. But you will only be able to use that piece of interactive software on a single machine in your network. As you gain experience and familiarity with the technology, you may want to run other types of interactive services that require inbound connections.

As companies become increasingly dependent on their networks and the resources they provide, it becomes more and more important for remote staff to be able to use the network as if they were onsite. The technology that makes this possible is VPN (for 'virtual private network'). VPN facilities are built into many firewalls and also into Windows 2000 and XP Professional. Essentially, a VPN uses encryption to create a secure 'tunnel' across the Internet so that outsiders can't eavesdrop on the connection or use the connection to gain unauthorized access for themselves. A remote staff member using the VPN connects to the network and is then authenticated with user name and password as usual. Once authenticated, the staff member has the same access rights as usual.

You will not be able to offer reliable inbound access via a VPN with a dynamic (that is, not fixed) IP address. However, there are some services available intended to help people with dynamic IP addresses who nonetheless want to host their own Web or other servers. Dynamic DNS services use an Internet standard (RFC 2136) to manage live updates. From the user's perspective, what happens is that the service installs a small bit of software on your computer, and whenever your IP number changes the software alerts the service, which immediately notes the change and updates its nameservers so that anyone looking for your domain is automatically routed to the new IP address.

These services do have limitations. Some cap the number of DNS queries they will accept for a single account in a given day; if you are routinely exceeding this you should probably have a more professional hosting arrangement anyway. In addition, if you plan to host a Web site on your own network using a dynamic DNS server when the broadband you have is a NAT service not intended for this purpose, you should check your ISP's terms and conditions carefully. If you are in violation of these, you could find yourself abruptly cut off if the ISP figures out what you're doing.

BROADBAND VERSUS UNMETERED DIAL-UP

Dial-up over either an ordinary telephone line or ISDN can also be networked around the office.

True flat-rate Internet access finally became available in the UK in 2000, and is available via ISPs such as AOL and Freeserve for a flat rate of around £15 per month. Unmetered dial-up shares one advantage with broadband – fixed cost. It is, however, one-tenth the speed of the slowest broadband connection, and if waiting around for Web pages and files to download causes a significant bottleneck and being instantly available to your customers via email is important to you, go for broadband.

The big advantage of broadband, besides speed, is permanent availability. A lot of people have taken 'unmetered' to mean 'unlimited', and this is definitely not the case. Heavy users – defined by many ISPs as more than 100 hours a month – of unmetered connections may find themselves cut off, warned, or surcharged. This policy is particularly aimed at those who engage in file-sharing, which can overload any network and which, unlike games, is often left unattended to run in the background. But it could equally apply to a business that keeps the connection open all the time. Some ISPs, for example, drop the connection any time it's been kept open longer than a set amount of time (usually at least a few hours), just to ensure that the connection isn't unattended, though they may let you dial immediately back. BT Openworld in particular announced usage caps on most of its services in late 2002, though not its ADSL offering.

The economics of the industry coupled with the fact that the really heavy users tend to be a relatively small percentage of customers mean that more such caps are likely to appear.

LINE SPEED, AND OTHER MYSTERIES OF BANDWIDTH

Many, many factors affect the speed with which your Internet connection works, and only some of them are under your control. The first and most obvious is the raw line speed – the speed at which your modem or broadband connection is rated. You control this by choosing your modem or service. With broadband, remember to take into account contention ratios (see glossary on p. 241).

Next is the speed with which data is transferred from the modem into the computer itself, either to be held and rendered in memory (like a Web page), or stored on your hard drive and then displayed (like email) or run (like a downloaded file). In Windows, end users can check this setting by looking at the port speed, which is to be found with the other modem 'properties'. In fact, it's worth checking because these settings often default to 9600, which was state-of-the-art in 1992. Set it to the highest available setting, and the computer will drop back to whatever speed it can manage.

For broadband, the transfer rate is limited by the speed of your USB or ethernet connection. Since even the older 10mb ethernet connection is many times faster than the fastest current broadband speed available, there's not much you can do to improve matters. USB transfers data at speeds of 12mbps to 480mbps, so even its slowest version is faster than the fastest currently available broadband connection (2mbps).

For many Internet-related activities the power and speed of the computer itself matters very little. But for browsing the Web this does make a big difference. Rendering Web pages takes processing power, and displaying them involves holding their data in memory, demands which are multiplied when the pages use fancy features like Java applets or Flash animations. The upshot is that someone who makes heavy use of the Web will notice a substantial difference between a fast PC with a lot of memory and a slow one with minimal RAM; the time spent waiting for pages to download can be a real bottleneck.

The number of people using the connection is also an important factor, since they all must share a finite resource.

There are some things you can do to manage the load on the connection. The most obvious is to start or schedule downloads of extremely large files – such as Windows service packs, for example – to run at night, when no one else needs the connection. Also, you can take advantage of the fact that your internal computers are networked – the connection to the Internet is almost always going to be many times slower than internal LAN connections. Web proxy software (such functions are, for example, built into mail servers like VPOP3 and Mailgate) can store Web pages so that a given page is retrieved only once from the ISP but then served to many users. Similarly, if you're going to distribute the same file (such as a service pack) to many users on the network, it's significantly faster to download it once to an internal server and have users retrieve or install it from there rather than have each user download it separately.

BANDWIDTH MANAGEMENT

It's very easy for users blessed with broadband to think of the Internet connection as 'free'. It's important to stress – via an acceptable use policy (see below) – that in fact it's an expensive resource that needs to be shared. If a lot of users indulge in bandwidth-hogging programs such as file-sharing (Gnutella and others), to say nothing of online games, they can easily consume all the available connection.

The temptation may be to set up an internal server with music and other material that users frequently download, since retrieval is always faster across the internal network. As noted elsewhere, however (see Chapter 7 on security), doing this can expose you to prosecution for copyright violations if a disaffected staff member decides to make trouble for you. You do not want to be the test case for a panicked entertainment industry anxious to make an example of someone.

In most cases, users who have these problems explained to them will stop using the programs causing the trouble. There are a couple of technological solutions in case there are some who don't. One is configuring your firewall (see Chapter 7) to block the ports used by the programs in question. As noted elsewhere (see Chapter 3) each program has a particular port that it uses and software manufacturers will typically tell you what they are. In the days when Napster, which had a central server, was the biggest file-sharing service this worked admirably well. Newer file-sharing services, however, have been designed with routing around firewalls in mind, and so they are more difficult to block in this way.

The second technological solution is known as packet-shaping. Installed as a software package, a packet-shaper allows you to analyse Internet traffic patterns and control them as you wish. You can, for example, cap the amount of bandwidth available to a specific user for a particular application and vary it by the time of day. (You can also, if you like, block an application or user altogether.) The ability to analyse patterns also lets you identify problem users and deal with them in the way that is appropriate in your company's culture.

EMAIL MANAGEMENT

In general, it's better to avoid the situation where employees use personal email addresses or free Web accounts to conduct company business. There are several reasons for this. First of all, if the staff member leaves the company – or even is off sick for a few days – email continues to go to the employee instead of feeding into the company's email system where it can be dealt with by someone else. Autoresponders can send back a notification that the staff member is missing; autoforwarding can send the message on to a replacement contact.

The free Web-based email services typically have limitations anyway that make them unsuitable for commercial applications. With email, these often take the form of storage limitations; Hotmail, for example, has a 2Mb limit, and if you exceed this (easily done if people are in the habit of sending you attachments) some of your mail may be deleted. Additionally, as email becomes an increasingly important tool of communication, you will find it vital to retain control of your email archives so they can be backed up and retained for future reference. A system where everyone has an individual email account on a different service using different software will be difficult to archive.

Ideally, therefore, all staff who have their own email at their desks will have company addresses bearing your own domain name. If you use a third-party service that hosts your domain and Web site and forwards email, typically you'll have several email addresses available as standard with the account and the option to pay for more or you'll be able to accept email to any address at your domain and route it appropriately yourself.

If you are still using dial-up or ISDN connections to collect email, there's an extra advantage in that the email server can control how often users dial up to collect email. If each person is doing this individually, the costs can mount up. With a server doing the rounds on a schedule, those costs are controlled. Because mail servers tend to be complicated to configure and maintain, however, there is a sort of 'halfway house' solution that many small businesses use: what's known as a 'mail transfer agent'. This type of software handles all the complexities of collecting email, often from multiple accounts, and directing it to the correct mailboxes within an organization. You might, for example, have three technical support staff who need to receive copies of all customer queries but want to use a single email address for support. A mail transfer agent (or a full-blown mail server) can do that sort of thing easily. It can also collect and send email on a schedule, limiting telephone costs if you're on dial-up. The one drawback is that a mail transfer agent does not store archives of the email it collects; these are stored in the client email software used by your staff. Backups are accordingly more complicated to manage.

However, mail transfer agents may be quite inexpensive – software such as VPOP3 starts at £50 for five users (£250 for twenty-five users), and offers add-ons such as fax server and virus protection (see Chapter 7). It also has facilities for creating junk email-killing rules. Mailgate, which starts at around £100 for five users, provides similar functionality but also supports internal email; both allow you to restrict downloading very large email messages until after hours. Both run only on Windows and work with either dial-up or broadband. For Linux, you are more likely to use one of the many mail servers available. Communigate runs on more than thirty platforms.

Further up the scale are more fully featured groupware products such as Lotus Notes (now owned by IBM) and Microsoft Exchange Server (or Small Business Server, which incorporates Exchange Server and a number of other applications besides). Both of these are complex pieces of software that manage a great deal more than email, such as shared scheduling and contact management. Users must use Microsoft Outlook to access Exchange Server. All these server packages, as well as any of the many Linux mailservers, tend to need a substantially higher level of expertise to configure, although all are probably now much cheaper than you might expect, just as raw software. However, the chances are you will need to hire technical help to manage any of these complex server packages, and you will need to add that cost as well as that of the hardware needed to run it and support proper backups to the raw cost of the software.

BLOCKING/CONTENT-FILTERING SOFTWARE

For the reasons noted in the section on pornography and copyright violations on pp. 169–71, many businesses worry about what their staff may access online and subsequently store on the company's machines. This is a legitimate worry.

Filtering is built into some firewalls and routers , but an entire class of software exists that's intended to block certain types of content. Much of this software is aimed as much at families panicked about what their children will see online as it is at businesses seeking to control staff use of the Internet connection. If you run your business at home, blocking material for your children may also be an issue – but in addition it is greatly preferable for security reasons to have a separate computer for children to play on so they do not use the one on which you run your business.

The most common concern is that staff may waste what ought to be productive time looking at material online which has nothing to do with the business's needs (whether or not it's pornographic or even illegal). People can get through an awful lot of time watching sports scores update or indulging in electronic shopping, and they look just as if they are working. There is the added concern of what kinds of material may get downloaded and stored on company servers or sent out via email.

Filtering software essentially blocks access to a list of known Web sites maintained in an internal database. Most such software will also let administrators add individual sites, so blocking popular ecommerce sites would be a simple matter. Many such programs also include functions to block chat rooms and prevent the disclosure of specific bits of information (usually intended to keep children from handing out personal addresses and telephone numbers).

The first consideration in choosing blocking software is how your business actually uses the Net. You will need to review, where possible, exactly what is being blocked and whether that impedes legitimate staff use of the Net. Some filtering software blocks leading search engines by default. Therefore, you should thoroughly test the software and ensure that it works on your system and meets your needs. Like anti-virus software, blocking software requires regular updates to ensure that it keeps up with the times. The Web is still growing explosively, and sites come and go all the time: you are aiming at a moving target. Since most of these software packages offer free trials, it's worth experimenting before making a final decision.

However, blocking software by itself may be too limited for what you actually need. We look in Chapter 6 at the risks of downloading files and opening emailed attachments. For this reason, packages like

McAfee or Norton both include content filtering as part of a wider privacy and security package with anti-virus protection. You should also ensure that staff understand there are some kinds of changes they should not make to the system. This is again an area where running a business version of Windows will help, as rights such as installing software can be reserved for the administrator. It's equally important that staff learn not to abuse the Net themselves by, for example, sending out unwanted bulk email.

One key decision you will have to make when choosing filtering software is whether you want it to be explicit that a site is being blocked and how. Some of these software packages display a blank page if a user attempts to go to a blocked site. Others put up pages of their own announcing that the site has been blocked. The blank page can be a problem: if users don't know a site is being deliberately blocked they can get very frustrated as they continue to try to access it. On the other hand, users may resent being told their access is blocked and some may take it as a challenge. In general, if you're going to use blocking software you should explain that this is being done and why.

Filtering software, as comforting an idea as it sounds at first, is a controversial and imperfect solution. The companies that develop it, generally US-based, can be secretive about exactly what they block and why. Most do not let users review their databases of blocked sites, although several Web sites exist to reverse-engineer and analyse these. The more purely practical problem for businesses is that the software may block access to sites staff need to access in the course of work. A user-configurable service known as ICRAfilter (for Internet Content Ratings Association) is supposed to solve this problem by making the lists transparent and user-configurable; it is what's behind the Content Advisor slider bar in Microsoft Internet Explorer.

The deeper problem with this type of software is that despite the manufacturers' claims it is not a panacea. No software is perfect. You will have to examine your own situation to determine whether it's right for you based on, among other things, what the logs show users have been doing on company time with company bandwidth.

PROXY SERVERS

A proxy server sits between your machine and the Internet and stores copies of Web pages you have accessed ('caches' in computer parlance). The reason is to speed up browsing: the next time you go to a page you've already visited, instead of fetching the page from the distant Web server you're given the copy in the cache instead. Local network speeds are always faster.

There are some types of pages for which this technique is not suited, such as constantly updating scores from sporting events or news pages that are constantly having new headlines added to them. There are also some Web sites that want caching turned off because their advertising rates depend on the number of visitors they get and caching makes that number smaller. But for much of the Web this is a valuable technique for cutting down on traffic, and because of this all ISPs have proxy servers in place. By doing so, they can get away with buying less bandwidth to their upstream Internet supplier, cutting their costs while at the same time giving customers faster service than would be possible otherwise.

At least, that's the theory. Many things can go wrong with proxy servers, even the ones that belong to ISPs. Dynamically refreshing pages can get erroneously cached. The cache settings can be wrong so that it actually takes longer for the cache to determine whether it has a copy of a particular page than it takes to get the page in the first place. Nonetheless, it's an important technique, and you will find that some firewalls come with proxy servers built in.

One final use of proxy servers is the phenomenon of public proxy servers on the Web. These effectively make your browsing anonymous so that you can visit particular types of sites without their being able to identify your ISP, email address, or the other details your system makes available to Web sites that look for them. Public proxy servers can be useful in situations where you need access to a Web site that blocks you based on your geographical location (which it determines from the IP address you present) or if for some reason you want to disguise the fact that you're visiting a particular site from the site itself. Some public proxy servers are designed to help users bypass national censorship regimes.

ISP CONTRACTS

The small business that signs its employees up with an ordinary ISP or with a commercial online service as domestic users is basically going to be stuck with that company's standard terms of service. If, however, you are signing up as a business customer with Web hosting and other services, you should make sure that a number of important points are clarified in your service agreement. Small businesses should be aware that the free Web space that comes with standard domestic ISP or online service accounts is not intended for commercial use, and that many ISPs do not allow you to register your own domain and use Web forwarding with their domestic pages – the free Web space is provided in part because it advertises the ISP when you hand out the URL.

If an ISP is hosting your Web site and you have a formal contract beyond the standard terms and conditions, the contract needs to specify who owns the intellectual property rights in the material on that site, who is responsible for updates, and how these will be carried out. Some services may allow you to upload new versions yourself; others may require you to send them the material, which they will make available within a specified period of time. If the service writes custom scripts or designs, ensure that you will be allowed to take these with you if you change ISPs. A similar caveat applies to registering a domain name: check in advance that you will be able to take the domain name with you if you change ISPs and how much it will cost.

You should always ensure that you have a full offline copy (and backups) of all the material on your Web site in case the ISP goes down unexpectedly: even the best ISP can be hit by a hurricane, and if your site goes down for an extended period, you may need to reconstruct the Web site elsewhere on another service so that your business can proceed uninterrupted. This is especially important if an outside supplier designed your Web site but is no longer involved: recommissioning it could be a lengthy and time-consuming process.

Outages and service levels should also be covered in the contract. Make sure you understand how much traffic is covered at what price, what level of service the ISP is guaranteeing, and what happens in case of a prolonged outage and whether you will be entitled to any compensation for loss of business.

ACCEPTABLE USE POLICIES

While you only have a few users, it's easy to communicate to them what they are and are not allowed to do with company email and Internet access. However, as your network and company grow, you may find it useful to think about and write an acceptable use policy that lays out those rules.

Policies, like system backups, are usually put in place because there's been a crisis. But it isn't strictly speaking necessary to wait for the crisis, and in the case of email, where things can go badly wrong in a few keystrokes, it's a good idea to implement an acceptable use policy before the crisis happens.

Acceptable use policies have their origins in the nature of the Internet as an academic and research network. In those days, such a policy's primary purpose was to make it plain that the public network was not to be used for commercial traffic. Then came 1993, and the conversion of the Internet into a commercial medium. Now, such policies specify what types of user behaviour are acceptable as well as what types of traffic may be sent out, and act to protect the organizations providing those users with email services.

Email raises a number of significant issues for a company, only some of which were raised by older methods of communication such as written letters, faxes, and telephone calls. Common issues across all these forms of communication are whether and under what circumstances company resources may be used for private purposes and what kind of behaviour is acceptable from someone who's representing the company. But email's unique characteristics – its infinite and immediate copyability, its storage requirements, and the security problems it poses – make it a special challenge. Each of these issues needs to be considered when drafting an acceptable use policy for email. In addition, employees should be warned against mass-forwarding virus hoaxes, chain get-rich-quick emails, and other Net abuses, as these can make the company look bad.

TIP Never buy version 1.0 of anything. Don't buy a new operating system until the first service pack has been released. And don't be the first person to install the service pack.

Probably the most important issue for any company is security. All the reasons why employees need to be reminded not to give out their passwords and to choose good ones are increased when a company has email. The problem is not just that someone might gain access to a particular user's email directory and be able to read the person's stored email; it's that someone gaining access to a user's email account may be able to impersonate that user and wreak havoc for both that individual and for the organization he or she represents. There are many legitimate circumstances under which someone might want to give someone else access to their email – if they're on vacation, for example, or out of the office doing other work. However, in most cases a better system for handling this sort of problem is to install autoforwarding or software that allows shared access to some parts of a user's email directory.

Privacy is probably the most contentious issue that needs to be covered in an acceptable use policy, which should spell out clearly the conditions under which employee email will be opened, read, backed up, stored, or disclosed to a third party. If, for example, your organization's view is that email should only be used for company business, and you regard all email as company property, this needs to be clearly stated. Many employees, lacking information to the contrary, assume that their email is private (even more private than postal mail), and divergent assumptions in this area can lead to nasty disputes, some of which have even landed in court. Even if company policy is to regard personal email as private, a system administrator is pretty much always going to be able to access users' private email, and any system that's properly backed up (which should be all systems) is by default going to retain copies of each user's email. In a legal case, these archives can be impounded by law enforcement. All of this needs to be explained to users, as there have been many reports of situations where users have assumed an embarrassing message has been deleted, only to find out weeks later that copies still exist on the backups. You should also specify how long you will store email.

The existence of forgotten copies raises another point: although email is a wonderful convenience and is an ideal communications tool, it also adds risk. Information that would have been difficult to remove from the premises when it was stored in the form of paper files can now be transmitted externally in seconds once it's available in electronic form, and it is very easy to make mistakes about the identity of the recipients. That staple of sitcoms, the mass-distributed embarrassing email, has been played out for real plenty of times, as in 1995 when Louis Rossetto, the chief of the ultra-savvy *Wired* magazine, found that one of his memos was leaked on the Net, from where it went to the front page of the *Wall Street Journal* just before the company's second failed IPO (Initial Public Offering). Employees, therefore, need to be reminded when a particular message is confidential, need to be trained in managing address books and group aliases, and need to understand the consequences of mistakes. One of the nastier, privacy-invading characteristics of the W32.Bugbear email virus circulating in late 2002 was its habit of seizing a piece of genuine email and sending it out to people randomly chosen from the infected user's address book.

Because email is a public and social medium as much as it is a private and business one, another area that needs to be considered is user behaviour by email. Any acceptable use policy should stress that users sending out messages bearing the company name are likely to be construed as representing the company. One option is to add a disclaimer to the message's standard signature: it is very common to see disclaimers reminding readers that the opinions given are those of the individual, not of the company. However, these often pass unread, and overly formal disclaimers can make a company look silly.

One solution to this sort of problem may be to encourage users to direct personal email to Web-accessible personal accounts with free services such as Hotmail or Yahoo!. While that isn't a panacea – company policy may be strict about employees transacting private business on company time – it does mean that users will have some privacy for their personal messages and also will not be identified as company representatives. However, you should make it plain that company email should be sent from a company address, for the reasons already noted.

But some education and/or training is also needed. Users should be informed of and know where to find out about common email hoaxes such as the 'virus' messages 'Good Times' and its many other incarnations and taught to avoid mass-forwarding email messages that claim they will attract payments to charity, or are petitions to sign. Users should also be taught not to circulate those messages further, however beneficent their intentions. Any policy you have also needs to make clear what kinds of commercial messages may be sent and to whom: if you want your company to have the good will of the Net (and continued service from your ISP), you should ensure that your users do not send out spam. No one is suggesting that email shouldn't be used for commercial purposes any more, but users need to understand that it's not appropriate to blanket the world with chain letters or emailed advertisements, no matter how many they themselves get. (What to do about junk email is another topic that can be usefully covered in an acceptable use policy, as users need to be warned that replying to junk email or following the 'remove' instructions may wind up verifying their address and getting them more junk. Hopefully you will be able to apply filters to whatever email service you use to limit the amount of junk users actually see.)

Any acceptable use policy should also consider the problem of harassment, whether inbound, outbound, or internal within the company. Users should know whom to contact if they need help in handling persistently abusive messages, and they should understand what constitutes harassment, and what the company's policy regarding abusers is.

An ancillary problem is that of files either sent via email as attachments or downloaded directly from the Internet. An acceptable use policy should remind users that in many cases it's more economical and efficient to send plain text (or, sometimes, to make such files available via the Web or FTP) than to attach word-processed documents, particularly if they're going out to large numbers of people. However, using these types of files may be inescapable in situations where remote co-workers are collaborating on a complex document that needs revision tracking. Ensuring that your company is not embarrassed by spreading viruses to other people is a major reason for installing anti-virus software and keeping it up to date (see Chapter 7).

An acceptable use policy should make it clear if there are types of files considered unsuitable (or even illegal) for storage on company computers. However, allowance has to be made for innocence: someone who has, say, a pornographic file in their email directory may not necessarily know what the file is if it's been sent, unsolicited, via email and it's been left undecoded. Several years ago, for example, a hoax message was sent out to several million users worldwide offering child pornography for sale and claiming that the message was sent to each of those users because their names had appeared on lists suggesting they were interested in that kind of thing. There was no list; there was no child pornography for sale as advertised; and the users who received the message were in no way to blame. Administrators should exercise extreme caution before jumping to conclusions in such a case. Nonetheless, the company has to be protected, and it should be made plain to users what constitutes illegal or unacceptable material and what the consequences will be of storing it or downloading it onto company machines.

Obviously no policy can cover all eventualities and, equally, any policy that's drafted needs to be fair, not excessively legalistic. That's not an easy balance, particularly when you're trying to avoid damaging the trust that exists between employers and employees: the point is not to create hostility. Nonetheless, because the consequences of the misuse of email can be severe, drafting an acceptable use policy can be an important part of working out what function email communication serves and training users, many of whom may be inexperienced, to handle it responsibly.

Finally, whatever acceptable use policy you decide upon must be seen to be enforced fairly across the company. Even if it means calling in the police on a fellow board member, it's important not to have one rule for secretaries and another for managers. Especially when it comes to material that is downright illegal and could put the entire company at risk.

6 Ebusiness

The Internet is not just the Web, and a Web site is not all you need to think about when you think about doing business online. The most important thing to remember is that adding an online dimension to your business may require some fundamental changes. Adding a Web site is not about writing code. It's about meeting the high expectations of Net users in terms of customer service and response times. To succeed on the Net you must adapt to the community standards of Net culture, just as you follow conventions in the physical world.

Because choosing a company to host your Web site is closely related to choosing an ISP and hosting a domain name, this topic is rolled into those, which were covered in Chapter 5.

WEB SITES: RETHINKING YOUR BUSINESS

Here's a strange anomaly. When you commission a brochure to advertise your business, you put a lot of thought into its design and you hire professional designers (if you don't already have them on staff) and printers and pick the papers and colours carefully. You know that the brochure is probably the front door to your business for many people. You also don't hand your accounts over to a friend with a copy of the personal finance software Quicken or do your own legal work based on a bit of research on a few Web sites. Even so: the most common mistake that many small businesses make, when faced with the desire to have a Web site, is to hand it over to the secretary's dentist's fourteen-year-old nephew, or the guy who edits the newsletter but knows nothing about the Web. Although the consequences of making a mistake in Web design may not be seen as serious, since you can start again without disrupting your daily business activities, why waste the time and effort and your hard-won reputation? It can take years to build up a good reputation on the Web; but only a few minutes to create a bad one.

Again, the industry is partly to blame for people's mistaken belief that a Web site ought to be easy. Web-page-editing software such as Front Page, online free 'communities' such as Geocities, and even ordinary office products like Microsoft Word all make it sound as though creating a Web page doesn't involve learning anything, and that all you have to do is type it in and upload it.

To some extent that's actually true. If you're a consumer at home who wants to put up the first pictures of the grandchild walking, those kinds of products will make it reasonably easy for you. More importantly, if you choose to ignore everything a decade of Web experience (and before that, decades of work with typography and graphic design) has taught people about what constitutes good design, it doesn't matter. You can underline your text (so people can't tell which bits are links and which are not, making navigation confusing), use unreadable colours, throw in blinking menu items and annoying noises, and it costs you nothing.

It's even true in a business sense if you get the right designer. There are companies out there who will create a Web site for you such that all you have to do to add content is type it into the forms they provide and hit a button. That ease of use and convenience, however, will come at a substantial price. It is not built into the average off-the-shelf shrink-wrapped box of Web editing software such as Dreamweaver or Front Page.

TIP Use standard, freely available file formats for any information you put on your Web site for public access. For ordinary documents, that might mean using plain text, HTML or its XML variants, or Adobe Acrobat PDFs; do NOT use Microsoft Word, PowerPoint, etc., unless there is a really powerful reason to do so.

If you are a business trying to use the Web to disseminate information about what you do or add a sales channel to your existing ones, you cannot afford to look like an amateur. For increasing numbers of people, your Web site is the first and possibly only contact they have with your organization. You should devote the same professionalism, care, and attention to creating it that you would put into creating any other kind of published material that bears your company's name and logo or into hiring the receptionist who greets prospective customers as they walk in the door or is the first contact for clients over the phone.

Most people who take the secretary's-dentist's-nephew route eventually realize that they need to think more professionally, either because customers complain or because they themselves gain Web experience and increasingly dislike what they have. This is when Web designers get called in: to do the second-generation Web site.

It's at this point that the second most common mistake gets made: the company often really doesn't know what it wants the Web site for.

You don't have to have a complete plan for every detail. But you do need to have some idea of what you want the Web site to do for your business. For example: do you want to increase your visibility in the marketplace? Or add a sales channel that's more convenient for customers? Give customers more information on products and technical support, reducing the burden on staff? Bring in new customers you can't reach now? All of these are perfectly reasonable goals. But each one may raise different questions about your existing business processes. A Web site is part of your business, and needs to be thought of that way.

Let's say that the biggest reason you want a Web site is to make it easier for customers to order the goods you sell. Obviously you hope that will ultimately mean more orders. But how are you going to fulfil those orders? Who is going to be responsible for answering email from customers? Web users expect speedy answers, and they expect them to come via the medium they use – that is, the Internet. They are very unlikely to welcome phone calls unless they're absolutely necessary, and printing out the email and placing it in an in-basket, letting it work its way to the top, and then answering by post will be completely unacceptable. (Not that it doesn't happen; but when it does you know the company has no idea what it's doing online.) Web users certainly don't want to be told that they have to make phone calls themselves to ask questions or follow up on missing orders.

In other words, you need to think through the consequences for your business if you get what you want from your Web site. If you already have a mail-order operation, integrating the additional Web sales channel won't be that difficult, since you already have facilities and staff for sending out orders and tracking their status. But you will find that postal, physical world, and even telephone customers are a lot more forgiving than those who come in via the Web. Web users expect immediate response and excellent customer service.

CHOOSING AND CONTRACTING WEB DESIGNERS

References. In choosing a Web designer, you have the easiest possible task in checking references: look at the sites that person has already designed. Are they attractive? Are they functional? Do they conform to the conventions of good Web design (see below)? Pick a reference site or two that belong to businesses not too different from yours and try setting yourself (or a moderately experienced Web user within your company) a few tasks you might like your Web site to enable someone to do – find out basic information about the company and its services or products, for example. Are they difficult to carry out? Is the site confusing to navigate? Is it slow and frustrating to load? If any of those things is true, find a different designer.

In addition, when you meet the designer, apply the same criteria you would apply to choosing a consultant (see pp. 211–14). The designer should not be turned on by a particular technology – Java, XML, Perl, .NET, whatever – but be interested in helping you solve a business problem. A Web site is a means to an end, and the designer's job is to help you implement that end. A good designer should not just be telling you what fancy features he can program, but should be asking you questions like the ones in the last section: what do you want the Web site to do for your business, and how do you plan to integrate it with the rest of what you do?

Ultimately, choosing a Web designer is much the same process as choosing a consultant or commissioning bespoke software (both covered in Chapter 10). The one thing that makes it far easier than either is, again, the ease of assessing their earlier work to see if they have the skills you need.

STATIC VERSUS DATABASE-DRIVEN WEB SITES

Chances are, your first Web site will be static – that is, the pages you put up will not change unless you write a new version and upload the changed pages. That's fine as long as the amount of information you want to make available is relatively small. But as time goes on and your Web site becomes more elaborate there will come a time when it becomes too difficult to update all the pages you have, or when the pages become too cluttered for visitors to your site to be able to find what they want easily. At that point, a Web developer may well tell you it's time to move to a database-driven Web site.

Say, for example, you have a Web site that lists all the current events your organization is running across the country every month. As long as you're talking about ten or twelve events nationwide, a static Web page is perfectly adequate. But supposing you're talking about hundreds of events every week? For users, it would be simpler to be able to pick the county they live in and get back a tailored list of nearby events in, say, December, rather than a gigantic single list. A database-driven site will let you give users that kind of personalized service. In addition, a well-designed database-driven site makes it much easier for you to add information: you add a database record instead of updating an entire Web page, with all the risks of error that involves.

Most of the major content sites you may be familiar with such as the BBC or the *Daily Telegraph* are database-driven sites; the items in the database may be a listing for a specific TV programme or a single newspaper article. Every time you click on an article heading on either of those sites, the page you ask for is generated dynamically – while you wait. On the BBC site, that process includes searching the archives for related content. The list of related stories you see alongside the article you requested is the results of that search.

The downside of a database-driven site is, of course, the expense, which may be considerable since typically the developer must create scripts and programs that meet your specific needs.

MARKETING YOUR WEB SITE

It is rare that you'll want to market your Web site by itself without making it part of the rest of your company's marketing efforts. However, you do want to advertise the site in such a way that Web users will find it. That begins, as noted in the last chapter, with picking a domain name that's relevant to your business and memorable. But it does not end when you officially launch your newly designed Web site.

The first and most important thing is to get your Web site indexed by the search engines so that users can find it, whether or not they're already familiar with your business. The way you do this is to go to the individual search engine sites and fill out the forms for adding links to their databases. It can take up to two months for some of them to index you, as some of them rate a page's value in terms of how many other sites link to it. You can speed up this process by paying the search engine to index it sooner, if you want to allocate your budget that way. For existing customers, you should include your Web address on all stationery and marketing materials you send out.

TIP When you design your Web site, bear in mind that it will be accessed by many types of people from anywhere in the world: investors, customers, suppliers, press, prospective staff, the merely curious. You do not have to cater to all these groups, but you must be aware that any of them can read the entire site.

Other strategies that have worked well include offering users discounts for recommending friends or becoming associates who sell merchandise via special links to your site. You may be able to swap banner ads with companies offering complementary services. Finally, if you sell information or software, you may be able to draw a lot of traffic to your site by offering free samples in the form of downloads, abstracts, or even full copies. Although many people worry that making material available for free on the Net will cost them sales, in general the reverse has proved true.

WHAT WEB USERS EXPECT

The Web in many ways has been like the early days of desktop publishing, when people put umpteen fonts in every newsletter just because they could. Yes, you can make Flash animations that fill your front page. Yes, you can make text blink. Yes, you can make your Web page green on yellow. Please don't do any of these things.

A Web site is like software, in that by the time you have designed and coded it you are too familiar with it to be able to judge whether it makes sense to an outsider (the same is of course also true of books, movies, and other intellectual endeavours). A Web site is also, of course, like software in that it is made up of program code that may contain errors.

Therefore, you should do what software developers do and test your Web site for usability, clarity, and technical robustness. Do not let the designer snow you with demonstrations that look great because the site is being displayed on a huge monitor over a very fast connection (or loaded even faster from a hard drive) by a demonstrator who is intimately familiar with the site. Conduct your own tests with a technically inept user (or users), a dial-up connection over a 56K modem, and a screen no larger than 15 inches. If it is still fast under those conditions, fine. More commonly, you will discover that the fast, easy site you saw is now transformed into a slow, clunky, confusing experience that needs to be revamped before being opened to the public. Also remember to look at the site in several browsers –

the designer is not supposed to dictate what software or hardware a customer uses to look at a Web site.

Designers often forget to test a site beyond the version of Internet Explorer they have installed, but it should be tested on a variety of platforms. The complete list would ideally be the current versions of Internet Explorer (5 to 6), Mozilla, Netscape (4, 6, and 7), the Linux browser Konqueror, Opera, WebTV, and WinCE/Pocket PC. Also take a look at the site on a Mac. If you don't, your customers will. In some situations, you may also want to request that the site be tested under WAP, the standard for mobile phone Web access.

The commodity in shortest supply on the Web is patience. This is still true even with broadband increasing the speed of people's connections by an order of magnitude. In fact, if anything, the higher speeds are making people even more impatient. Your front page, therefore, should load quickly, contain the most important things someone is likely to be looking for. Overall, your site should have a clean, readable design that conforms with not only the formal standards defined by the World Wide Web Consortium, which oversees the development of the Web, but the informal ones that have grown up through community use. As an example of the latter, consider that in most browsers the standard way of indicating that a bit of text is a hotlink to further information is to underline it. That's not true of every site you'll visit; there are plenty of Web sites that are designed not to use those underlines but to show the text in a different colour or even font. However, it's true that all browsers do this much of the time. Therefore, someone who is experienced and designing a Web site with usability in mind will not underline text just for emphasis: it confuses the user as to which text is linked and which is not. A Web site that breaks this unwritten rule looks amateurish and immediately sends a message to users that the company behind the Web site has no idea how to do business online.

Similarly, if you have a navigation menu with a series of items, it ought to go without saying that having those items blink makes it impossible for a user to spot which one to click on to get to a particular part of the Web site. (In fact, in general the blink tag is considered a pretty duff idea.) Sadly, however, it isn't always obvious. Other common conventions you'll run across include being able to click on the logo at the top left corner and have it take you to the site's home page – things you may never notice until they don't work.

These basic mistakes are not generally made by professional designers (and if yours makes them get someone else). The same cannot be said of Flash-animated front pages, however, which seem to be beloved by many large and some small European businesses. Newer versions of Flash do make much more economical graphics and so they are not quite the bane of the Web user's existence that they used to be. However, it is a major error to assume that everyone either has or wants the necessary plug-in to display them. You should not have a front page that has a Flash animation and nothing else. You should always have navigation buttons or menus that can be used by people who do not have Flash. Doing otherwise is like requiring people coming into your shop to watch a video at the front door with the door handle only accessible after it's completed. The classic ecommerce site front page is that of Amazon.com or eBay. Both have the most important item – the search button – at the top, are full of information about new goods for sale, are personalized and yet load very, very quickly.

TIP Do not base your assessment of the speed and usability of your new Web site on the designer's demonstration. Get the least technically competent person in your organization – or recruit a friend and relative – and give them some routine tasks to complete using your Web site over a dial-up connection on an ordinary PC with a screen no larger than 15 inches (CRT). If your Web site is intended to sell goods, get the person to put through a purchase; if it's intended to offer information about your company, ask the user to find the basic facts you want customers to be able to retrieve. Watch them try to complete the tasks. How frustrated do they get? How slow is the site to load? Do the navigational aids actually help them find their way through the site?

It adds to the difficulty of designing a good site that the Web is constantly changing, both technically and stylistically. Technically, the early 2000s are seeing the Web change from a rather static system (HTML) to a more interactive, dynamic one. In the old Web, HTML (HyperText Markup Language) is used to create Web pages. Designers use HTML tags to code portions of text, images, audio and video clips; the tags tell Web browsers how to display the content. XML (eXtended HTML) takes the concept further, allowing industry sectors to create their own sets of tags so that data can be exchanged between disparate applications. Microsoft Office 11 (the version after Office XP) saves files in XML, and the format is gradually making inroads into mainstream computing as well as the Web.

WHAT ONLINE CUSTOMERS EXPECT: DO'S AND DON'TS

One reason so many small business Web sites are ineffective is that often they are commissioned by people who use the Web very little themselves, and don't understand the Web audience's expectations.

One such expectation is that the goods just ordered will be delivered within a day or two. This is not like mail order, where people may be willing to wait as long as a month for their orders to be fulfilled. If that kind of delay is built into your ordering system, then you must tell customers about it while they still have time to back out of the order. They may still go elsewhere, but they will do so with much less frustration and anger towards your company and are more likely to consider coming back another time. If you were a customer of an outfit that made you wait a month for your goods, would you be anything but frustrated? Would you return, or would you look for a better retailer? One thing about the Web is that it's just as easy to buy from your competitor as it is to buy from you. That is, assuming the competitor understands how to run a Web site.

What follows is taken from real-life examples.

DON'Ts

1 Web users expect that if you need to correspond with them you will do so by email. Do not, for example, reply by post 'because the person who does the email is away for two weeks'.

2 Web users expect that if you say an item has been shipped it will be with them in a day or two. Do not fail to specify if the item is being shipped from somewhere such as, say, Singapore, from where shipping will clearly take much longer.

3 Do not wait until after the order is complete to tell the customer that shipping may take up to twenty-eight days.

4 Do not send customers email in HTML-encoded format only. If you do, you will disenfranchise some of your customers from using your service.

5 Do not penalize your customers for errors such as mistakes in product codes, particularly on expensive items. That may be a reasonable policy with telesales, where the customer has the opportunity to check with a live human that the right thing is being ordered, but on the Web subtle errors of design can make accurate ordering difficult. Operate a fair returns policy.

6 Do not bill consumers' credit cards for goods until they ship.

7 Do not pester customers with follow-up marketing email unless they opt in to receive such offers. Any marketing email you do send should include instructions on how to opt out of receiving any further mailings.

DO's

1 Deliver quickly, or if you can't at least supply quickly an estimated time of arrival and update the information if circumstances change (you should give the Web users the choice of email or Web-based tracking, if you can).

2 Give clear instructions on whom to contact and how (email, phone, fax) in case of a problem.

3 Make the company's main address and phone number easy to find on the Web site.

4 Answer email promptly and relevantly. If you can't answer quickly, put in an autoresponder to let customers know their email has been successfully received, and include an estimate of how long they can expect to wait before they get their answer. Then send the answer by that deadline and make sure it is a relevant response to whatever their problem is. It is extremely frustrating to write a detailed explanation of a problem and get back a canned response that asks you questions you've already answered in your original email.

5 Include on the Web site a clear statement customers can read *before* buying that lays out your returns policy, what support they can expect from you, what the shipping charges and approximate expected arrival times are, and any other terms and conditions or extra charges relevant to sales.

6 If your site is supposed to apply a membership discount, see that it actually does apply the discount when the transaction goes through. If the system is set up to reject invalid discount codes, make sure the user is notified that the discount does not apply.

7 Post copies of your policies to cover privacy (what you will do with customer data, if applicable), copyright (which parts of your site you regard as protected and what limits you wish to impose on their reuse by others), and terms and conditions for sales (if applicable). The usual standard is to include a fine-print menu bar at the bottom of each page that links to these policies, along with links to basic information about the company.

ACCESSIBILITY

In the physical world, we put ramps at the front of public buildings and at intersections and add sound to traffic lights for blind pedestrians. In the online world, catering to those with visual impairments – an increasingly large percentage of users as the population ages – is equally important. It is important not to block off a large portion of your potential clientele by making your site inaccessible.

Doing so does not require massive effort on the Web designer's part, mainly because today's computers can meet the Web halfway. The accessibility options in Windows make it possible to increase the size of fonts and make keys easier to manage for shaky hands. In addition, most Web browsers let the user turn off the designer's choices and substitute the user's own, a valuable function if what you need is a large, readable font (many, presumably young, designers opt for font sizes that are extremely small on many screens). Finally, screen access software can actually read the screen in synthesized speech to blind users, enabling them to understand and operate the Web site without needing someone to guide them.

TIP Test your new Web site with more than one browser – 90 per cent of Web users may use Internet Explorer, but 10 per cent of hundreds of millions of people is still a lot of people to alienate by refusing to allow Mozilla, Netscape, or Opera users to see your Web site.

However, your Web site must help for these technologies to be of any use. The World Wide Web Consortium, which oversees the development of the Web, has taken on accessibility as a major issue. This means that the technology exists to embed text descriptions of graphics that screen-access software can use. One of the traditional objections to designing a Web site to work only with Flash was that Flash didn't support such embedded text. With the release of version 5, this is no longer true (although there are other reasons to limit the use of Flash).

It's fairly simple to test your Web site for accessibility: turn off graphics in your Web browser (in Internet Explorer, the option to do this is in Tools | Internet Options | Advanced | Multimedia). Then try using your Web site to perform some common tasks, such as getting information about your company or putting through a transaction. If you find it difficult or impossible without graphics, so will screen-access software.

This is not to say you shouldn't use graphics or have video clips on your Web site. It's just that these should not be required for navigation or for carrying out the transactions your Web site is there for.

MAILING LISTS

One of the most common uses of email is to keep customers and other interested parties apprised of new developments within your company. Even a small specialist catalogue retailer may have a mailing list of hundreds of thousands of customers who opt to receive monthly updates. Compared to the old days of print newsletters, email is an amazingly low-cost and effective way to build a community around your areas of interest to keep your business growing. The software to manage this size of mailing list is readily available on the Net. Customers can subscribe or unsubscribe via the Web or email and be added or dropped without human intervention. Depending on how you set up your mailing list software, they can even discuss the company and its products and offer each other technical assistance if that's appropriate.

Like any other Internet service, you can host your mailing list yourself using your own software or pay a third party to host and manage it for you. If you do decide to host it yourself, check with your ISP whether there are any terms and conditions you must meet; the last thing you want is for your ISP to think you're a spammer. If you have a very large mailing list, managing it yourself from your desktop may be a problem as your Net connection (even if it's broadband) may be too slow. You will also find there are free mailing list host services on the Net, but be aware that all of them add advertising for their services to your messages.

There are certain rules you must follow, both because the data protection laws impose certain requirements and because Net community standards can be unforgiving towards anyone who violates those standards.

First of all, ensure that everyone on your mailing list has actively opted in. Don't add them automatically if they buy something from you and demand that they actively unsubscribe if they don't want to receive the mailings – it's annoying and time-consuming to have to keep unsubscribing from lists you never asked to be on. Instead, offer a box for users to check or uncheck if they want to join the mailing list. Offer clear instructions at the end of each message and on the Web site for anyone who wants to unsubscribe so that it's easy for them to do so. As European data protection laws tighten up, opt-in will become the default standard, so you might as well implement it now and not have to worry about revamping your mailing list later.

Second, if you only offer one format for your bulk email, make it plain text. Outlook by default sends email out in what it calls 'rich text'; that means formatted as a Web page (HTML encoded). For anyone using older email software or mobile phones or other limited devices, that may mean they can't read the message. Many people simply don't like HTML email for reasons of their own. Plain text is readable by everyone. If you feel you must offer HTML and/or PDF or other versions, also offer plain text as an option. Besides its convenience for users, plain text is much easier for you to produce, as what you see is what you get and no fancy coding is necessary.

The third point – and this applies to individual messages sent out to smaller groups of people as well – make sure you use blind carbon copy (BCC) to hide the list of recipients' names and email addresses. If you don't, anyone on the list can see the full list. Hiding the list protects the privacy of the recipients and ensures that none of them can copy the addresses and use the list for their own purposes. It also protects the list from spammers of the type who send out junk email advertising questionable get-rich-quick schemes, as they harvest email addresses for their lists anywhere they can.

Finally, keep it simple. People don't want to fill out complicated forms in order to get what they perceive as at least partly advertising. Keep the sign-up form down to a single line asking for the email address; if you offer options such as several different newsletters or formats, use a set of check boxes for those. Make sure the privacy policy (see p. 131) posted on your Web site includes a statement about what you intend to do with the personal data you collect.

LEGAL MATTERS

Several pieces of legislation cover issues raised by electronic commerce and general use of the Internet and related technologies. The UK regulations implementing the Electronic Commerce Directive were published in July 2002 and came into force in August; these regulations cover various aspects of electronic commerce. The Electronic Communications Act, passed in 2000, provides for a register of suppliers of cryptographic services and legalizes electronic contracts. The Regulation of Investigatory Powers Act, also passed in 2000, deals with a number of law enforcement powers; in terms of electronic commerce the most relevant is the right of access to encrypted data given a court order. Finally, the Anti-Terrorism, Crime, and Security Act, passed in the wake of the 11 September 2001 attacks in the USA, requires telecommunications service providers to retain certain types of traffic data for possible later use by law enforcement.

All these bills add up to a confusing interconnected web of laws covering electronic commerce and data whose full impact won't be understood until the supporting regulations are finished. Proposals for the ATCS rules suggested that data – which means traffic data that the data protection laws previously required to be destroyed as soon as it was no longer needed for billing purposes – would be retained for as long as two years. This traffic data would include login records, email headers, Web site accesses (though not specific URLs), and the like. Data retention is strongly opposed by ISPs, as the cost of implementing it will be considerable.

For small businesses, these pieces of legislation are probably not a major issue for the time being. However, the way these laws develop may change some of the decisions you make about where you host your ecommerce facilities, and you certainly need to be aware of what kinds of data may be seizable by law enforcement as part of your security review.

It is especially unclear how the data retention rules will be applied to the many smaller organizations and individuals who given broadband will host services that could be classed as 'public telecommunications systems'.

The final set of legislation that applies to ecommerce is of course the Data Protection Act, whose provisions were last revised in 1998. If you are dealing with consumers, you must tell them when you collect their personal data what you intend to do with it, and you must get permission from them if you plan to change this use. Most American sites have adopted the custom of posting a 'Privacy Policy' to cover this. This is less necessary in the UK because you are bound by the data protection laws. To write your own, read some sample policies from other people's sites. You may need to get legal advice. The Office of the Information Commissioner (as the Data Protection Registrar was renamed in 2001) has resources to help you determine what types of data processing are legal and under what circumstances you're required to register.

Computer-related crimes are covered by the 1990 Computer Misuse Act, which prohibits unauthorized access to computers; it's been used to prosecute virus writers as well as those who crack into other people's computer systems. The UK is a signatory, along with many other countries, to the Cybercrime Treaty (2000), which seeks to help law enforcement fight high-tech crimes such as computer fraud, the digital distribution of child pornography, and copyright infringement.

INTELLECTUAL PROPERTY ISSUES

Intellectual property law in relation to the Web affects you in three ways: first, as a Web user; second, as a Web content provider; and third, as the purchaser of Web design services. Many companies limit what's available on their Web sites because they are afraid the material will be copied and distributed – effectively, stolen. At the same time, it's very easy to violate copyright yourself by reusing material without realizing it's protected. Finally, if you hire someone to design your Web site, you must ensure that the agreement you have with that person specifies who owns what.

The third of these problems is the simplest. Generally speaking, you should retain copyright in any material you provide, and your payment to the designer should award to you the copyright in the pages and designs – logos, graphics, and so on – that the designer creates for you. However, if that person writes programs to make your Web pages work in a certain way, such as Web forms to enable you to edit and add content easily, the designer may insist on retaining the copyright in those programs. That's logical from the designer's point of view, since that sort of functionality is likely to be something they will sell to other customers as well. If the designer also hosts your Web site, those programs may not work on another server in any case. But these are matters you should hash out when you make your agreement with the designer.

One of the problems with the public nature of the World Wide Web is that many people think that any information made available over it is in the public domain. Plenty of myths persist, including the comforting but wrong notion that as long as the material is marked with a copyright notice indicating its origins it's completely legal to reproduce it. This is, of course, absolutely not true, and many sites bear notices explaining their copyright policy, an idea you may want to copy for your Web site. If you do, remember to take into account that you may have both public (such as press releases) and proprietary information on your site.

You should always make sure that anything you use on your Web site – text, images, video, audio – is material you have the right to use. You should also be careful how you use the technique known as frames, which lets you keep a static menu bar while varying the rest of the page. A few years ago, two Shetland newspapers went to court over framing. There will doubtless be more cases before the law in this area is fully clarified, but in general you should assume that the owners of advertising-sponsored sites will object if you link to their material in such a way as to cost them hits which translate into ad revenues. The Web's entire design is based on the idea of linking related material, but if you do have any doubt about links you want to include in your site check whether the site you want to link to has a linking policy. Some do. However, link licences – that is, a requirement that users get formal permission from a site's owner before linking to it – are contrary to the spirit of the Web, and if you demand that people get such permission you will look foolish.

A common question that comes up is what to do about press write-ups of your company or products that you may want to include on your site. Many companies believe – wrongly – that because the write-up is about them they have the right to distribute it. It's certainly true that if you hand out a few paper copies probably no one will notice, but you should get permission for large-scale paper distribution – or for placing such material on the Web. Wherever possible, you should link to the press write-up on the site belonging to its original publication. Apart from anything else, that looks more impressive. If that's not possible because the material isn't placed on the Web or is available only briefly, you should request permission from the publication. They may in turn send you to the writer if that person is freelance rather than staff.

The other side of the equation – whether and how much you should worry about other people copying content from your site without permission – is equally tricky. Much of the content you put on your Web site – product information, company background, and so on – is public information, for which protection is irrelevant. If your chief business is selling expensive reports or newsletters, protecting those becomes an issue as soon as you use electronic distribution because they're so easily copied. Various schemes have been tried for protecting these, and so far none is perfect.

With good quality images, which are far harder for the average person to create than text, most content owners' solution has been to post only versions whose resolution is too low for high-quality reproduction, or simply not to post them at all. The limitations of the equipment we use to access the Web foster this choice anyway, as too large an image won't fit on a PC's screen, and dial-up connections, which are still fairly common, at least among home users, are too slow to make large images acceptable anyway. As time goes on and bandwidth and screen size increase, however, this may change.

Certainly, for professionals, being able to ship images around via online connections speeds up delivery times to the point where a photographer with a digital camera, a mobile phone, and a Mac had pictures of William Hague's wedding announcement on newspaper screens within eleven and a half minutes. With multimedia messaging now a reality on mobile phones, low-resolution digital pictures can take as little as seconds to get from snap to worldwide distribution.

That situation, however, brings us back to the issue of identifying images' owners. In the old days, you had the negatives. Today, when your photograph begins and ends its life as a bunch of bits, it's difficult to prove it's yours. In addition, software such as Photoshop makes it comparatively easy to alter images any way the user likes. Like sampled music, this also poses a challenge to traditional ideas of copyright.

This is not to say that technology companies and others haven't been working on solutions. They have, but none is ideal. Corbis, for example, sells both traditionally licensed and royalty-free images on the professional side of its Web site; buyers search the site on keywords and are shown low-resolution versions of the images. They pay according to the resolution or size of the final image, and download it then and there. On the consumer side of its site, Corbis offers smaller, free versions of the images for personal use, but marks them visibly with the word 'Corbis' in the background, turning them into advertisements for the service. That works as a deterrent – to using the images at all, in many cases.

The other solution is digital watermarking. This technique involves encrypting information such as the name of the copyright owner, the creator, the date, and the source or buyer and hiding it all unnoticeably in the 'noise' in the picture file. Digimarc, for example, marks material so that it's identifiable and traceable.

Digital watermarking sounds good, but has two flaws. First is the fact that there are plenty of folks out there dedicated to cracking such systems, many of which have already been shown to have technical limitations. Some of these systems can, for example, be defeated by methods as easy as saving a file in a slightly more compressed format, discarding the same noise in which the digital watermarking is hidden. In general, the consensus is that so far these systems promise more security than they can deliver. The second problem is that even at their best digital watermarking systems don't block copying; they merely make it provable and traceable. While it may be comforting to think about being able to prove that the images distributed across the Net are yours, that doesn't give you back control over the images.

Even without all the challenges posed by the Web, copyright in images is a much more complex matter than copyright in text. For one thing, while the image itself is typically owned by its creator or the outfit that commissioned it, there may be additional copyright interests in a photograph's subject. For example, if you photograph a sculpture, while the copyright in the photograph belongs to you, the copyright in the sculpture itself belongs to the original artist and then to his estate for seventy years after his death. In practice, that means getting permission from both copyright holders to use the photograph.

The whole area of licensing images to use online is a difficult one. As yet, there is no standard licensing scheme to cover such uses, nor is there a standard licensing scheme to allow you to copy images off other Web pages for reproduction, either on the Web or in print. The exception, at least in common practice in newspapers and magazines, is to use screen grabs of whole Web pages, which have, after all, been placed in public view. If the page is protected by a registration scheme, particularly if it's a subscription site, it's probably wise to ask permission for any widespread distribution. Copying parts of a page and using them in your own page – such as grabbing an image off someone else's page and using it intact or as a background graphic on your own page – is technically very easy but is generally frowned on unless the page's owner has explicitly given permission either individually or in a stated policy on the page. Linking to a page, however, ought to require no explicit permission, as it's the concept on which the Web's design was based.

Unless the image you want is specifically royalty-free, ask before using it on your own Web site or in a company brochure. You may of course save or print a copy of the Web page for your own personal use without first getting permission.

DOING BUSINESS INTERNATIONALLY: VAT PITFALLS

Early Net pioneers believed that the Net would prove to be the great leveller: that it would give small businesses the chance to compete on an equal footing with large ones. To some extent that's true, but they reckoned without conflicting tax regimes. If you're doing business on the Web, it's a concern because when you set up your site you are de facto setting up in business worldwide – the Internet is a global medium. If you don't want to or can't deal with customers from outside the UK, you should state this clearly on the front page so you don't waste people's time.

TIP When's the last time you ran a checker over your Web site to make sure all the links still work?

VAT regulations pose a serious problem for small companies doing business over the Net. Despite long-standing plans for harmonization across the European Union, rates vary, rules vary, and even the threshold above which registration is required varies from roughly €35,000 to €100,000. For those struggling to build up their businesses, VAT is something that can easily be overlooked until it's too late.

The UK rules governing VAT on ecommerce changed on 1 July 2003. Until then, electronic and broadcasting services were deemed to attract VAT in the supplier's home country. This has now changed so that these services will be deemed to be supplied in the customer's country. However, EU businesses will continue to charge the rate due in the supplier's home country to private individuals and non-business organizations in other member states. As of 1 July 2003 businesses must also charge VAT to EU-based customers on digital downloads such as software and services. This applies even if the material that's downloaded is zero-rated when it's sold in the form of a book, magazine, or leaflet. You do not have to charge VAT on services exported outside the EU.

The new rules also close a loophole that has given non-EU, particularly American and Canadian, companies an advantage, in that they did not have to charge VAT on goods and services. Non-EU-based businesses are now required to add VAT, although they still have a slight advantage in that they are allowed to pick a single EU country to register in.

The difficulty for small EU-based businesses is that the laws may be harmonized but the national interpretations are not. An EU company selling goods or services into another EU country is supposed to register and file returns in the other country once its sales there reach a certain threshold. So, if you're an online CD retailer based in the UK, where VAT rates are at 17.5 per cent, and you're selling into a high-tax country such as Sweden, where VAT is at 25 per cent, you have a price (or profit) advantage over indigenous competition. Hence the protectionist requirement to register as soon as sales become significant. In many countries registering requires the company to have a locally based fiscal representative. None of the return forms are similar, nor are the invoicing requirements, an adminstrative burden that falls disproportionately on small European businesses.

Therefore, if you start doing any significant volume of business with customers in other EU countries, check on the current state of the law and think about what the VAT implications are, what you'll need to buy, how you're going to pay VAT on what you buy, and how you're going to get it back. Particularly in relation to situations where you're going to incur local VAT in another country, you will need somebody who will spot the warning signals when a deal is struck. You do not want to find out too late that you should have registered. The penalties for not filing in a timely manner can be severe.

Besides VAT, some jurisdictions will require a non-resident business to pay tax on profits from a branch located in that country. It's not clear yet whether a server operated to trade in such a country would amount to a branch; in some cases it might. It's easy to assume that small businesses couldn't reach the minimums involved, but a Scottish company, say, trading in lightweight, expensive cashmere sweaters wouldn't necessarily have to sell very many before hitting the limit.

British consumers are supposed to pay customs duty on any package containing goods worth more than £18. However, the onus is on the delivery services to collect the money, and as the volume of arriving packages has grown, the number getting through duty-free has gone up dramatically.

One consequence of all this is that you may find that your most important competitors are not in the UK at all. If, for example, you sell DVDs, you will find your prices and margins squeezed by online retailers in Canada, who pay much less for their stocks. Postage on DVDs is trivial, and Customs charges rarely apply since even two-disc sets are likely to come in under the £18 threshold. If you are planning to set up to sell online, therefore, before investing in an ecommerce site survey the competition, remembering that your biggest online competitors are often going to be very different companies from the ones you compete with offline.

TIP If for some reason you must put Microsoft Word files on your Web site, make sure all revisions have been merged first. Otherwise, journalists and geeks will have much fun publicizing what you changed and speculating why.

7 Security

As cryptography expert Bruce Schneier has observed, 'Security is a process.'

Remembering that security is not a product you can install and forget about is vital. Risks to your network change constantly as your circumstances change and as new threats are discovered. For that reason, you should schedule a regular – say, once a month – review of your security and include in it a review of your disaster recovery plan (see Chapter 8). It sounds like a lot of work when you've got so many other jobs to do, but it is absolutely necessary if you want to retain control of the systems that support your business.

The moving target is only part of the difficulty of ensuring good security; the other part is the fact that in general people are poor at risk assessment. Just as people can be hysterically worried about the risks of a mobile phone's giving them brain cancer (either non-existent or very remote) while smoking a pack of cigarettes a day (for which the risks are well established), computer users respond to media panics about teenaged hackers while ignoring the much bigger risks of disaffected former staff with inside knowledge and passwords.

That is not to say that there is no risk. The Internet is populated by an army of small-timers whose entertainment in life seems to be wandering around the Net rattling doorknobs and keeping a count of the number of systems they can get into. Most of them are not particularly technically skilled, contrary to media portrayals. They are, instead, what's known as 'script kiddies' – young people, mostly male, who have picked up some standard and well-known cracking tools and are trying them out. If they fail with their limited roster of tricks, they move on. The collection of people who are technically skilled and capable of mounting a clever attack is really very small.

The best known of those often do not succeed because of their technical skills but because of their ability to con staff into helping them by giving them often apparently useless information about the inner workings of a company's system ('social engineering').

Therefore, just as with planning for disaster recovery (which is covered in the next chapter), you need to make a realistic assessment of what your biggest risks are and plan around them. Don't get so unnerved by press reports of hacker attacks across the Net that you lose perspective. You are far more vulnerable to attack from inside your business than from outside. If, for example, the entire amount of data a competitor would need to copy and undermine your business would fit on a floppy or portable storage device, that data is accessible from anywhere on the network, and your networked machines have no passwords and are accessible to anyone who wanders in, you have more urgent problems than hackers across the Net. In the scenario just outlined, a disaffected employee could walk out of the building with a copy of the entire business in a shirt pocket.

Things will get much more complicated in the near future, since the same up-and-coming technologies such as XML, which will support the development of truly interactive Web services that offer the advantages of having direct connections to customers and suppliers, will bring new risks with them. There certainly are advantages in streamlining procurement, but there are also risks in that you may wind up revealing more about your business to those partners – and perhaps your competitors – than you realize.

SECURING YOUR SYSTEM

There are three reasons why it's important to secure your system. The one you've probably already thought of is that others may read or copy information from your machines. That could include anything from confidential information on products and projects in progress to financial records, personal email, and legal documents. Unless the uninvited visitor can use the information he finds to damage your commercial interests, usually it's not someone's viewing the information (as disconcerting as that is) that is the biggest risk. Much worse is the possibility that the information can be changed or deleted without your knowledge (here again, backups are important).

The second reason is that even if you think you have no data on your system that's going to interest anyone and the only people attacking you are script kiddies, break-ins can eat up valuable time while you check your system for damage. Someone breaking into a weakly secured system can make as much of a mess in your computer system as someone can make in your physical offices by breaking a window, climbing in, and strewing flour all over the place. Any time you suspect someone has broken into your system you will need to take the time to audit everything thoroughly and make sure the attacker has not deleted or modified anything, or left behind software to make it easier to gain access next time (a 'back door').

The third and most powerful reason is the risk that someone cracking into your system can use your computing resources to launch attacks against other machines across the Net or to send out viruses or to pose as you in transactions you wouldn't want to have associated with your business. Someone else impersonating you by using your machine to access services and other machines on the Net is, in many cases, far more damaging than the simple acquisition of confidential information. As more and more of our business, especially banking, is conducted online, the need for system security will only increase. It is for this reason that it is so important, for example, to run anti-virus software and ensure that your system stays clean. You do not want to be identified as the source of a virus. It is as irresponsible and anti-social to allow viruses or Net attacks to propagate from your system as it is to knowingly go out in public with a dangerous, communicable disease and risk infecting others.

The same characteristics that let you see the entire Internet from your computer mean that the Internet and its many computers can also see your computer. In some cases, such as when you want to use your machine to host a Web site, that's extremely useful. But in others, such as when someone installs software on your machine without your knowledge, it can be extremely dangerous. The well-publicized attacks on leading electronic retailers such as Amazon.com and Yahoo! in early 2000 and the 2002 attacks on some of the most important computers that run the Internet came about because software was installed on 'innocent' machines that set them to sending out constant probes to those services, flooding them with junk (these are known as 'distributed denial of service' attacks).

The more of the time your computer is connected to the Internet the more of the time your computer is available to the outside, making your risk greater. However, there are some mitigating factors. If you use standard dial-up, the chances are that you are assigned an IP number dynamically (see p. 60) when you log on; this means that although someone might be able to gain access to your computer during an extended session, they are unlikely to be able to find it again easily as it probably won't be at the same address. However, if a Trojan (see p. 148) has been installed on your machine it will run whenever you're logged on. Those using the NAT version of ADSL or cable broadband will find that their ISPs have built some security protection into the services. Those using the non-NAT version of ADSL must provide their own security and install a firewall. Although this is more work than having BT install and manage your routes, in general experts recommend non-NAT in part because it means you control your own security. It's considered a bad idea to rely on the security of strangers. You should add your own firewall to the security the ISP provides.

With or without your own firewall, you need anti-virus software. There are a number of reputable vendors – Sophos, F-Secure, Grisoft, to name just a few. Anti-virus software is not like other software, in that you cannot install it once and have it work effectively forever. Because new viruses are appearing all the time (see pp. 158–62), your anti-virus protection must be updated regularly. Therefore, when you buy anti-virus software you are really buying a subscription for a specified length of time, usually a year.

One of the reasons security is so difficult is that with 90 per cent of PCs running the same operating system, email, and office software, today's computers are like a field of cloned sheep, all prone to the same diseases. For example, if you don't use Word you're not vulnerable to Word viruses and if you don't use Outlook, email-borne viruses that exploit the known format of your address book can't spread by sending themselves to the names on your contact list. Most small businesses, however, do use standard software: they may benefit more from standardization than they lose in risk, if only because standardization means they can easily exchange data with others working on the same projects and temporary staff need less training.

Even so, you can resist letting your software decide where to put your data and create a directory structure that suits you by using custom installation routines. For example, instead of letting every piece of Internet software create a 'My Downloads' subdirectory of its own, tell them all to use a central directory; instead of letting every piece of office software create its own data directory, create a central one. Controlling how your data is organized is important in making it easier to keep regular backups of those important files. You can also store especially sensitive data on a disk in a removable drive, such as a Zip drive, and take the disk out of the drive when it's not in use, making the information physically inaccessible not just to over-curious hackers but to over-curious staff (but remember to make backups of the disk).

On shared computers, allowing ecommerce sites to 'remember' you may let others using the same machine and user account access your ecommerce account without your knowledge. Users should get into the habit of logging out if they're going to be away from their machines (or set the screensaver options so that it turns on after a brief idle period and requires a password to restart). You should also remind staff not to share user accounts even with other staff.

FIREWALLS

A simple guideline: if you can't reel off from memory your IP address, your DNS server address, and your subnet mask, and don't know what an IP port is or how IP addressing works you should not try to configure your firewall yourself. Firewalls are actually very simple, wholly logical devices with a detailed set of rules – but creating those rules requires a solid understanding of what you're doing. Firewalls are not toasters.

However, you should have a firewall that you control even if your business is protected behind broadband that's supposedly secured by the ISP. Ultimately, you are responsible for your network and the use that's made of it.

Firewalls in the computer world, like their non-computer counterparts, act as a barrier between your computer system and the Internet. They perform two primary functions. First, they block unauthorized outsiders from accessing your system. Second, they can help control the use your staff make of the Internet by blocking certain types of services. Firewalls provide a central point of access control between your computer system or network and the Internet. As such, they implement the security and access policies you've decided on.

That's what they do. Just as important is what they don't do. Firewalls cannot protect you against hostile staff members (or former staff members) who divulge confidential details over the phone or copy data onto floppy disks and physically take them off the premises and give them to competitors. Firewalls, even if they have anti-virus capabilities built into them, cannot protect against viruses brought in on floppy disks or via email (unless your firewall has anti-virus software built into it). Firewalls cannot protect against theft of equipment, social engineering attacks, poorly or malevolently written software used in interactive Internet applications, or any other type of attack that does not go through the firewall. Finally, in most cases they cannot block malicious software that exploits an already open connection or port.

TIP Firewalls cannot protect against attacks on your system that do not come through the firewall.

The advent of broadband has made firewalls extremely important because that permanent Internet connection leaves you permanently vulnerable. You could make this analogy: dial-up is the equivalent of leaving the front door open while you pop next door for a pint of milk; broadband is removing the door.

Firewalls must form part of a coherent security policy. You do not buy the firewall and build your security policy around it; you decide on the policy and buy the firewall that comes closest to implementing it.

Firewalls may be built into your router (wired or wireless), but many experts prefer to buy them as a separate box, and there are a number of companies such as Sonicwall that make inexpensive boxes of this type aimed at small businesses. Most such boxes are expandable as a network grows. See below for an explanation of how firewalls filter Internet traffic. For some services, you may need to position a box outside the firewall – for example, if you host a Web site you want that machine to be publicly accessible, but you do not want anyone to use that machine as a gateway into the rest of your system. More expensive firewalls can accommodate what's known as a 'DMZ' (demilitarized zone) machine or even network for that reason and if you are going to run servers exposed to the Net you will need this function.

CONFIGURING A FIREWALL: MR SPOCK TECHNOLOGY

The simple rule is, never allow all outbound or inbound connections. Lock down all the internal to external and external to internal connections and then open them selectively on a case-by-case basis. If you open something, open it for a reason and only so long as it's necessary. Firewalls are the ultimate in logical devices: if you give them a rule, they will apply it consistently and without fail. So the key is to give them the right rules.

Configuring a firewall is creating the set of rules that is going to govern online access. Take a simple spreadsheet and list the machines on your network against the types of connections you might want/need to allow – email, DNS, Web, and so on. Tick the boxes for the connections you need so you wind up with a logical table showing all the connections. Then implement that as a set of rules for the firewall. A rule is not in and of itself a complex thing – it opens a specific port (belonging to a specific application, see glossary) and may also specify to which machine traffic of that type is to be forwarded.

The important trick is controlling the set of rules in the future. To do that, the recommended method is saving the known good set of rules to disk. Then, if you make a temporary change to allow a particular type of connection, rather than trying to change the configuration back you can restore the known good set of rules. If you have a fully routed non-NAT network, you may have seventy or a hundred rules in a firewall. At that level, it's easy to make a mistake when removing a temporary rule that breaks the configuration – and you may not know about it until it's too late. If you want to keep the new rule on a permanent basis, save the new set to disk and make that the default known good set. If you have frequent temporary changes for some reason, make reapplying the known good set of rules part of your monthly 'housekeeping' – the regular routine of making your disaster recovery checks.

To do the actual work of implementing the rules you will need the specific instructions for your firewall and the port numbers for the applications in question; look at the section on ports in Chapter 3 (see pp. 49–51) for an explanation of how to find this out. In some cases, you may want to choose software on the basis of what ports it needs to have opened. NetMeeting, for example, was originally designed for use over an internal network, and it demands a huge number of open ports. If you want to use it over the Internet, do so through a VPN (virtual private network, see pp. 149–50). Do not scatter-punch holes through your firewall on a random basis and do not open big blocks of ports; choose software that behaves responsibly in this respect. Manufacturers of Internet software should be able to tell you which ports their products use if you ask.

You also need to be aware of unexpected 'gotchas'. For example, a number of laser printers now have mini Web browsers embedded in them so you can print across the Internet. Those can be used to launch denial-of-service attacks; block them in the firewall. As more and more formerly 'standalone' peripherals are Web- and network-enabled – to say nothing of video and audio equipment and even appliances – there will be more and more such connections waiting to trap the unwary.

In most cases, assuming you've bought your firewall from a known manufacturer, testing the firewall means examining the rules. If, however, you want to put through a more direct test, there are Web sites (http://www.grc.com) that will do a basic scan for open ports on the machine you connect to it with. For more thorough testing, either you get a knowledgeable friend to try to break in from the outside, or you buy specialist software such as ISS or GFI's Languard (or take advantage of their limited free trials) to scan your network. In most cases, examining the rules carefully is the most important test.

HOW FIREWALLS WORK

The explanation of ports in Chapter 3 should give you some idea of how firewalls work: essentially, they allow you to selectively open or block the ports that applications need in order to communicate with your system. A piece of hostile software such as the well-known program Back Orifice, once installed on your system, opens a port that listens for anyone who's looking for an active Back Orifice client. Once such a connection is made, the person at the other end can do pretty much anything he wants on your system: delete or change files, operate the machine, and even control its resources more intimately than the person sitting at the keyboard. A correctly installed firewall may not be able to prevent Back Orifice from being installed (if, say, an uneducated member of staff installs it without really understanding what they're doing), but it can block the ports the program would use to communicate.

This kind of protection is becoming increasingly important as malware becomes more sophisticated. The latest tricks used in mouting a distributed denial of service attack (see p. 163) are clever enough that a machine may be infected with the software an attacker can use to control that machine without the owner's ever having consciously downloaded anything. Today's attackers may, for example, hack into an insecure Web server and hide an IRC server there or use a stolen credit card to buy what's known as a shell account – that is, an account that allows old-style text-based access to low-level Internet services. The addresses of these sites are then stored in software (a 'Trojan') that may lurk in JavaScript on a Web site or may be distributed via any of the techniques used for distributing viruses (see pp. 158–62). Once a machine is infected by the Trojan, the software connects to those stored addresses behind the scenes and awaits commands. The infecting software may even set the infected machine to scan ranges of numbered Internet addresses to find more insecure machines they can infect. It is for this sort of reason that it is socially irresponsible not to secure your own systems even if you are not worried about the risks to yourself or your business.

One important function of a firewall is logging what kinds of connections and traffic have passed through or been blocked. Looking at such logs shows that even computers with nothing of interest on them do get attacked from the outside. Again, what is at risk is not simply the information on your system, but the resources of your system that can be used to launch attacks on other machines across the Net. You should not, for example, leave your email server open so that someone from outside can use it to send email. That is known as an 'open relay' and such open connections are beloved by spammers for sending out junk email. Having an open relay can get you dumped by your ISP for violating its acceptable use policy, causing you potentially immense hassle and loss of business while you try to restore your Internet connection.

TIP The cost of security systems to prevent attacks will always be less than the cost of the consequences of a successful attack.

However, when we say a firewall blocks certain types of traffic, that does not necessarily mean that a firewall can identify the content of that traffic. A firewall blocks the traffic by keeping the port an application uses closed or, when IPSec rolls out, by detecting that traffic is not authenticated. Unless it is specially designed to do so –

and most aren't – a firewall does not normally filter content. If you want, say, to stop staff from accessing pornography over the Web, you will either need to install blocking software such as NetNanny or CyberPatrol, or educate staff as to what you consider to be acceptable use for the company Internet connection and network resources. See Chapter 5 for a discussion of acceptable use policies and more on blocking software.

SUPPORTING REMOTE/MOBILE USERS

One of the most useful techniques that broadband opens up for small businesses is virtual private networking, the ability to securely connect staff working at home or on the road to the company LAN. Essentially, what a VPN does is to create a secured 'tunnel' – an encrypted data stream – across the otherwise public Internet. Remote users dialling in via a VPN log into the network and are authenticated like any other user, and thereafter can work just as if they were on the premises. Basic VPN connections are included in Windows 2000 and XP Professional; more configurable versions with better security are built into many firewalls.

Users dialling in directly are securely connected in any case. But being able to use a VPN means that they can use their own Internet connection, whether that's dial-up, a wireless hotspot in a cafe, or the broadband they have at home, to access the network, saving substantially on telecommunications costs and in many cases achieving higher connection speeds.

One important issue that often gets forgotten is hand-held computers and mobile phones. Increasingly, these are computers in their own right, and they also must be authenticated when they join the network like any other device. When they do, they should automatically be backed up. If all your most important customer contact numbers and recent email messages are in your mobile phone and it gets lost or stolen, then what? Software is readily available on the Net to back up such devices, and hardware is beginning to appear to make it easy to keep updating a backup copy of your phone's SIM card when you're travelling. Just remember to separate the backup from the actual phone so that if the phone gets stolen you still have the backup. Orange, with its Smartphone, now offers a single-button backup service, and hopefully more mobile network operators will follow suit.

Because PDAs and mobile phones are thought of as 'lifestyle' devices, they are often not included in a company's security policy. But if they are used by staff in the course of work they may contain valuable data that can easily be lost. Newer machines, for example, may allow you to read company documents in ebook format and run presentations directly from the phone or PDA, making them little different from carrying a very small laptop. Most such devices have very little security enabled to protect the information inside; their use and integration into your security system needs to be thought out carefully.

If you or your staff are on the road and use Internet cafes and other public locations to access the company network, there are some additional caveats. It sounds paranoid, but make sure no one's reading over your shoulder when you enter ID numbers or passwords if you're accessing important accounts in a public area. If you've been on a trip where you've had to use terminals in such places, it couldn't hurt to change your password when you get home. In addition, always make sure you correctly log off the company network and/or sites where personal financial information is stored, so that even if the terminal's next user finds a way to explore your just-completed transactions he or she won't be able to actually get into your account.

Make sure devices that can be are password-protected, especially if they are set up to automatically log into a company network over a secure connection and be accepted as a trusted part of the network. If you sell a laptop (or desktop, for that matter), make sure that not only the data is removed but the passwords and user IDs are, too, including any passwords that may have been applied to the BIOS, hard drives, and any other system pieces. This protects not only you but also the buyer, as in some cases if the BIOS password is lost the machine locks up and becomes unusable without a major and very expensive replacement system board.

SPECIAL RISKS OF WIRELESS

People who pay great attention to the security of their wired networks nonetheless often forget that when they add wireless access it opens a whole new area of risk. Unlike a wired user, someone wishing to snoop on your network via your wireless connection or 'borrow' some of your bandwidth can do so without your necessarily being aware of it. Remember: it's radio. It broadcasts to any receiver that can pick up the signal.

At setup, 802.11b access points and routers will offer you the option to set up an SSID (Service Set IDentifier), which you should accept. Set the SSID to something that is not your company name, the manufacturer's name, street address, or anything else obviously and easily guessable. If the option is available, disable broadcasting the SSID, so that anyone wishing to use a wireless card to access your network must configure the card with the right SSID in order to be able to do so. Change the default password on the router/access point so that outsiders can't come in and reconfigure it; those who are interested in such things know all the manufacturers' default passwords.

You can also make it harder for someone outside the office to use your wireless connection by siting the access point well away from windows and outside walls. The closer the access point or router is to a window the more likely that coverage will extend to the street outside. If your company starts to grow, you may even want, as part of your ongoing security checks and reviews, to periodically run software available from the Net to scan your site for access points. As prices come down further and further, it would be very easy for someone to install an extra access point without your even realizing it.

Finally, enable WEP (Wireless Encryption Protocol), the facility built into 802.11b equipment to encrypt the data stream while it is in transit, preferably to a key strength of 128 bits (the minimum offered is 40). As you may know from reading press reports, WEP has been cracked. Nonetheless, using it is a great deal better than using nothing, and turns eavesdropping on your network traffic from something anyone passing by with an 802.11b card can do into something that requires a lot more sophistication.

Place the wireless part (including any mobile devices staff use to tap in) of your network in the DMZ that is the buffer zone between your network and the Internet created by your firewall and use a VPN to let those users access the wired computers and other devices on your network. That way, if someone does crack into your wireless network they won't have access to your entire system unless they can be authenticated correctly by the VPN. It's a lot of layers to think about, but wireless, despite its huge convenience, poses many additional risks that are easily forgotten. This is especially true if you have not disabled the 'Everyone' group (see p. 80). If you do not have a DMZ built into your firewall, put the wireless access points outside the firewall and consider buying a second firewall to protect them.

The downside to doing all this is that it becomes much harder to configure a new card or add a user, or to debug a connection when something goes wrong. Generally speaking, the first reaction when that happens is to turn off all the security. If you do that, remember to turn it back on again. If you do so step by step you should be able to identify whatever the problem was.

SOFTWARE – UPDATES AND PATCHES

Periodically you will read about some new hole that's just been discovered in a piece of commonly used software that could open a system running the software to hackers and other problems. This is why security is a process, not a product: things change. A good example is the January 2003 Internet slowdown caused by the SQL Slammer worm, which took advantage of a hole in the SQL Server that was discovered in July 2002.

These announcements are not things to ignore, even though you shouldn't panic immediately either. Typically, a patch to close the newly discovered hole will be released fairly speedily. However, it is up to you or to your IT administrator to find the security patches and apply them. That means not only installing the patches, but keeping backup copies, as if you ever have to reinstall the software you will need to reapply the patches. For products like Windows 2000, Microsoft periodically releases service packs, which usually include all the security patches rolled out to date; in those cases, you just need to keep the most recent service pack plus any updates issued since that service pack.

Some caution should be used when updating the software. Obviously, you will make sure your backups are up to date before installing the update. If possible, take a look at the relevant Usenet newsgroup or search the technical sites to make sure that the patch isn't causing problems on the systems it's installed on. It happens, and you don't want to be the one it happens to.

A recent trend in software is auto-updating, in which the software takes advantage of a moment when you're online to go and check for updates and install them for you. The latest and most complex such initiative is Microsoft's Next Generation Secure Computing Base (formerly Palladium), intended as a platform for 'trusted computing.' In one respect it makes sense: it sounds more efficient for the software to ensure it incorporates all the latest security fixes than for it to rely on a possibly distracted user or system administrator to remember to go and look for them. Despite the convenience, there are real risks to allowing your software to do this. For one thing, you can easily lose track of what's been installed on your system, potentially making it unmaintainable. If you rely on auto-updating for anti-virus software, check periodically to ensure these updates are taking place as they're supposed to. Also remember to check the software maintenance policy for your firewall.

SECURITY FOR ECOMMERCE AND THE WEB

A Web site is public. If you store information in the storage space allocated to your Web site, you must regard it as public. In 2002, the news service Reuters got sued when a journalist guessed at a URL and downloaded a company's financial results early. The company in question argued that because the URL hadn't been posted the journalist was in violation of the Computer Misuse Act. In fact, it was silly behaviour by the company. Assume that even if the information is not publicly flagged on your Web site, if it's there someone will find it. It's noted elsewhere that you should not in general use proprietary formats such as Word and PowerPoint to post documents – use the more widely readable Adobe Acrobat format PDF instead if you must retain the formatting – but an additional reason is the risk posed in, for example, Word if staff forget to merge final revisions. (This actually happened in 2000, when the online bank Egg posted its final results with last-minute changes to the text clearly visible.)

If you are going to accept customer orders online with payment by credit or debit card, you are taking on a whole new set of risks. These days, many ecommerce packages offer secure facilities to accept sensitive information such as personal details, all using encryption to create a secure channel (known as SSL for Secure Sockets Layer) so the data is protected in transmission against snoops. Hackers do sometimes gain access to a site and alter its front page to one of their own choosing, but if you have taken proper precautions this need not endanger your database of customer information – again, think in layers.

Protecting data in transmission by itself is not enough. You must think through how you are going to handle this information once it reaches your servers. The last thing you want is the damage to your reputation and ecommerce sales of a security breach. Make sure that your database of customer transactions is not held on the Web server or on a wirelessly connected machine; it should not be accessible at all from outside the company. You can even write the daily transactions in a file and transfer that to another machine that holds the long-term records. You can further protect the machine that accepts the transactions by putting two network cards in it with no routing between them; one that is accessed from the outside by customers and the other connected to the internal network.

TIP Watch out for hidden browsers in networked devices such as printers that can be used from outside your organization to launch attacks.

Better still, outsource this part of your ecommerce operation to a specialist in financial services. Typically, such a specialist has more experience and can offer a more secure operation and faster recovery from snafus. It is also likely to be insured. Finally, if something does go wrong, it's their bad PR, not yours.

Some other common ecommerce mistakes. Do not send customer passwords and IDs (and still less, credit card numbers and expiry dates) to them via unencrypted email. While it may be handy for the customer to have the record, the risk that the information could get intercepted and used is very real. If you need to send customers a password – for example, if they forget their passwords and request it to be reset so they can regain access to their accounts – send a temporary password and force them to change it at their next logon. Remind customers never to give out their passwords, and make it plain that you will not ask for them.

As ecommerce has grown in scope, the biggest and most successful companies have become targets of various types of spoofing attacks – and if you promote your services, as some small companies do, on auction sites like eBay or Amazon you need to be aware of them. Never respond to email purporting to come from one of these large services asking you to 'confirm' the details of your account by clicking on a link in the email and entering your details in a form, especially if that form asks you for your account password. If you are worried, go to the site itself and log into your account and check the details or ask for confirmation via the support system built into the site. The Web sites linked from email of this type are almost always spoofs designed to trap the financial information of the unwary. If you have a vendor's account with a good reputation you are potentially a target for someone wishing to profit from that reputation to offer goods, take the money, and default, leaving you with all the problems. For small businesses these umbrella sites offer a good chance to help interested potential customers find them; but they also offer risks you should be aware of.

Similarly, never give out the password to your company computer or any online service you use to someone who phones and asks for it, even if they say they're staff and sound credible. If you think there's a genuine reason why they might be contacting you, ask for the person's name, and call them back using the company's published phone number. If it's someone claiming to be a staff member of your company and you don't know them or recognize the voice, get a phone number and say you'll call back. Then check the person's name and the phone number you've been given with official company records.

A number of organizations offer schemes you can join that will allow you to put a logo on your page to signify you've been accepted as a responsible electronic retailer. In general, these schemes mean less than you might expect to Net users. It is much more valuable to focus on giving great customer service.

A CRYPTOGRAPHY PRIMER

Cryptography's importance in computer security can't be overstated: it is used, for example, to protect customer credit card details in transit between their Web browser and ecommerce sites, and can be used to protect confidential email and stored data, and authenticate electronic contracts. In general, you do not buy cryptography by itself; you buy products that have cryptography built into them. Currently, the strongest cryptography available on the mass market uses 128-bit keys; essentially, the longer the key (128-bit instead of, say, 40-bit) the tougher the cryptography is to crack.

What follows explains how today's cryptographic systems are used in security applications. Some security system vendors will refuse to divulge details of the algorithm they use on the grounds that keeping them confidential helps guard their systems against attacks. The most important thing you need to know about cryptography is that you should resist accepting those refusals, which are often referred to as 'security by obscurity'. Security by obscurity certainly works when the item being kept secret is the combination to the lock on the front door. But how that lock works should not be obscure – how can you tell if the design is sound? Similarly, when it comes to cryptography, the best way to be sure an algorithm has no easily exploitable flaws is to let experts try to crack it and review how it works, a process known as cryptanalysis.

Until recently, cryptography was the sole province of governments and the military, if only because they were the only organizations who could afford the necessary 'big iron' hardware. The advent of cheap, mass-market computing power began to change that situation, while the Internet has created a new demand for cryptographically enabled software because it supports ecommerce but was not built with security in mind. Emailed communications of all types are open to view by the administrators of all the systems they pass through, while packet sniffing and other techniques can give hackers access to confidential information such as credit card details and passwords when these are passed between Web sites and their visitors.

The revolution in cryptography began in 1978, when two researchers, Whitfield Diffie and Martin Hellman, proposed what is now known as 'public key cryptography', a technique particularly suited to spontaneous communications between strangers across a public network. Unlike older forms of cryptography, which depended on the transmission of a secret key between the parties before communications could begin, public key cryptography, first widely distributed in the form of a free program called 'PGP', depends on a complementary pair of keys, one public and one private. The private key you keep secret; the public key you distribute as widely as possible. Anything encrypted with one of the keys can only be decrypted with the other, so that the system provides both of the two important functions of cryptography: authentication (anything encrypted with your private key can only have come from you) and confidentiality (anything encrypted with your public key can only be read by you). If a sender encrypts a message with his own private key and the recipient's public key, the message is authenticated as coming from him without change, and can only be read by the recipient.

In practice, because public key cryptography is rather slow, for large amounts of data the public key technique is used to encrypt and send the other correspondent a secret key to be used only for that session. The session key is then used to encrypt the data (and decrypt it again on the other side of the connection).

Public key cryptography is also extremely important in authenticating electronic contracts and giving Internet users a way to verify that a message has come from the person who purports to have sent it and has not been tampered with en route. Typically, the cryptographic software 'signs' a communication by appending a mathematically derived digest of the message using the sender's private key. Someone wishing to check the authenticity of the message can do so by decrypting the digest using the sender's public key and then performing the same mathematical function and comparing the results. This sounds like a lot of work, but software automates the checking and in practice it's very easy for the user. PGP is still offered as a commercial product to plug into email software. The infrastructure to accept digital signatures is likely to develop slowly over the next few years.

TIP Do not 'store' the current backup tape in the drive. Rotate tapes and other backup media regularly.

The use of strong cryptography in peacetime (Internet) applications spread slowly in part because governments (especially the US and UK governments) tended to view it as a strategically important military weapon that needed to be restricted. Big political battles were fought during the 1990s to allow encryption to be used freely. In most countries, the regulations have given way in the interests of providing security for electronic commerce. You can, in the UK, be compelled to produce cryptographic keys if law enforcement agents demand access under the Regulation of Investigatory Powers Act.

VIRUSES

Viruses are programs that replicate themselves. They may or may not include a destructive payload – that is, functions that delete files or do other malicious damage to your system. Formerly, the most common way for machines to pick up viruses was via infected floppy disks. These days, the most common method is via email. Either way, you should clean up viruses that infect your system, first because you never know what damage they may do, and second because they are designed to replicate themselves and so you may be spreading the infection to other machines and systems. Spreading viruses is a very good way to damage your company's hard-won good reputation.

Viruses, including subtypes known as 'worms', are programs. They must be contained in executable code – programs, identifiable as files ending in .EXE, .PIF, .BAT, or .COM – in order to infect your system. Plain text therefore cannot carry a virus although Word and Excel files may carry macro viruses. There are many hoax viruses that circulate on the Net claiming to be warnings about dangerous viruses; most include a note that the warning has been confirmed by Microsoft, AOL, IBM, or some other major company or government department. You should always check with one of the pages that indexes hoaxes before forwarding an email of this type, particularly if there is a long list of former recipients (a clear sign that it's been mass-forwarded by people who are not technically adept). Other types of files that cannot carry viruses are picture files (such as .GIF, .JPG, .TIF) and sound files (such as .WAV and .MP3), although it is of course possible to infect the players. However, today's virus writers have found a way to take advantage of people's trust in these types of files via email software.

Mass-market email software, such as Microsoft's Outlook Express, has done a lot to make email consistent and easier to use. However, as part of its effort to hide complexity from users, it has also made it easier for virus writers to take advantage of the unschooled.

Internet email is transmitted solely as plain text. In order to send binary files, such as word-processed files, pictures, sounds, and programs, across the Internet they must be translated into plain text. The most commonly used standard for this is known as MIME, and when you attach a file to an email message what is really happening is that your email software encodes the file for transmission. Mass-market email software decodes the attached file and turns it back into its original form, automatically, so that what the user sees is an email message with a little icon to click on to open the attached file. But because the email software also hides email headers, it is very difficult for unsophisticated users to check whether the file they're opening is genuinely safe or not. The best solution in most circumstances is to run anti-virus software, and keep it up to date. New viruses are released all the time. Most good anti-virus software includes an automatic updating facility, and if you have broadband the updates should be unnoticeable to users. It is false economy to install anti-virus software and not pay for the updates.

Anti-virus software is, however, only one element in the battle to protect your system. Although good anti-virus software does include some generic detection ability, most scanners depend on identifying known bits of program code ('signatures') to spot viruses. A very new virus may not be included in even the latest update. It is therefore always wise to look for a second opinion if you have reason to suspect a file you're about to open might be infected. Several reputable companies run Web-based free services that will scan either a hard drive or a single file for you; for a quick check they can be extremely useful.

It is also important, however, to educate users about the risks of attached files, and not to open files they weren't expecting, even if those files appear to come from users they trust. Virus writers have become very sophisticated at constructing messages that appear to be genuine and safe. It also can't be said too often how important it is to have up-to-date backups of your data. However, one problem with virus infections is that if they are not quickly identified and cleaned up, the virus may also infect the backups. This is another reason why it is vital to run anti-virus software and keep it up to date – you want to spot any virus that enters your system as quickly as possible and prevent it from doing any damage. You should also ensure that users' email software is configured *not* to automatically decode and run attachments.

The email headers in Figure 6 (*right*) are taken from an email message containing a virus that was circulating among the committee managing a tennis club. These headers are typically hidden from end users (you can access them by right-clicking on the message in Outlook and choosing Properties), but they clearly indicate cause for concern about opening the file attached to the message. There are two

From xxxxxxxxxxxxxxx@compuserve.com Thu Aug 15 21:56:09 2002

Received: from siaar1ab.compuserve.com (siaar1ab.compuserve.com [149.174.40.10]) by technetium.cix.co.uk (8.11.3/CIX/8.11.2) with ESMTP id g7FKu5J14270 for <xxxxxxxxxxxxxx@cix.compulink.co.uk>; Thu, 15 Aug 2002 21:56:05 +0100 (BST)

X-Envelope-From: xxxxxxxxxxxxxxx@compuserve.com

Received: (from mailgate@localhost) by siaar1ab.compuserve.com (8.9.3/8.9.3/SUN-REL-1.3) id QAA25947 for xxxxxxxxxxxxxxx@cix.compulink.co.uk; Thu, 15 Aug 2002 16:56:04 -0400 (EDT)

Sender: xxxxxxxxxxxxxxx@compuserve.com

Received: from Wqcky (pc-62-31-51-70-ch.blueyonder.co.uk [62.31.51.70]) by siaar1ab.compuserve.com (8.9.3/8.9.3/SUN-REL-1.3) with SMTP id QAA25844 for <xxxxxxxxxxxxxxx@cix.compulink.co.uk>; Thu, 15 Aug 2002 16:55:45 -0400 (EDT)

Date: Thu, 15 Aug 2002 16:55:45 -0400 (EDT)

Message-Id: <200208152055.QAA25844@siaar1ab.compuserve.com>

From: yyyyyyy <yyyyyyyy@aol.com>

To: xxxxxxxxxxxxxxx@cix.compulink.co.uk

Subject:

MIME-Version: 1.0

Content-Type: multipart/alternative; boundary=I27gGZn55m

--I27gGZn55m

Content-Type: text/html;

Content-Transfer-Encoding: quoted-printable

--I27gGZn55m

Content-Type: audio/x-wav; name=hspace.bat

Content-Transfer-Encoding: base64

Figure 6

Headers from an email carrying a virus; the most significant portions are shown in bold.

significant indicators. First and most important: although the message says the file is an audio file – that is, something that cannot carry viruses – the name of the file ends in .BAT. This means the attached file is an executable program file, which is masquerading as an audio file. The attached file is almost guaranteed to be a virus, as it's hard to imagine a legitimate reason for this kind of disguise. Second: although two lines list a compuserve.com address (From, Sender) as the sender, a few lines further down another (also From) lists an aol.com address, which in fact is the true source of the message. The faked From line at the top is the one your email software will pick up to show as the sender. It's not unknown for legitimate messages to have different 'from' and 'reply-to' addresses, but we already know this is not a legitimate message. The file attached to this message, when run through a virus checker, was identified as carrying the Yaha.E (also known as Lentin.G) worm.

Yaha.E is representative of today's viruses: it is stealthy and difficult to both identify and remove. If you open that attached file, the virus runs and infects the system. On execution, Yaha.E picks a random string of four characters and uses them to name its files, making it difficult to search for. It also alters the Windows registry to force every program that executes to go through its hook first, so that if you find and remove the program file (typically stored in C:\windows\recycled or c:\windows\recycler) your system is effectively disabled. The anti-virus software vendor F-Secure does, however, provide a simple tool for removing it. It is a perfect example of why anti-virus software is so important to run: prevention is a lot quicker than cure.

For instructions on what to do if you discover your computer is infected with a virus, see Chapter 8 on disaster recovery.

COMMON TYPES OF ATTACKS: TECHNICAL DETAILS

To understand how to secure your system, it's important to understand what you're securing it against. What follows are some examples. Bear in mind that TCP/IP was originally designed to create a robust network – but a trusted one in which all the users were academic researchers. It was intended to help people share information, not block it, and as a result security has generally been left for users to implement on their own systems.

'Denial of service' attacks are attacks intended to stop users of the target system from using their own system. Junk email, for example, in sufficient quantity could be thought of as a DoS attack if it fills a mailbox with limited capacity and thereafter blocks genuine email from arriving. The DDoS attacks referred to on p. 142 which were carried out against some of the Internet's major retailers blocked those retailers from operating by sending them floods of poorly formed IP packets that flooded their systems, rendering them unable to respond to genuine requests. Because the stream of packets came from hundreds of different hosts, the retailers couldn't simply block a source address. Any machine permanently connected to the Internet may be vulnerable to such an attack. It is important both to protect your system (by limiting what kinds of traffic are allowed in) and to protect others by ensuring that your system is not turned into an accomplice (by ensuring that unauthorized users can't install and run hidden software on your system). One type of DoS attack is known as the 'ping of death'; it uses Ping to send a fragmented IP packet that exceeds the maximum legal length (65535 octets) and will crash the target machine. Discovered in 1996, by 1997 operating system vendors had patched their software to block this particular problem. However, the existence of this technique is the reason many larger commercial Internet operations began to block Ping (and have continued to do so).

So-called 'SYN flood' attacks are denial of service attacks that takes advantage of the fact that TCP devices on the Internet trust each other and do not perform authentication or verification of each other. SYN flood works by sending out multiple messages requesting a connection (SYN) with faked source IP addresses to the target computer. The computer then allocates memory for the connection and sends an ACK (acknowledge) message to the faked IP address. That message will time out (because it's been sent to a faked address) and the computer will resend it, keeping the memory allocated. This repeats until the computer runs out of memory and can't create any more TCP connections or it crashes (or both). Some servers limit the damage of this kind of attack by limiting the number of opened TCP connections; there are also a number of other techniques (requiring a response before allocating the memory, for example) that prevent this type of attack from being successful.

Packet sniffers are programs that monitor a network connection, capturing and analysing the traffic that goes past just like a wiretap on a telephone line. There are many legitimate uses for packet sniffers; network administrators, for example, use them to detect bottlenecks and other network problems, and you yourself may decide to install one for this reason. However, a packet sniffer installed by an attacker or inserted between the two halves of a TCP connection may be used to capture information about your network and its traffic, such as passwords, the contents of email and Web sessions, and the pattern of correspondents. Of course you should ensure that an attacker can't put a packet sniffer on your system. A valuable protection against eavesdroppers is encryption, which is used to protect sensitive data such as credit card information in transit between a Web browser and a Web site and can also be used to protect email via a plug-in for your software. But encrypting the actual data is only part of the answer, since the pattern of who you communicate with and how often can be even more revealing than the content of what you actually say. The best solution to packet sniffers is preventive: ensure that your system is secured so that one can't be installed by an attacker without your knowledge.

Packet sniffers are far more of a risk with wireless connections, of course. Software is widely available on the Net to scan for access points and take snapshots of data passing. Some of this is purely for entertainment – one bit of software, known as Etherpeg, picks graphics from Web pages downloaded over the air and in a crowded 802.11b-enabled conference room can put together a fascinating mosaic.

These examples are not in any way intended to be comprehensive; they are merely intended to illustrate how fundamentally insecure the

Internet protocols are and why all users and system administrators must take responsibility for their own security.

THE PLAGUE OF JUNK EMAIL

Junk email may not seem like a security problem. In one sense, spam is relatively trivial: you can delete it pretty easily. But it's an incredible waste of resources. Apart from the extra disk space and bandwidth junk email consumes, real email can get lost in the noise. If users are dealing with email services that impose limits on the amount of email that can be stored in an inbox at any one time (this is especially a problem with free services), junk email that isn't cleared regularly can actually block out real email entirely. But it is a security issue in the sense that it's an unwanted intrusion.

There are basically two types of junk email: unwanted bulk email from companies you have actually done business with, and even more unwanted junk from companies and individuals you would never dream of doing business with. In the latter category go the (originally Nigerian) scams about acting as an intermediary to help someone get millions of dollars out of their country and the ads for credit repair, colon cleansers, get-rich-quick schemes, and so on. With email of this second type, you should not believe statements in the email that say you've been selected to receive the email because you've signed up for it or your name is on a list.

How you deal with junk email depends in part on which type it is, as well as how much control you have over your system and what facilities your ISP provides. There are essentially three points at which junk email can be removed: at the ISP, on its arrival to your system or servers, and on its arrival at the end user's email software.

A number of ISPs offer spam-blocking services either on their own (like AOL) or with a partner such as Brightmail. While this kind of setup can work very well, it's important to remember that by giving your ISP the right to judge what is and what is not junk you are taking the risk that it will block material you actually want. However, it has to be said that many of these services are effective. A Net search should give some idea whether the ISP has been caught overstepping its bounds.

Exactly what software is available to block junk at your server depends on what server you have and what operating system it runs on. Generally speaking, if you run any widely available server – Exchange Server, Lotus Notes – or any of the UNIX offerings you should be able to find something. Most such software, like anti-virus software, runs on a continuously updated database of known spam sources and IP addresses, and therefore a number of these products either require or support a subscription to a service such as MAPS (Mail Abuse Prevention System) that regularly updates the database. You should also be able to add your own selections to the list. Essentially, the software acts as a gatekeeper to block unwanted messages and attachments. Besides checking for email from known spammers, it filters messages based on email headers and transport information. These products are usually priced on a per-server or per-mailbox basis.

At the user level, good email software should support filtering beyond the rather crude and time-consuming method of hitting the delete key whenever an unwanted message arrives. If you want to design your own set of rules, there are some useful sets of tricks to help weed out whole categories of junk – you can't simply filter on the source addresses because these keep changing. Start by setting up a separate folder for the junk you filter out, so you can check that your rules aren't so broad that they're catching genuine email. Set up filters that look for phrases that are common in junk email but rare in legitimate email, such as '!!!!!', 'call now for your free', or 'remove in the subject'. You can filter out most Asian spam by using the settings that identify the character set in the email headers, such as 'charset="ks_c_5601-1987'. Software such as Outlook Express and Eudora Pro support user-defined filters, which are also useful for organizing and categorizing email so you can deal with it more efficiently in a logical order of priority.

There are a number of third-party services and add-ons that will delete junk email for you. Add-ons for popular software such as Outlook include SpamCop, which pools user reports of junk so that everyone benefits, and SpamAssassin, which also works with several other email clients such as Eudora. The company that makes Mailgate also distributes a piece of free software called SpamWeasel, which inserts itself between any email client and your POP3 mailbox, diverting material it identifies as junk into an archive you can review later. Other services maintain a 'white list' of correspondents. The first time someone emails you, the service sends back a request that requires a human response; once that person answers the challenge he or she is added to the list of known good correspondents. This kind of service can be very effective, but it is not suitable for businesses that must accept customer email. In all of these cases you should be very careful to review exactly what the system is identifying as junk until you are sure that legitimate email isn't being trapped by it.

There are some additional ways to protect users from junk email. Email addresses are often harvested from the Web, Usenet, and AOL chat services. If you have occasion to use those in the course of business use a separate email address for those activities from the one you use every day for email from colleagues. You may still have to monitor that account (especially if the junk is being attracted by a customer service or sales address posted on your Web site), but it all helps.

With the worst junk, it's generally considered unwise to follow the instructions that purport to remove you from the list for future mailings. It's more likely that responding will validate your address for future resale and use. However, if the email comes from a legitimate business, following the removal instructions does work, even though it's an annoying waste of time to have to do it for junk you never requested in the first place.

By late 2002, the overall volume of junk email had become so large that even the Direct Marketing Association began campaigning for legislation to block it. The problem – and the reason such legislation isn't generally considered a good solution – is that much spam comes from outside the areas that have the legislation. Junk emailers based in Korea, Russia, or Nigeria, or hit-and-run spammers who use either fake return addresses or free trial accounts on major services such as

Yahoo! or AOL don't care what US or UK legislation says. It is also very difficult to draft legislation that defines junk email without also capturing a number of types of legitimate email.

PRIVACY PROTECTION: GETTING RID OF WEB JUNK

One problem with allowing users to install free file-sharing programs on company machines is that some of them come with add-ons that bring with them vastly increased amounts of advertising and surveillance. Known as 'spyware', these programs are supposed to bring in revenue for the software developers by selling advertising space. But their impact is to double the amount of junk you have to wade through to get work done, and some of the tracking they do of personal preferences can be quite sinister. Many Web retailers hate these programs because they often pop up ads for competitors when users visit their sites. Other advertisers are simply so profligate that they're annoying (like X10, which does give you the option of blocking its ads for thirty days by going to a link on its Web site).

Ad agencies like Doubleclick collect information about users' Web usage in order to target ads more effectively. Although they say the data is not personally identifiable, many of these services do assign a unique user ID to each machine, which is used to track preferences and interests based on browsing habits. In some cases you can opt out of this tracking so that although you still see ads, they're generic instead of targeted.

You can check your system for spyware via the free program Ad-Aware (http://www.lavasoft.de). Be careful, however, about letting it delete the programs it finds – turn on the backup options and if possible do a quick Net search to check whether the software you're removing has any special troubles associated with it. Some, such as the alternative domain name software Newdotnet, can disable some parts of your Internet connection if removed incorrectly (and sometimes even if removed correctly). Repairing the damage requires you to edit the registry, a low-level bit of hands-on work that should be attempted only by experts since the registry is where Windows stores all the settings needed to make your computer work.

Because all this is a time-wasting nuisance that consumes bandwidth, it's simpler to stop users from installing unauthorized programs by not granting them administrator rights over their own machines (see p. 78) and/or via your acceptable use policy (see page 109). However, free file-sharing programs are not the only source of spyware; some software that purports to block unwanted pop-up ads also brings with it ads of its own. The other common sources are free programs advertised to manage downloads and some Internet phone software. Often the spyware modules are billed in the software's installation routine as money-savers offering discounts. Online indexes catalogue hundreds of programs that carry such modules.

If you do want to get rid of pop-up ads there are, however, software programs without these troubles that do this successfully. Look for Proxomitron, which installs itself as a proxy (see pp. 107–8) and speeds up Web use substantially.

With all software, read through the licensing terms and check what the stated policy is concerning what types of data they collect, and what they do with it. If you do not like the terms, do not install the software and, in order to push people to behave in responsible ways, notify the originating company of your decision and the reasons for it. If you have a firewall installed that includes outbound blocking, it should stop spyware that lives on your computer from sending out monitoring data.

PORNOGRAPHY AND COPYRIGHT

You may not think of someone's downloading pornography as a security risk, but it can be, quite apart from the wastage of resources such as staff time, disk space, and bandwidth. Engaging in widespread but common activities such as sharing copyrighted material online and using unlicensed software can also put your company at risk.

Most pornography online is not illegal; but some of it is. The Internet Watch Foundation (http://www.iwf.org.uk) acts as a clearing house for reports from the public. If on investigation the IWF finds reported material to be illegal, it issues an advisory to ISPs to remove the material from their servers and notifies the police. The problem for a small business with staff who download pornography is that unless you monitor what's being downloaded you won't know if any of it is illegal. Any time a machine goes in for repair, if illegal material is found by a service repairman who reports it to the police, you could be prosecuted. That's what happened in the case of pop star Gary Glitter. In such a circumstance, the police investigation is unlikely to be limited to just the machine taken in for repair. You could find your whole system carted away for an indefinite period of time, enough to put a small company out of business. A secondary consideration is that stored pornography could open you to a sexual harassment claim.

TIP When you redesign your system, redesign your security from the ground up. Don't fudge by patching the old system.

A third is that pornography has been used as a vehicle for a variety of scams. In one case, a Web site asked visitors to download a special 'image viewer'. In fact, the downloaded program was a Trojan that dropped the dial-up connection to the regular ISP and silently redialled a premium-rate number in Moldova. Other malicious programs also entice people to run them by masquerading as pornography. Though viruses also masquerade as screensavers, audio files, and documents sent by colleagues, pornography represents a wholly unnecessary risk unless you're in that business.

Copyright violation isn't the same level of risk as pornography, but it has some elements in common. As noted in the discussion on software licences (see pp. 31–4), if you run your business on unlicensed software you may find that consultants are unwilling to help you. In addition, the organizations that monitor software overuse encourage employees to report companies that run commercial software they haven't paid for. A company that's been reported is usually offered the chance to audit its systems and bring them into compliance. Failure to do so can lead to a dawn 'Anton

Piller' raid and public prosecution. Again, this is the sort of thing that can put a small company out of business.

File-sharing services such as Gnutella and KaZaA pose slightly different risks. If your Internet connection is dial-up via modem or ISDN, file-sharing is unlikely to be a problem because you're not continuously connected and the speeds are too slow. Once you have broadband, file-sharing becomes much more of a temptation. For a small business, it poses three problems. The first is that file-sharing is typically two-way. Users designate a drive or directory that is shared with everyone else using that service. As the software indexes all files of certain media types (usually audio and video, sometimes programs and text) in that directory or drive, uneducated users may inadvertently make confidential company information available to the public. We've already talked (see pp. 101–2) about the consumption of resources such as storage space and bandwidth.

A potentially dangerous factor is the fact that the entertainment industry is becoming ever more aggressive about going after the most active file-sharers, particularly those who make large collections of copyrighted material available to others. On most file-sharing services, someone who devotes the resources can trace such users, and increasingly the entertainment industry is proposing to do just that, going after the users of such services rather than the companies that write the software and/or provide the servers. You do not want your small business dragged into a prosecution intended to make a worldwide point about copyright theft, even if you disagree with the current trends in intellectual property law.

These are, therefore, all issues to consider when you devise your acceptable-use policy as discussed on p. 109.

WRITING A SECURITY POLICY

The reason to write a security policy is that until you know what you want to protect and to what level of security you cannot make any decisions about what kind of security to implement. As the section on firewalls explains, you cannot simply install a firewall and expect it to solve all your problems. Many of the most powerful attacks on organizations have nothing to do with the Internet at all but use the technique known as 'social engineering' to convince human staff to hand over information to someone they shouldn't. A firewall merely implements a portion of the security policy you've decided upon.

Some items are common to all security policies. You should give a general overview of why the policy is being put in place, what is covered by the policy, what is not covered, whether there are any exceptions, the scope – which operating systems, machines, networks, people are included – and who is in charge of the policy's operation. If the policy represents a big cultural change, you will need to get across to users why it's necessary.

Users should never give their passwords to anyone no matter how knowledgeable they seem. Users should not post their passwords on their monitors on Post-it notes where they may be seen by outsiders visiting the company. In companies large enough so that not all staff know each other, anyone being asked to divulge information such as that contained in database records, their own IDs and/or passwords, or even employee names and phone numbers should check that the person making the request really is who he says he is. The fact that someone phoning in knows the codes to work the database and appears to be a company staff member is not sufficient evidence. Get a phone number and check before phoning back.

Other items in your security plan depend on how your business works. For example, you might decide that all email attachments should be scanned for viruses on arrival using one of any of the anti-virus products on the market.

Finally, you must enforce both your security policy and your acceptable-use policy and be seen to do so, even if it means firing someone at board level (or calling in the police) because that's the action you have stated will take place if a particular violation is found.

8 Disasters: Planning for Recovery

'Can we please have more warning of unscheduled downtime in future?'

Client email to consultant

First: when a disaster happens do not panic.

Second: plan *now* for that moment so you won't have to.

It's often said that there are only two kinds of users: those who have lost their data and those who are going to lose their data. The fact is that even though today's computer hardware is extremely reliable you should always have a plan for what to do when some part of your infrastructure fails. That plan, like your security arrangements, needs to be continuously updated as circumstances change and regularly reviewed at least once a month.

Disaster planning should not be limited to your computer system but should include all parts of your business, from how you'll keep going if the phones are out to what you'll do in the event of the sudden loss of a key staff member. What will you do if the electricity goes off because someone's driven a pneumatic drill through the mains cable out in the street? Fires, floods, thefts, malicious damage, even terrorist attacks – these are all dangers to plan for. Identify the key parts of your infrastructure and plan how you will handle the situation if those fail, even if you can't foresee everything.

TIP Do you know where your backups are? Are they sitting in a box on top of the server? Or, worse, in its drive? If it gets stolen, where will they be?

The standard statistic in this area is frightening: according to PriceWaterhouse, 90 per cent of all companies that experience a computer 'disaster' and have no survival plan go out of business within eighteen months.

Obviously backups of your computer data are a key element of any disaster recovery plan. But they are not the whole game.

This is a good time to think through what third parties you depend on. Do you have a computer consultant and is that person the only one who knows the passwords for the account with your ISP or understands how your network is configured? Do you depend for key information, services, or products on a sole supplier? What happens if that supplier is the one who has the disaster?

As part of your planning, you should take a walk through your premises and let the most pessimistic side of your personality take over. Is the server situated uncomfortably close to a pipe that could leak on it? Are you storing the backup copies next to a radiator so they'll be damaged by the heat?

These questions should sound familiar to anyone who completed one of those checklists that were all the rage in 1999, when people were panicking about the Year 2000 problem. What was silly at the time was not the panic itself but how short a time it lasted: if your business was at risk if your computer got its dates tangled on 1/1/2000, you are at risk tomorrow if your computer fails or is stolen.

After the 11 September 2001 attacks in the USA, for example, because they had recovery plans in place many of the businesses that had offices in the World Trade Center were up and running again within a few days either at satellite offices that were already in existence or at premises rented in the attacks' aftermath. In fact, the World Trade Center attacks were a perfect example of how dangerous it can be to have too much infrastructure centred at the same single point of failure. Communications, broadcasting, power, and even the intended coordination point for emergency services were all taken out when the buildings collapsed.

The important principle is simple: you are trying to ensure that your business will be able to continue with minimal interruption no matter what happens.

DATA AND SYSTEM BACKUPS

In terms of your computer system, the key element of any disaster recovery plan is backups. There are two parts needed for any backup strategy: (1) working technology that actually backs up the data; (2) safe storage of the media holding the data.

The first question is: what qualifies as a backup? If you want to take a hard line on the matter, you'd say that the only thing that qualifies as a backup is one that no-fail absolutely will be usable under all conceivable circumstances. Depending on your situation, that may not be feasible with just one type of backup; you may find your best shot is layers of alternatives that can be called in depending on the situation.

To a hardliner, a backup that's stored on-site doesn't count. Fire, flood, theft, or a bomb scare could all deprive you of access to it: you cannot assume access to your office or even your building. So a backup is a copy that's stored off-site.

To a hardliner, a backup that's written on an unstable medium or one that is not guaranteed to run in widely available standard hardware does not count. That means CD-RW is out (because many CD drives cannot read them), and so is writable DVD (because the standards have yet to settle down and the drives are not widely available), and tape. Yes, tape backups are very common and inexpensive, but they are fraught with problems. The tape may stretch. The drive may have slowly gone out of alignment so that the tape can't be read accurately on a different one, even though it's the same make and model. The make and model you need may no longer be available and newer drives may not be compatible. Floppy disks, well . . . they are standard and they are everywhere. But floppy disks can fail, and the disks written in one machine are not always readable in another, and the capacity is very small. If you must use floppy disks, make two copies, and have them written by two different machines on your network. Zip drives, especially those that take the larger capacity disks, may not be available. CDs don't have these problems: the medium is stable and the drives to read them are everywhere.

Plus, they are cheap so you can make multiple copies and lodge them in several different places.

You will probably also want to have a second type of backup that's handier if you need to restore a file or two that get damaged or lost, or that compensates for a single machine failure by making the data available to a second one. So, for example, you may want to ensure that the main data file for whatever software runs your core business is mirrored on several different machines and that all those mirrors are updated throughout the day. Or you may want to keep a dynamically updated laptop or a copy in an easily grabbed form in case you need to leave quickly in an emergency – higher capacity Compact Flash, perhaps (making sure the PC Card adaptor for the Compact Flash card is with the laptop, of course). For a contact list, a backup could be as simple as a daily printout sent home with a staff member. It would take time to key it all back in, of course, but you would still have your customer list.

An additional possibility for live on-site backups is either an external hard drive (you can get very fast 160GB external FireWire drives now for a few hundred pounds), a networked device like a SnapServer, or, for the more technically adept, a RAID (redundant array of inexpensive disks). In a crisis where you have to leave the office, grabbing an external hard drive and taking it with you wouldn't be too difficult.

With the advent of broadband, storing off-site backups via an Internet service has become a realistic and convenient possibility, and there are a number of companies that offer such a service. These may range from as little as $7 (just over £4) a month for 100MB of critical data, to $24.95 (£15.50) a month for 10GB. You will need to decide what type of backup you want – critical data, all data and important system files, full backup – and test not only that the service's software works the way you want but that the backups it creates work the way you expect and restore correctly. Many such services offer a thirty-day free trial, and you should take advantage of this to test them thoroughly. The big advantage to the online services is that you can access them from anywhere, including from on the road with a laptop you've just discovered is missing a key file. The disadvantage is that you are relying on this third party to provide an essential service. You should, as far as you can, check on the stability and longevity of the company that hosts the service.

It can't be said often enough that it's not enough just to create the backups. You need to test – regularly – that you can restore a system using them. The last thing you want to find when disaster strikes is that the backups you've told the newly imported consultant you have are in reality copies of the backup software or haven't been working for four months. If that happens after the consultant has begun restoring your system from scratch, you will have lost all your data. When you run your backup software, check any error messages that appear very carefully. If you do not know what they mean, find someone who does and fix whatever the problem is promptly.

Testing that your backups restore correctly and can be read on different hardware is part of the regular review you should conduct of your disaster recovery plan.

BACKUP STRATEGIES

This is an area where Microsoft and personal computing designs have seriously let both businesses and consumers down. Making regular backups should be a default built into the operating system, not an optional extra. PCs should include a backup device as part of the specification. Operating systems should make backups mandatory – and they don't (although Apple's OS X supports an automatic online backup via its MacUnlimited service). That places the onus on you, the unwilling IT administrator, to ensure that everything that is critical to your business gets backed up. The lack of failure-proof disaster recovery systems in most small businesses is a big reason that many consultants advise their small business clients not to computerize their accounting systems. If you lose your customer list, you can work out ways to regenerate it. If you lose the last nine months of invoices, your business is dead. Therefore, your backup strategy must form part of your purchasing decisions.

Many people with small systems think it's easier just to back up the data on their machines and simply reinstall the software if they need to. If that is your strategy, you need to bear a couple of things in mind. First of all, it's rare for software to remain exactly the way it comes out of the box. Most software these days is highly customizable, and most users take at least some advantage of that fact. If you're going to reinstall the software from scratch, be aware that you will also have to duplicate the configuration. With many packages that's easily done – Microsoft Word, for example, stores all of its configuration in the global template file NORMAL.DOT, and as long as you back up that file along with copies of any custom document templates you have created along the way, you should be able to duplicate your customized installation of Word with ease. With other packages, however, it's not so easy and you may have to allow time to restore their settings. This is one area where it's worth doing an online search and/or asking other users because often there are ways of backing up a configuration that aren't mentioned in the manual. That can save you a lot of time and aggravation.

TIP Don't make a problem into a disaster. Most disasters start as little niggles and one 'fix' leads to another until someone does something catastrophic – like getting carried away at an auction. Especially, if you have a consultant whose job it is to take care of the server, don't tinker with it without checking first.

Second of all, if you're going to reinstall, you're going to have to ensure that you have master copies of all your software in a safe location, off-site, along with all the CD keys, registration numbers, passwords, and any other information needed to unlock the software for daily use. If some of it was downloaded from the Internet, don't assume that you're going to be able to find the same version again: time goes by, new versions get released, and the old ones are sometimes withdrawn. You should therefore ensure that you have backup copies of the original downloads. Given this, it may be as much or more work to do data-only backups and plan to reinstall software as it is to do full backups of your entire system.

However, there are other potential pitfalls of relying solely on full system backups, notably that some software will not restore to a computer that is even only slightly different from the one used in the original installation. As hardware manufacturers change their product line-ups with increasing frequency, you may well find it impossible to get an exact copy of a server if one's gone down. In such a case, reinstalling from scratch may be your only option to get a system that functions correctly. Again, the way to find out is to do a test restore sometime when there's no panic on and you can test your strategy in relative calm.

REDUNDANCY

Anything can fail, not just your computer. And not only your computer can be stolen or damaged. Keep spares of key components around. Things like ethernet cables, hubs, power leads, USB cables, keyboards, and mice are all inexpensive enough that it's worth having extras, just as you keep spares of toner and inkjet cartridges, paper, and other necessities. Being able to swap a spare from the cupboard can save you hours on an important deadline if something fails.

The best protection against server failure has traditionally been the mirror – an identical server kept up to date with the same software and data which is ready to go if the first one fails. This used to be a hugely expensive option available only to large corporations, but by now hardware costs have dropped enough to make it a possibility even for a small business. The problem comes in ensuring that the software that runs your business will support it. For example, Small Business Server only allows one server, so a mirror isn't a possibility although servers can be added to run pieces of the software (such as Exchange Server). If you need to run mirror servers, you will have to move to Back Office.

Redundancy does not necessarily mean having two of everything. The backup for your fax machine, for example, may be the shop down the street that sends faxes for a specified fee per page. The backup for your broadband is most likely going to be either an ordinary modem and phone line or an ISDN line. What redundancy means is simply that you have more than one way of doing things, so that you have an alternative if the first-choice method fails.

REHEARSE

Whatever your recovery plan is, rehearse it. Check the details *regularly*. Is the shop down the street you can send faxes from still offering the service? Does the dial-up account you plan to use as a backup if the ISP that provides your broadband falls over still exist? (Some free services delete accounts that haven't been used for ninety days.) If you've updated your installation of Windows with a new service pack, have you saved a copy with the other master disks? You should remember to update your plan whenever you make a change to your system or business processes.

Similarly, you should try out your plan for restoring your computers in a dummy run. The time to find out you're missing a password or aren't sure how to configure a bunch of settings isn't in the middle of a crisis but in advance when things are calm. You should also test your backups regularly. It's sad but true that a common problem in a disaster is the discovery that the regular backups do not restore correctly. Make sure yours do not fall into that category.

TIP If you haven't got the equipment necessary to rehearse a complete restoration of your server from scratch as part of building up your disaster recovery plan, rent it. The cost may even be recoverable, since some business insurers require comprehensive disaster recovery plans and either won't insure you without them or may be willing to renegotiate your premiums if you can show them you've tried your procedures and therefore know they work.

Also make sure your staff know what the plan is and whom to contact if there's a crisis. The disaster plan should not depend on one key person who may be away or unavailable when the details are needed. Obviously you don't want to give every staff member every password and serial number, but ensure that the information that would be needed in a crisis is stored somewhere safe and that the people responsible for retrieving it in an emergency know what to do.

IN CASE OF VIRUS INFECTION

As always, the first thing is not to panic.

The second is to make sure that the problem really is a virus. In some cases, this is easy: the virus may announce its presence by, for example, scrawling words across your screen or popping up a bit of text. In such a case, search for information about the virus via either Google or one of the anti-virus software vendors' information sites, and follow the instructions you find for removing it. In other cases, though, the symptoms are quite subtle, and may be easily confused with ordinary software or hardware failures. Stop and think whether you've recently installed any new software or hardware that could be causing a problem. If you have kept a log of changes to the system (as recommended on p. 190), it should be easy to pinpoint if any changes were made just before the trouble started.

If you run anti-virus software, the next step is to download the latest update and see if it finds a virus. Most vendors of anti-virus software react very quickly when a new virus is discovered, especially if it's widespread.

If you don't, you can either download and run a scanner or trial version, or point your hard drive at one of the Web sites that will scan for viruses for you. When the user who sent the email message whose headers appear in Figure 6 (see p. 161) did so, the site found thirteen virus-infected files on his machine. However, this was after he'd already sent out scores of infected messages to other members of a club committee so that many other unprotected machines got infected.

The key thing before taking any action if you do have an infected machine is to ensure that you have correctly identified the virus. They are all different, and they require different technical strategies for removal. Many virus-like symptoms – for example, the machine slowing down and cutting out – may in fact be caused by other hardware or software problems. However, if you can trace the problems to opening and running a specific attached file, that's probably a clear indicator that you have a virus – and if you still have the attached file in question you can scan it to make sure and identify the culprit.

Make a new set of backups of any crucial data before proceeding. Making a new set means that you don't risk contaminating the old backups if they are not yet infected with the virus and it also means that any data you've created since your last backup is copied.

Be careful, however, about installing or running anti-virus software over an existing infection; at the very least make sure you read the software's user manual and installation instructions carefully. It may be a better strategy to find a tool specifically designed to remove the virus you have; vendors often release these for free. Ideally, you should use an uninfected machine to download the tool onto a floppy disk and use that to clean the infected system. Then install the anti-virus software, making sure to let it scan your entire system for infected files you may not know about. Once your system is clearly clean, you can proceed with greater confidence.

Without using a scanner and just going by symptoms, it's very difficult to identify a virus. Obviously the first suspect is whatever virus is in the news this week. But most virus information libraries are organized by virus name, not by virus symptoms, and many are not indexed by the search engines, making it difficult to identify what a particular infection is. Some viruses, such as Yaha.E, use random names for their files, making it impossible to do a simple hard drive search. However, many leave standard text file markers, and if you really want to confirm the scanner's findings you may be able to search on a known string of text that appears in those marker files.

Do everything you can to identify the virus you have before installing anything; back up your data onto a fresh set of disks or a separate location (in case the data is infected) before attempting removal; and read as much as you can about the tools you're going to use before you install them.

Bear in mind that the best anti-virus software cannot identify viruses that have appeared since its last update. If the anti-virus software hasn't been updated for more than three years, it will not be able to detect the month-old virus that's doing the rounds this week. Most anti-virus software will warn you if it is out of date and recommend you update it. If you do not know how to update your anti-virus software, call the vendor and find out.

UNINTERRUPTIBLE POWER SUPPLIES (UPS)

Checking the battery in your UPS should be one item in your regular review of your disaster recovery plan – time how long the battery lasts and make sure it's larger than it takes the machine it supports to shut down safely. If you do not have a UPS, consider carefully whether you need one. UPSs are not designed to keep you working if the power goes off; they are designed to help you make an orderly shutdown and ensure that your equipment is not damaged and you do not lose your data. Keeping working is a separate problem that needs to be solved in a different way.

Unless you're going to go out and buy your own generator, one thing you can't back up is your source of electrical power. You can, however, limit the damage an outage is going to cause with a UPS. These heavy devices, which even their manufacturers agree qualify as the most boring pieces of IT equipment in anyone's catalogue, run long enough to let you shut down your system in an orderly way if the power goes out.

If you've ever knocked a plug out of its outlet by accident and had the machine work perfectly when you restart it afterwards, you may wonder why a UPS is necessary. But the loss of power that takes down a machine will take with it the files you're working on, losing you data and possibly corrupting both the files and the programs themselves. Worse, hardware can be damaged – especially if there's a surge when the power comes back and you've left the equipment switched on. A UPS between your computer system and the mains supply also acts as a conditioner, ensuring that any spikes, surges, or high-frequency noise are smoothed out.

A computer runs on DC – direct current. The power supply inside the system unit (or outside it, in the case of a laptop) takes the AC – alternating current – power that comes from the wall and converts it to DC. A UPS looks much like a mini-tower computer, although it's much heavier. Inside it are a rectifier battery charger, battery, inverter, and voltage monitor. The current comes in from the wall and passes through the rectifier, which converts it to DC. A small trickle passes to the battery to keep it charged, and the rest goes into the inverter, which converts it back to AC – now a clean, perfect AC – and feeds it to the computer's power supply. In the event of a power failure, the load draws current from the battery. A series of lights on the outside of the box usually tells the user how much battery life is left.

Power protection devices must be chosen to match the load they're going to run. The trade-off is that more power means more expense, but a device that's not rated high enough can't power the load you need it to run. So the first step in deciding what to buy is finding out how much power is needed. This is pretty easily done, since several of the manufacturers (notably APC, at http://www.apc.com) have calculators on their Web sites that let you list the devices you want to supply with backup power and tell you what capacity you need and how long it will last given the load you've specified.

TIP In a computer crisis, stop, take your hands off the keyboard, and think before doing anything that might make the problem worse. VERY IMPORTANT EXCEPTION: anything to do with liquid. Anything wet – coffee, tea, water, soft drinks – combined with the electricity that is coursing through your system can damage your computer beyond repair. Act very fast to disconnect everything from the power source. (In the case of a laptop, also disconnect the battery.) Do not reconnect the power until the machine (or even keyboard) has been thoroughly cleaned and dried. Otherwise, you might as well just start arranging the funeral.

If you want to do it yourself, it's still pretty easily done: most computer equipment has a plate on the back specifying the number of watts it draws. Add up the wattage of the various devices you want to cover – computer, hard drive, broadband modem, perhaps – and that gives the total power requirements of the load. A complication is that computer manufacturers talk about watts and kilowatts but power protection manufacturers talk about volt-amps (VA) and kilo volt-amps (kVA). You can always also ask the UPS manufacturer to make recommendations for your specific load; but remember to allow for expansion of your system and recalculate any time you add a new device that has to be supported. It's better to overspecify and gain extra time than be caught short.

Many UPSs come with bundled software that integrates with your operating system to monitor battery life and manage safe system shutdown. Exactly what equipment you cover with your UPS depends on your configuration and what items are essential to your business, and that's something only you can decide. Remember that workstations may also need UPS support particularly if they work on a shared database. Obviously you don't need to include laptops, since they already have batteries that can keep them going in a power outage. Few would choose to include a printer because even if the printer's memory is wiped it's easy enough to send the file again. Finally, if you have a laser printer *do not* plug it into a UPS because the way it draws power can cause the UPS to overheat and shut down.

MOBILE USERS

Remember the one about the Ministry of Defence laptop stolen from a car? That could happen to anyone on any given day. Mobile users, because they're disconnected from the company network most of the time, must carry their own data stores. But laptops and personal digital assistants (PDAs) are more fragile than desktop machines, and they lead a higher-risk existence: they get banged around and dropped, and are much more vulnerable to theft. The upshot is that anyone travelling with a laptop should also carry some kind of backup facility. This may be online – a daily link to an online data storage service or back to the office over either dial-up or a VPN. Or it may be via any one of a number of highly portable options, such as high-capacity Compact Flash cards (1GB models became available in late 2002), so-called Pendrives or their many clones (which plug into any Windows machine USB slot without extra drivers, fit unnoticeably on a keyring and hold up to 1GB of data), portable MP3 players and hard drives (whose capacity may be 20GB or more) or, sometimes available for more recent model laptops, writable CD-ROM.

Ideally, if you have a laptop, you want both an online backup and a portable one. The online one (either an online service or a VPN to the home network) you'd want to restore your laptop's entire working environment if the one you're travelling with gets lost or damaged. The portable one you'd want to carry the projects you're working on and any presentations you're supposed to make. If, for example, something goes wrong with your equipment just before you're due to make a presentation, there might not be time to pull down an online copy onto a local machine but you can plug a Compact Flash card into a PC Card adaptor and then into just about any laptop. Some new projectors even have PC Card slots for just that sort of use. Similarly, you can plug a Pendrive into a USB outlet on just about any modern Windows machine and have it work. Given these technologies, you could arguably even travel without the laptop and all its messy accoutrements.

UPGRADES, MOVES, AND OTHER UPHEAVALS

In many ways, even a planned upgrade or move is a lot like a disaster. At least, it needs to be treated as one in the making: whatever backup and recovery plans you have, this is the moment to make sure they are up to date and that everything is backed up safely before you start. Remember to update your Emergency Repair Disks in Windows, too. Even the largest businesses have been known to bungle upgrades by rolling them out too widely, too soon, with inadequate testing, and no way back to a known good state.

For upgrades, in general the best strategy is almost always to continue to run the old system while the new one is installed, configured, and tested on a spare backup copy of the current data to make sure it works correctly. If possible run the new and old systems in parallel for long enough to ensure the new one works correctly before phasing the old system out.

Moves are more fraught than upgrades, if only because you can't carry them out without taking down your servers for a time (unless you install all new equipment in the new location). This is especially a problem for things like Exchange Servers, where taking them down takes away your ability to receive email. Make sure you carry out full online backups of such servers before you shut them down.

TIP Most people do not think well in an emergency. Do your thinking in advance.

Begin by making a timetable of the move, starting with the endpoint – the moment when you want the network to be fully functioning again – and a list of all the resources that need to be available at the destination in order to bring the server (especially) and other machines back up in their new location. Since a lot of businesses plan moves over weekends so the business interruption will be as unnoticeable as possible, that endpoint is likely to be first thing Monday morning. Then work backwards. What time do you need to start setting up the servers? How long do you need to allow to physically transport the machines from one location to another? When will the new location be ready, accessible to you, and with electrical service, phone, and Internet connections all up and running, cable installation work complete? There's no point in taking down a functioning server and moving it into a building where the power won't be turned on for another two days, so make sure your information on the state of these necessities is kept up to date. From your endpoint you can work backwards to figure out when you need to start turning off the network.

While you're making your timetable and list, develop a contingency plan for what to do if the preconditions you need for moving the system aren't met.

If the move is more than a few machines, take a floor plan and assign numbers (or colours) to the rooms and spaces on the floor plan and label the machines according to which room they're going in. Make sure the movers have copies of the floor plan and that further copies are available at both the old and new sites. If all the equipment is delivered to the right locations, it will make setting your network back up much faster.

Also ensure that the movers – whether hired professionals or helpful friends – are careful when moving the machines. You'd think it would go without saying, but as comparatively robust as computers have become they can still be damaged beyond repair in a move. If possible, pack them in the original box and packaging material they were delivered in. Ensure that all machines, including rack-mounted servers, are secured before the truck drives off. If you wind up driving the machines yourself and don't have the original packaging, pad them and wedge them securely or use the car's seatbelts to hold them in place. Make sure your insurance covers damage or loss of equipment during the move.

9 Getting Help: Technical Support and DIY

The moment will always come with any computer system when you need help. Either something breaks, or you have trouble installing new software or hardware, or you get sick of not being able to get the system to do something it was supposed to when you bought it. At this point, you have several options: try to find out how to fix it yourself; call technical support; get some training; live with it until you replace the equipment; or call in a consultant or hire technical staff.

This chapter assumes you're going to try one of the first four of those options, and we're going to take them in that order of increasing desperation. Hiring and managing consultants and technical staff is covered in the next chapter.

Trying to find out how to fix it yourself generally these days means searching the Internet for technical information; if you are even somewhat technically able this is often faster than calling technical support. This is especially true if the problem may relate to the interaction of equipment from several different manufacturers, as the manufacturers themselves are unlikely to have tried every combination. The first section of this chapter therefore looks at how to find technical information on the Internet. The second looks at how to get the best out of technical support when and if you do call. The third looks at training. The final section looks at when you should conclude that you can't live with the equipment any longer.

TIP Do not buy a system for which support is scarce unless there is an overwhelming reason to do so; if you do, you can find yourself locked into a single supplier, a situation that is much better for the supplier than it is for you.

WHEN THINGS GO WRONG: FIRST STEPS

First, don't panic. Take your hands off the computer and stop and think before you do anything to make the problem worse. If you have an ongoing relationship with a consultant and you can't identify the problem with a few simple tests, call the consultant. Depending on the terms of your contract with that consultant, this may or may not cost you money. But if you make a small problem into a large disaster, it will certainly cost you many times the amount you'd save if you were able to fix it successfully yourself.

Second, if this is the first time this problem has occurred, ask yourself and everyone else: what has changed? It is extremely common for weird and mysterious network faults to be the result of adding new software or hardware (or, often, both), or someone's tripping over a cable and unplugging something vital, or someone's making an unannounced decision to alter a configuration or replug a cable. This is where three pieces of advice can save you a lot of trouble. First, whenever possible, keep a log of the system changes you make so it's easy to roll back the last one. Second, only ever change one thing at a time, and don't go on to change the next thing until the first one has been cleared as presenting no problems. If restarting a particular machine is disruptive, it can be very tempting to do several things at once – say, add a FireWire card and an extra monitor and replace the network card, with new software needed for each one. But if you now have a problem, which new component is causing it? Third: do not make system changes when you're in the middle of a major project or facing an important deadline unless you absolutely have to. If your system is working, do not risk breaking it at a crucial moment. Wait to make changes until the pressure is less.

Most technical support calls follow a set routine. First, they ask you to check all the connections. Is everything plugged in correctly? Is everything turned on? Is the software loaded? What version are you running? These are things you can check before making the call (perhaps even obviating the need for the call), so you might as well, and it could save both time and money (if you must pay for technical support). While you're checking these things, make the list of details recommended at the beginning of the section on calling technical support (see p. 198) – if nothing else, you can add it to the pile of documentation for your system that you're keeping as part of your disaster recovery plan (see Chapter 8).

If you can identify the problem just by asking around, the solution is obvious: undo whatever was changed. If you can't identify it by that means, the next step is to start a process of elimination to test the various pieces. A standard part of diagnosing a problem is to change one variable at a time. For example, if you have a scanner that won't power up, first check that the AC power cord is correctly connected at both ends and that the outlet is turned on (if it has a switch). If it still doesn't work, try substituting a different AC power cord. If that changes nothing, try the scanner again with the original power cord at a different outlet. And so on. (For networks using BNC coax you use a variant of this, which is to divide the network in two, put a terminator at each end of each section and see which one works – this is where utilities like Ping, discussed in on p. 69, come in handy. Repeat with the non-working half until you locate the problem.)

Once you've eliminated each variable one at a time, whatever's left is most likely to be the problem.

With software that crashes or refuses to run, the strategy is a little different but similar: close down all the other programs that are open and try to repeat the steps that led to the crash so you can identify exactly what makes it happen. If the software now refuses to crash, the problem may be an interaction between it and another program. Your system may be able to help you: in the business versions of Windows you can consult the Event Viewer (accessible through Administrative Tools in the Control Panel), which will give you some (possibly incomprehensible) technical information on what happened. Read any error messages you find and write down what they say before clearing them off your screen. These can give valuable clues (and you will need them if you call technical support). If a file name is mentioned as the cause of the error, locate the file on your computer and see if you can work out which program it's associated with. (In Windows, ALT-ENTER or right-click | Properties brings up information about the file's origins.) Often, you can identify the source just from seeing which program folder the file is located in.

Remember that software interactions can be complex, and the software that's causing the problem may not be the program you are using at the moment the error message appears. The trick is to read all the information in the window that appears – in Windows the name of the file involved may appear in the title bar of the error message window. A 'memory could not be read' error message that appeared in one case whenever any multimedia application (and a few that weren't in that category) was closed turned out to be related to the scheduling module in an audio recording program. Removing the scheduling module solved the problem. There was nothing wrong with the other applications. Misidentifying the source of an error like that and removing harmless software can cost you a lot of time that could be saved by paying greater attention to the logging information you already have available.

Often even hardware problems are really software problems: a bug in the driver, perhaps. If hardware or software is newly installed and giving trouble, the standard first step is to restart the computer in case something simply didn't load properly the last time. If that doesn't work, the usual next step is to delete the device or software that is causing the problem and reinstall it from scratch. (Make sure any program data and configuration is backed up before you uninstall, of course.) Doing this will fix a surprising number of problems. There is, however, one real problem with the ease-of-use of USB: it can be very hard to debug. A driver that causes your system to crash when it's loaded doesn't load when the device that needs it isn't connected. This means that either you can't find the driver to delete it or you can't get to it because your system has crashed, an infinite loop solvable only by either rebuilding the machine's software from scratch or leaving the driver installed but never using that device.

If these strategies don't work, the next step is usually to look on the manufacturer's Web site for software updates. The problem you have may be a common one, and it may already have been fixed. Even if your problem isn't a common one, this is usually the next step technical support will recommend. You should of course make sure that the update is intended for the version of the software or hardware you have – check not only the model/version number but also the country. An update for, say, the US version of QuickBooks will not apply to the UK version. If you can't find a Web site for the manufacturer – which does happen with some smaller hardware operations that sell in the UK solely through distributors – try typing the name of the manufacturer into Google (http://www.google.com) along with the words 'distributor UK'. With any luck, you'll find a Web site for the company that handles the item.

In some cases – especially hardware that's broken on arrival – you are best off going back to the shop where you bought the goods. If, however, you're trying to put together a complex system like a network, unless the shop has well-trained specialists on its staff and technical support for putting together the things you buy was included in the purchase price, you're likely to run into a dead end. This is where buying machines intended for businesses, with warranty and technical support to match, or using smaller specialist suppliers that understand your needs, can pay dividends.

FINDING HELP ON THE INTERNET

Let's assume you've tried all the above strategies, and it still doesn't work, or that you're trying to work out how to do something that isn't in the manuals.

If you're searching for information about a particular piece of hardware, try typing the manufacturer's name, the make, and the model number into Google. Model numbers are almost always unique from manufacturer to manufacturer, and you should get back a list of very tightly targeted hits.

When you use the main search engines, throw in as many unusual words as you can that are likely to appear in the final document to help eliminate irrelevant junk. Don't just type in 'Outlook' if, for example, you're having trouble figuring out where Outlook stores its data for backups; type in something more like 'Outlook data directory location backup'. (If you type that into Google you'll get a couple of hits near the top that give you instructions on how to back up email stored in Outlook or Outlook Express.)

It pays to familiarize yourself with the help files of whichever search engine you use most. Try clicking on 'help' or 'advanced search' to get pointers on how to target your searches. If this seems like too much work, remember that any tool requires a little effort to learn, and that as a child you probably spent a few hours learning how to find things in a library. For example, on Google, you can force the search engine to include common words it would normally discard such as 'and', 'the', and most prepositions by adding a '+' in front of the word. Similarly, you can force Google to look for a whole phrase such as 'virus scanner' by surrounding the phrase in quotes. Tips like these can make your searches far faster, more effective, and much less frustrating, and the way you learn about them is by reading the help files. Each engine has its own quirks and design differences.

Once you've been spoiled by a well-designed search engine, you can get very frustrated very fast by the cut-down search engines included on many corporate sites. There is a way around this on Google: you can limit your search to a specific site. If, for example, you want to search the massive Microsoft site for a particular bit of technical information it's often faster to go to Google and enter 'site:microsoft.com <search terms>'. The engine will use the terms you enter to search only on the Microsoft site. Unfortunately, some of the time you do have to use the much less helpful corporate mini-searches. Sites that require registration are essentially walling off their content from the search engines, and others have their sites designed in such a way that they don't get adequately indexed.

One set of techniques that pops up on many search engines is Boolean operators. Based on a branch of algebra, Boolean searching sounds more complicated than it is, and it is worth learning because it is so widely used. The most common and simplest operators are AND, NOT, and OR. Searching on 'scanner AND graphics' requires both terms to appear on a page for it to be returned as a hit. Using that should get you hits that talk about scanners and graphics, without a lot of clutter from virus scanners. Searching on 'scanner OR graphics', on the other hand, will get you pages that have either term or both.

Searching on 'scanner NOT graphics' will get you back a list of pages that talk about scanners (virus, email, science fiction), but will exclude pages that include the word 'graphics'.

Boolean searches also allow you to specify a phrase by surrounding it with quotes; only pages with all the words, in the order specified, next to each other will be returned. Additional operators you don't find as often include ADJ, NEAR, FAR, and BEFORE, and all of these specify the relationship between the terms (ADJ stands for adjacent, so it means the words are next to each other, but in any order). A good explanation of Boolean operators and how to use them is at Lycos (http://www.lycos.co.uk/help/boolean.html), where you can use them to build complex searches that return very tightly targeted hits.

TIP If it's not broken, don't 'fix' it.

Ultimately, picking a search engine you're comfortable with and learning the best strategies for that specific engine is probably the best strategy for general searches. But you need to learn where to look for specific types of information, and ultimately that will come with experience and increased knowledge of both the Internet and the kinds of information you frequently search for.

Not all of the Web is searchable. Besides registration-blocked sites, any site can be deliberately kept out of the search engine indexes by including a file called robots.txt in the directory where the Web pages are stored. Using a standard syntax this file can instruct the search engines' indexing software ('spider') to ignore any or all pages in the site, rendering a page as invisible as an ex-directory phone number. In addition, interactive features such as calculators and dictionaries, databases, and archived material are often not searchable by normal means. A number of specialist search engines claim to have cracked this; details of such engines are available from the invaluable Search Engine Watch site (http://searchenginewatch.com).

In addition, the Web is notoriously ephemeral: some estimate the average Web page stays up no more than seventy-eight days. With older computer products, this can be a real problem, as some companies remove all reference to them from their Web sites when they go out of production. For this type of material, you have two strategies. For hits turned up in a Google search that have broken links, click on the 'Cached' option that appears at the bottom of each description; this takes you to the page that's now gone, saved in Google's cache. For material that's expired from Google's cache, head for the Internet Archive (http://www.archive.org), which has been archiving the Web on a continuous basis since 1996, and allows comprehensive searching through its 'Wayback Machine' either by URL or by date.

But the Internet is more than the Web, and it's a mistake to think that the Web is the only source of technical information – or that the only material of value is that posted by manufacturers. It's always worth looking up what users are saying on opinion sites and discussion boards about the products you're considering buying. Why not benefit from their experience?

Going back to one of those Google searches, click on the 'Groups' tab at the top of the screen. Your search has now been repeated on Usenet, a huge collection of tens of thousands of worldwide bulletin boards known as 'newsgroups' where everything under the sun is discussed. Many of those newsgroups are dedicated to technical matters, and you will again often find the educated opinion of experienced users. If you look at nothing else from the newsgroups, it's still worth searching with the added term 'FAQ' in either the Groups tab or the main one. Many newsgroups have lengthy explanatory documents (FAQs – Frequently Asked Questions) compiled by the most knowledgeable contributors that are solid backgrounders on technical subjects such as cryptography, Windows 2000, and how to get the best results out of scanners. These are an invaluable – and free – resource. For topics you revisit regularly, you may want to join one or more Usenet groups and read them regularly; it is easy and cheap to do this over a broadband connection, though you will need newsreader software, which you configure to access the news server at your ISP. Newsreaders are built into browsers, but for daily use look for a dedicated piece of software that includes threading and supports rules and filters the way your email software does.

Similarly, some technical subjects have IRC channels dedicated to them, though the easiest way to find these is by searching the Web using any of the above techniques and adding the term 'IRC' to the list of keywords. Besides Usenet and IRC, many umbrella sites (such as Yahoo!) include chat rooms and bulletin boards where users congregate and offer each other technical help.

With all these user-to-user channels you must exercise some care in assessing the advice you receive. You can pick up a great deal of good advice from them, but you can equally find yourself being advised by someone who is LCW – Loud, Confident, and Wrong. In general, however, the FAQs from well-established discussion groups can be trusted, because they have typically been refined and improved over time.

GETTING THE BEST OUT OF TECHNICAL SUPPORT

OK, so you have to call technical support. Hopefully, you've done the preparatory work so you can explain the problem clearly. Unfortunately, by now you're probably already frustrated and annoyed, and if you're calling manufacturer technical support their blithe presumption that you are an idiot is only likely to make you more so.

End users and technical support are a marriage made in hell. For every technical support person who asks you to check your computer is plugged in and who knows nothing more than the information that can be found by searching in the company's knowledge base there's a user who doesn't realize that the reason the monitor is beeping is because they've left a stopwatch under it. The result is a huge amount of frustration and, sometimes, a disaster instead of a minor problem. If you can, make sure your backups are up to date before calling technical support.

To get the best out of technical support, the first thing to do is to assemble the information you're going to need in a thorough and organized fashion, as noted above. Sometimes, just the process of doing this will help you solve the problem. In most cases, you will need to know the operating system version (including any service packs you've applied), the processor type, and amount of RAM. If the problem is hardware, you'll also need details of the hardware you're having trouble with (plus the version number of any software drivers). If it's software, you'll need to know what version you're running.

Put together a description of the problem that lists the steps you took before it happened. Note details of any error messages that appear, and any other symptoms that seem relevant. When you call or email technical support, try to be as thorough as possible in explaining what happened. If you did something you know was stupid to cause the problem – clicked on an email message that in retrospect was clearly carrying a virus, or aborted an operation whose instructions warned not to do so – tell the technical support people up front. They can't help you if you won't give them the information they need. However, do consider the implications of the advice they give you before acting on it. If they say to reinstall their own software or download a more recent driver, remove the device entirely, and install it again from scratch with the new driver, fine. If they tell you to reinstall Windows, that's going to require you to reinstall everything from scratch, so investigate whether there are other alternatives first. In a situation where you're unsure that you're being given good advice, write down the steps you're being told to perform or request that they be sent to you in an email message or fax, and take time to think (and update your backups) before proceeding.

Of course, that shouldn't be necessary. But the reality is that just as technical support personnel tell horror stories about the stupidity of 'users', user stories of incompetent tech support are commonplace. There's the supposedly expert Windows support person at a major computer manufacturer who didn't know what 'SP' was (it stands for 'service pack', an important update to Windows). There's the guy whose laptop got busted when a tech support person (presumably assuming the machine was a desktop) told him to bang the keyboard on his desk to get the crumbs out of it. There's the guy whose SCSI card problem escalated into total loss of data when a tech support person insisted his troubles could only be cured by reformatting his hard drive.

When things go wrong the downside for the users is much, much worse than any consequences for the support people. Take, for example, the story of the accounting firm that called in a consultant because the company's hard drive wasn't working correctly. The consultant asked if the company had backups: there they were in the safe, a neat row of disk boxes, all carefully labelled. Accordingly, the consultant performed a low-level format to rescue the hard disk . . . only to find when he began to restore the firm's data that all the backups were of the original DOS disk rather than the data. With all its data lost, the company went bust shortly afterwards, a situation that could have been prevented had the backups been checked first or had the company bought a new hard drive instead of formatting the old one. Or had either the users or the consultant asked the right questions.

So do call tech support when you need to, but give information that's as complete as possible, and do everything you can to ensure that you have *working* backups in place and a way of working if the advice gets you into worse trouble than you were in to begin with.

TRAINING COURSES

At some point, looking at the prices consultants charge and despairing at the number of IT people who do not understand your business, you may be tempted to try to train up a staff member to administer your network. This undoubtedly has benefits – for one thing, it really is convenient if you don't have to call an (expensive) consultant every time some small thing goes wrong with your IT system. However, there are some pitfalls to be aware of.

For one thing, many training courses are of necessity somewhat general. A course on Windows 2000 and networking basics, for example, will give you an introduction to the networking capabilities of Windows 2000 but is likely to give only very limited hands-on practice. It is, in other words, easy to learn just enough to create real problems upon your return. There is no substitute for hands-on experience and a lot of it; a course or an exam, however successfully completed, is only a start. All the caveats that apply to your trying to fix your IT yourself – making sure you know how to reverse whatever changes you implement, making sure you document what you do, first testing the new configuration on a limited portion of the network that is not doing anything mission-critical – apply in spades to the newly educated, possibly over-confident staff member just out of training.

TIP Always write down the current settings before you change any of them, so you know what to go back to if something stops working.

The prices of commercial training courses are in general set with an eye on deep corporate pockets. Expect courses to start at £300 to £400 a day (plus whatever the loss of your staff member's time costs you). Be as specific as possible about what you want when you talk to the training organization so they can match the course to your staff member's abilities, existing knowledge, and desired curriculum as accurately as possible, and shop around before settling on any specific course. Often, suppliers of the key software you use will be able to recommend a training partner.

Besides commercial organizations, courses in a wide variety of computer and networking related subjects are available from the adult education programmes run by colleges all over the country, and these may be very reasonably priced, though less intensive. If your staff member is aiming to gain standard accreditations such as MCSA, MCSE, or CNE, ensure that the training courses selected are designed with passing the exams for those accreditations in mind. If you are funding the training, it may be wise to agree with the staff member a contractual period he or she is required to stay on at your company in return. Leaving to join a dot-com start-up isn't as popular as it was in 1999, but technical knowledge is still a valuable commodity.

Even with more ordinary software, such as office suites or

customized databases designed to run your particular type of business (law practice, dentist's office . . .), you may want to invest in staff training. Even though IT manufacturers never stop saying their new products will give no trouble, learning a new product is rarely straightforward. Allow staff time to adjust whenever you make major changes to your system, and don't make those changes when there's a pressing deadline unless you have to.

For this kind of training, the first place to start is the manual if there is one. Increasingly, software comes only with online help files. Commercial software often comes with an initial tour that shows off the main features, and 'training wheels' in the form of wizards, balloon text that appears if you hold the mouse over an icon or menu choice, and templates. While these are fine for looking up what a particular feature does, they don't generally work as well for teaching you when and how to use it to complete a particular task. For some types of software, you may want to buy supplemental books staff can consult. For other types, such as customized software for your business, you should pay the developer to write a (however brief) manual staff can refer to. (This is of course an added cost, but worth it.) However, these user aids are not adequate to teach someone how to administer, say, Windows 2000 Server.

Other training options include audio cassettes, videotapes, and computer-based training (CBT). Each has advantages and disadvantages depending on the type of user you have and the situation in which the products are going to be used.

TIP Who's in charge of ensuring your backups get made and stored off-site? Who deputizes if that person is ill or on holiday?

In making a selection of training method, the first question to consider is the computer literacy – or lack thereof – of a given system's users. People who are already uncomfortable with technology may not react well to computer-based training packages, even though CBT seems like a logical way of showing someone how a program works. People in this position are likely to feel more comfortable with familiar types of materials – books, for example, which can be laid flat on the desk in front of the PC and used as step-by-step guides, or classroom courses that feature live humans. On the other hand, very bright, computer-literate people tend to be bored by classroom courses, and may be happier using media where they can set their own pace.

Most classroom courses are generally designed for 'average' users, which means they're too slow for the people who tended to jump ahead of the class when reading textbooks in their school days, and yet may be too fast for the least experienced technophobes. Trainers do try to accommodate various grades of user – small classes mean they spend some time helping each trainee get to grips with the exercises – but within the scope of most courses they can't do remedial teaching. As classroom courses tend to be expensive, it's important to make sure you've got a good match between the type of course and the skills and aptitudes of your staff member.

At the same time, it's important to think about what your users actually need to learn. In the case of a DTP package, for example, they may not need to learn everything the package can do as much as they need to learn how to produce specific materials, such as a company newsletter, letterhead, or memos. Sometimes the solution to this sort of thing may not lie in training at all but in customized macros or style sheets, supplemented with a page or two of instructions for their use.

The other disadvantage to training courses is that knowledge acquired by one staff member in classroom courses isn't easily transferable to other staff. CBT packages, audio and video tapes, and books all have the advantage that they can be passed around a company and reused; also, they are still available later for new staff to learn from.

Ancillary to that is the matter of location; opinions vary widely on this one. Some people find it easiest to learn something new when there are no other demands on them; these people are happier with off-site training where they won't be interrupted. Others find losing whole work days too disruptive, and are happier with on-site training, particularly using techniques where they can set their own pace or learn just what they need when they need it.

Most companies will want to use a mix of methods. Also, it's worth being a little bit creative about training. It shouldn't just be about learning the features of the company software packages. Today's computers have put onto everyone's desktops tools that formerly would have been reserved for highly skilled people. Giving the people using the computers some of those skills helps them make the most of the IT investment. So besides product-based courses, look at courses that teach business writing and the literacy skills that secretaries used to supply, as well as design and even typing.

There are two main kinds of CBT packages: simulation and concurrent. A simulation tutorial is exactly what it sounds like: it simulates the computer environment the user will be working in, and teaches the user how to perform the necessary tasks through exercises. The problem with this approach is that the simulation is never around when you need it most: when you're actually working. Generally speaking, people are better at remembering things they've learned if they are learned as part of doing real work. Simulation CBT is sterile, and the lessons it teaches tend not to be retained well.

However, there are certain circumstances where simulations are important. You don't, for example, want to turn a novice loose on the company's live financial data or its mission-critical network. Simulations prevent the user from doing any damage by limiting the number of features they work with at any one time and by sequestering them from the real system, and they require far lower hardware overheads. However, the constraints that keep the user from making errors also have a cost, since there's no way to learn from such a system how to recover from mistakes, probably the most important thing a novice needs to learn.

Concurrent systems load on top of the program you're using and guide you through what you need to do. In some cases, the software is an extension to the Help system that gives you added information. In others, as in Intuit's Quicken finance products, little balloons pop up to tell the user what to do next to complete a given task – useful, since it can be difficult to remember what the next step is when the help screen vanishes behind the window you're working in. You turn the balloon help off, feature by feature, as you become confident that you've got the hang of things. Some software ships with part of the menu system switched off, to give beginning users a simpler interface.

Do not confuse training with technical support. Aside from the fact that many support hotlines take a long time to answer questions and may charge for the privilege, teaching users isn't what technical support is intended for. It's fair to call technical support if the documentation on a particular feature is poor, or if a user has a specific question, or if something is repeatedly crashing or clearly broken; it's not fair to expect technical support to teach people to write macros, or to take a novice through the complexities of setting up a network.

One other option is videotapes, which are now available to teach even such complex subjects as installing Exchange Server. The best thing about videotape is that you can see what your screen is supposed to look like as you move around it and enter commands. A real limitation, though, is that it may be difficult to assemble all the necessary technology in a single place. A training room equipped with a VCR and computer that employees can book into might be one solution; another might be allowing employees to take tapes home. But even then, tapes are awkward to refer back to because they can't be easily indexed.

THE POINT OF DIMINISHING RETURNS

There comes a point in the life of any technology when it's just not worth the trouble any more. Identifying whether a particular machine or bit of software has reached that point is tricky.

In general, for business use, software reaches that point when its manufacturer ceases to support it. As noted earlier, Microsoft has promised to support its products for five years from the date of release. This means NT is supported until the summer of 2003, Windows 2000 until at least July 2005, and XP at least until 2006. There may, of course, be reasons why you decide to stick with a piece of software anyway – perhaps there is nothing else that does the same job. But over time that software is going to be more and more of a problem as it becomes increasingly antiquated. Application software in that category, for example, will have to be tested every time you propose to upgrade your operating system software to make sure that it will still run. If using that software means you never upgrade your operating system, there will be many genuine improvements you miss out on. In addition, if you run other mission-critical applications on an unsupported operating system, particularly if those applications include your accounting system, you may run into problems because most accounting software must be updated every year to take account of legal changes.

With hardware, obviously you will need to replace a machine that is actually stolen. If a particular component in a machine breaks, you may or may not want to replace the component rather than the whole machine – you will have to look at the relative cost of the two, plus the amount of time it will take to configure a new machine to do the old one's job. With equipment that is working, the rule of thumb is to replace it when there are too many things you need or want to do that it can't handle. These days, obsolescence takes much longer than it did in the early 1990s. With interim upgrades to hard disk and memory, an ordinary machine can easily last five years or more. If you use roaming profiles and a hierarchical system of distributing computer power around your company, as suggested on p. 76, you can make upgrading your computer equipment quite economical while ensuring the most powerful machines are in the hands of those who need them most.

The rule of thumb for when to upgrade hardware is the specification you need to run the software you must have to run your business. If you do work that is graphics-intensive, like design or publishing, or work that is processor-intensive, such as frequent and massive spreadsheet recalculations or database queries, you may well need the latest and greatest. But if what's stressing your system is that the amount of Internet research you do means you keep 438 browser windows open at all times, then what you need is probably not a new computer but some extra memory and disk space. Be careful about this type of upgrade, however. You can easily spend more on new components than a new system would cost you. In addition, recent increases in system speed have as much to do with increased memory speed and bus performance (the speed at which data transfers between the processor and the rest of the system) as it does with increased processor speeds. It is no longer as easy as it was for a while to simply drop a new processor into an older machine, although you will get the same benefit from components such as faster CD writers and DVD writers with either a new or an old machine. If you upgrade, you may be able to keep some of your old hardware as backups. For example, if you upgrade to a much faster CD writer you may want to keep the old one for use in case the new one fails.

TIP Remember to review your maintenance contracts when you buy new equipment so you don't wind up continuing to pay for support on equipment you no longer have or on equipment that would be cheaper to replace.

It's become fashionable to claim that little has improved in computing in the last ten years. It's true that the pace of change has become less obvious than it was a decade ago, but it's still substantial. You may realize noticeable benefits from upgrading hardware that is more than five years old. A 1992 laser printer managed four pages per minute; the 2002 version does twenty. A 2003 computer may have ten times the disk space, eight times the memory, and six times the speed of its 1997 predecessor. A 2003 CD writer churns out a full data CD in four minutes. The changes are incremental, but over time they can add up to a substantial improvement in productivity.

Most computer systems have at least some flaws that users stop seeing because they've become so inured to working around them. It's time to replace the machine (or at least reinstall all its software from scratch) if the flaws add up to the point where if one more thing fails the machine is unworkable. For example, the combination of an inability to read a CD-ROM drive and a failed network card installation is lethal. It is also a good time to upgrade if the amount of time required to fix the number of things wrong with a particular machine would actually cost you more than a new machine would.

One way of avoiding problems is to make sure that anything you buy is compatible with what you already own or plan to use it with. Microsoft, for example, publishes lengthy compatibility lists for its operating systems, and you should check these in advance. This is particularly true for Windows NT/2000/XP – you cannot assume that just because something works under 95/98/ME it will work with the other flavours of Windows. While something may work even if it's not on the hardware compatibility list, it may not, and you can waste countless valuable hours trying to make it work. Where possible, stick to the list, which is available on Microsoft's Web site.

What to do with old machines you've decided are no longer worth keeping is always a difficulty. There are organizations that recycle old machines, some of which will even collect the machines from you. Old computers typically aren't worth much, but you may be able to sell them second-hand through eBay or local classified ads. If you go down this route, however, make absolutely sure you have wiped the system clean of all your data and software you are not including in the purchase. If you do include software in the purchase, you must give the buyer the system disks and documentation, and you will be giving up your licence to use that software.

10 Getting Help: Hiring Consultants and Technical Staff

One of the most difficult things is hiring an expert on a subject you don't understand very well yourself. How do you pick good IT staff out of the morass of jargon coming your way from the people you interview?

This chapter looks at hiring help either as staff or in the form of consultants and how to manage those critical relationships. Knowing when you're out of your depth is important; equally, however, you must understand the amount of control you give up when you put an outside consultant in charge of your IT, and be aware of how much trust you are placing in that person and his company.

The last section has some help on assessing whether what that person is advising you to do is sensible, economically and technically. It is sad but true that certain types of cash-rich professional firms made up of well-educated, smart people who know very little about IT – lawyers, doctors, dentists – get exploited simply because they do not understand what they're buying.

HIRING STAFF

As a rule of thumb, you will need one full-time technical support person per fifty users. You should probably begin considering hiring such a person when you have around twenty-five staff. Do not try to hire eighteen-year-olds who 'know a lot about computers'. Hire a grown-up with experience of business networks.

Probably the most common piece of advice for hiring either full-time technical staff or consultants is to look for technical qualifications such as MCSE (Microsoft Certified Systems Engineer) or Novell's

CNE (Certified Novell Engineer). Plenty of techies will say that those are not any indication of competence, and that's at least partially true. But while it is perfectly true that someone can pass these qualifications and still be incompetent, it is much easier *not* to pass those certification exams and be incompetent. Even so, certification by itself is not enough. Technical staff need to have relevant experience on top of those qualifications. Wherever possible, you should check references and talk to the referees and look into the details on the CVs they give you – standard fare in any kind of hiring, but essential in technical areas where it will be difficult for you to assess the outcome personally if you are not yourself technically skilled.

If you already have people who are knowledgeable about IT in your company, get them to talk to your prospective new employee. They may also be able to suggest a practical test such as 'breaking' a system in a known way, then watching the prospective staff member grapple with the problem. It's not just a question of whether the person can solve the problem; you or a technical person you already know and trust can learn a lot about an applicant by watching how they approach the challenge.

Even if you're not a technical guru, it can be helpful to ask candidates simple questions, just to see how they would deal with non-technical users. This is especially important if the position you're trying to fill is in technical support or at a help desk. The situations you present in these questions might range from a machine's refusing to power up or a user's being unable to print in Excel (though printing successfully in everything else), to the PC's 'hanging' while a user types an address into an email message. Getting the right answer isn't necessarily the most important thing. It is more crucial to check the candidate understands how to approach an unknown problem, break it down, and attempt to fix and/or explain it. What kinds of questions does the candidate ask in trying to isolate the failure? What kinds of answers does he or she come up with when facing a confused, possibly panic-stricken user?

For similar reasons, some systems administrators pepper candidates for support and helpdesk positions with technical questions until they find a subject applicants don't know about. Then they watch to see how the applicants behave when they're out of their depth. Can they reason from what they already know to add to their existing store of knowledge?

In small businesses, however, technical knowledge by itself is not enough. People must fit in personally as well as professionally in a small team. You may want to consider conducting the second half of interviews over a couple of pints in the pub or in some other less formal setting, where the candidate's true personality is more likely to emerge. You should not assume that all technical personnel are of necessity socially incompetent; but you do want to make sure they can fit into a small team.

At the same time, it's important to get away from the stereotyping that's often applied to technical staff – and this goes for consultants, too. Don't assume they're all the same and that you can just throw them together as if they were an endless series of identical twins. Most are under a lot of stress: they are working in a very tense environment trying to do extremely difficult things with absolute accuracy, often under managers who do not understand what they do or why it's difficult. In that high-stress environment, it can be especially frustrating if someone is added to the team who is not technically competent, as it just adds exponentially to the workload. Ensure, therefore, that whoever you hire has the respect of any existing technical staff and that the personalities mesh. You could, for example, send candidates around the company and let them ask questions, first briefing the staff and making sure they aren't working on anything commercially sensitive or classified. Then, later, find out what kinds of questions the candidates asked and how they came across.

If technical experts seem arrogant and obnoxious, sometimes that's because they live in a society that for the most part does not value their hard-won knowledge and expertise. These are often people who have been 'jokingly' called 'sad' to their faces when they've demonstrated a particular bit of skill, and who are routinely assumed to have no human interests outside of work. Don't call them geeks, even if they use the term among themselves as one of high praise. Many find it offensive, and you will not win any friends by doing so.

HIRING A CONSULTANT

There is no hard and fast rule as to when to hire a consultant. However, it's safe to say that it's very easy for even a very small business to get to the point where strategic decisions are necessary before its network continues to grow haphazardly in what may be the wrong direction. In the long term, spending some money on consultants at the beginning of your networked life may save you considerable time, money, and crises.

The key to getting what you need out of a consultancy relationship is to understand what it is you're outsourcing, so you can be reasonably sure the solution that's being recommended to you is appropriate. As much as you have to be able to trust the technical staff you hire to work for you full-time, you have to be able to trust consultants even more. When you hand the job of designing and maintaining your IT system to a third party who does not work for you, you are handing that person more control over your business than if you had given them the key to your office and left them alone in it.

For this reason, when you hire a consultant, do ask for references from client companies and do take them up. In addition, just as you would get quotes from several builders before embarking on a major extension project, for bigger IT projects you may want to ask more than one consultant to review your system and make recommendations and give sample costings. Expect to pay for that level of detail.

When you do this kind of comparative exercise, the key point is that the prospective consultant should understand how your business works and what your business processes are. To help the prospective consultant, therefore, you must know yourself what you want IT to do for you. You do not necessarily need to be an expert in IT for this, but you must recognize that if you are not an expert you may have no idea what is actually possible, what's easy or hard, what a particular technology does, or which technology will offer the best return on your capital investment. These are the things you want a consultant to tell you. Give the consultant a wish list by all means, but if the consultant tells you that some items on your list are unlikely to repay their initial cost and you can establish that the consultant is competent with those technologies, listen.

TIP Do not pay more in support per year for a piece of hardware than it would cost to buy a spare one and stick it in the cupboard. This is especially true of simple boxes such as hubs, where there's no configuration or software involved.

The key is to remember that you are buying a business solution, not just technology, and the tools you are offered must fit your business needs. You should be trying to convey to the consultant what you want to be able to accomplish with a sense of which capabilities have the highest priority, so the consultant can make recommendations that fit the bill. Ideally, there should be a feedback process between you and the consultant so that you wind up with an appropriate specification. You must help your consultant by not hiding key elements of your business strategy, even if you're keeping those secret from your staff. If, for example, you plan to split the business into two, or close down a site, you must tell this to the consultant you have asked to recommend an IT strategy; a report based on your existing situation may be wholly the wrong approach.

The crucial point is that you want to see how the person addresses the problem. At initial meetings with prospective consultants, they should be asking you what do you want to achieve, what your aims are, and what your business processes are. They should not be telling you, for example, that Linux is really cool and Microsoft is crap. What matters is what tools are the right ones for your business. A consultant with ideas that are too rigid is the man with a hammer to whom every problem looks like a baby rat.

When you are making your final decision, do compare its implications with the original wish list you started with, as the gap between the two may send conflicting messages to a consultant trying to work with you. For example, if you say you require rock-solid reliable Internet access at all times, don't be surprised if the consultant recommends a leased line, even though it is smaller bandwidth at ten times the cost of ADSL. The reason: leased lines are the only permanent connections at the moment that come with a service-level agreement you can call on in an outage. You may decide that's too expensive, and that's your right. But then the logical implication is that unbreakable Internet access isn't as important to you as you thought it was. This could become an issue if you then complain that you need constant Internet access if your ADSL goes down for a week; getting it back on will be down to BT and your ISP, and the consultant will have no way to get it turned back on any faster. You must read any consultant's report you commission very carefully to take account of these kinds of issues. If you do not understand why a particular recommendation has been made after reading the report thoroughly, ask.

The matter of how much of a consultant's advice you decide to take is always contentious. Even if your consultant has the needs of your business at heart, you may disagree with some of the advice you're given, and the consultant may take exception to this. Whether this is reasonable depends on what the advice is and what the consequences are of not taking it.

Let's say, for example, your problem is that your network is unreliable. Your consultant tells you that: (1) the coaxial cable connecting your machines is making the network fragile because if you trip over the cable and break it all the connections go down; (2) it's impossible to control backups because your network is all peer-to-peer with no server; (3) your broadband can't be properly shared around the office because you've ordered the home USB ADSL service instead of the business ethernet one; and (4) you're running the home-oriented flavours of Windows. The consultant tells you to improve the speed and reliability of your network and facilitate backups by ordering a specific type of new business machine, replacing the coaxial cable with ethernet, and switching to an ethernet-based version of broadband with a router to share it around the office. If, at that point, you reject every suggestion he makes, don't be surprised if that network consultant refuses to help you install complex software to run on your unreliable kludge. The consultant knows, even if you don't, that maintaining such an inherently flaky system will be a nightmare.

In another example, perhaps you've decided that your network is too slow, and you want the consultant to speed it up a bit, and the consultant tells you that rather than spend money on his time you should replace your existing machines with faster ones. The reason may not be obvious to you. But from the consultant's point of view, the old machines may be so slow that his time working on the machines will be mostly spent waiting, with very little improvement actually possible in the end, meaning that you could spend the same amount of money but get both the consultant's efforts and the newer machines and their improved performance, overall a better deal for you (as discussed in Chapter 9). You can easily establish whether this is the case by costing the new machines and the difference in the consultant's time.

These situations are all tricky. The most important part, therefore, is to keep focused on your business, and remember that the consultant's job is to help you use IT to further your business goals.

Finally, do not expect your consultant to be able to solve your internal political problems. Sometimes they can: if a board is divided on the right approach to IT, a consultant's recommendation may help everyone move forward. However, if one director waits until the others are away and hires the consultant to implement his favoured solution, you have much deeper political problems than anything even the best consultant can solve with IT.

AGREEING TERMS: CONTRACTS

In a long-term relationship with a consultant, usually you will want a written agreement. This needs to cover issues such as turnaround times on technical support and lay out who is responsible for which parts of your system and what the agreement actually covers. You should review what's covered periodically as prices and specifications change. It makes no sense, for example, to pay for support on an item like a hub, which is now so cheap that it's easy to have a spare in a cupboard. Equally, however, it makes no sense to avoid paying for support on complex servers if you simply do not have the in-house expertise to fix them if something stops working. Much of the time, a consultant assisting you with technical support will be able to do so remotely by using your VPN to connect to your network and perform diagnostics. The agreement will specify whether the price agreed includes travel and related expenses, and who pays for materials required (usually you).

The contract should include service levels in some detail. It's common to include turnaround times such as four hours, but it's important to specify whether that turnaround time means the length of time it takes for the consultant to send someone or log in remotely or to complete the repair.

If any of the software you use is no longer supported by its manufacturer and the consultant is offering to support it, you should of course ask how they're going to do it. There aren't going to be new patches to install, and if there are bugs the manufacturer isn't going to help fix them.

If the consultant supplies customized software, you also need to agree terms on who owns the software, when and under what circumstances it will be updated, whether you get copies of the code, and whether you have the right to get someone else to update it if you need to after your agreement with this consultant expires. The contract should also specify who owns the documentation and materials the consultant writes for you. You will of course want to own the rights to documentation specific to your system, but it is reasonable for the consultant to retain the right to reuse the material for similar projects elsewhere.

If the consultant is carrying out a major project for you, the agreement should include agreed milestones and dates by which they should be reached, and staged payments. The agreement should include a note of how and under what circumstances the specifications of the project may be changed by either you or the consultancy, along with a confidentiality clause.

Most of the contract should be the familiar clauses from any service agreement, such as payment terms and indemnification.

BESPOKE SOFTWARE

It is relatively rare these days to need to commission truly bespoke software, and for small businesses that's a good thing: it can be hideously expensive. A more common scenario is customization work on an existing application. This could be anything from a complex macro for Word that saves staff hours of time in carrying out repetitive but complicated tasks to a complete database application. It's important to remember that 'buying a database' only means buying the capability to build a database; to get it to do anything useful you have to design how it's going to store information. Errors in design can make it impossible to extract the information you need out of the database, so expert help can be vital. Setting up macros, putting in and organizing directories, and creating templates are all simpler things that experienced users can do for themselves but can be very difficult to get right and time-consuming and expensive to learn how to do for inexperienced users. Any consultant you hire should be able to either supply or recommend someone to supply this kind of service. Customization work has the added advantage that the bulk of technical support comes from the commercial software's manufacturer and you are not locked into a sole supplier.

Development costs are affected by who is going to own the source code of the resulting software and whether or not the developer is free to sell the same software elsewhere. Generally, the more restricted the supplier is in reusing the code he's written the more it will cost you: if the developer can't sell the software to other customers all the development costs will fall on your shoulders. In addition, the developer is unlikely to make any improvements to the software unless you commission them.

In general, you will find that commercial software is a much, much cheaper route to go, and you should always look there first, even though you may need to change your way of working to suit the new software. You will need to factor in time: say you're losing ten minutes a day of staff time on a task that would cost £3,000 to automate using customized software. That adds up to about forty-five hours a year. Is it worth it? If, on the other hand, you have tasks whose automation would save a couple of salaries and a PC or two, the equation looks very different.

When it comes to finding a consultant, the Association of Independent Computer Specialists (AICS) vets its members and requires them to adhere to a Code of Practice, and is intended to help businesses find good-quality computer-related services. Other likely ways are to get recommendations through your own trade association, through your relevant trade magazines, or from the British Computer Society. One of the best places to find consultants and developers, though, is online.

As a corollary to this, ask how long the supplier has been in business, and try to stick with suppliers who have been around for a while – say, five years. Remember that unless you are commissioning something very simple, such as a couple of macros, you are entering into a long-term relationship with a professional adviser. Just as you do in other fields, be sure to pick someone you feel comfortable with and who you think understands your business and what you're trying to do.

TIP Do not implement IT to a level that exceeds your business's commitment to IT. That means, for example, that if your business revolves totally around your IT and the business would fail if anything went wrong with the implementation, you need someone at board level who understands and appreciates the level of the business's dependence on IT. Similarly, if you give everyone down to the secretaries access to the Internet you must have a clearly written acceptable use policy laying out what they can and cannot do with it, and you must be seen to enforce that policy fairly even if it means calling the police in if a business partner is caught downloading child pornography.

Besides asking for customer references, ask to see examples of work the developer has done before, preferably for customers in a line of business similar to yours. This isn't just because it shows the developer has a track record in understanding the problems you have; it also affects you directly, since most developers save time and your money by building new work using experience and blocks of code from the old. Reusing code lets them spread the costs across several clients.

Ensure that any software you commission is thoroughly documented so that if you later have to hire someone else to update it that person can understand how the code is structured. You should also insist on user documentation that helps your staff understand how to use the software. Try to avoid developers who are sticky about allowing you access to the source code; this may be important at a future date if the developer is no longer available.

In addition, ask for a detailed specification before coding starts, make sure you understand it fully, and agree it with them, along with an installation plan with specified delivery dates, staged payments based on completed milestones, and hardware specifications. You also need to consider how the software will be supported, and what the supplier's turnaround time will be in case of bugs that need to be fixed.

CUSTARD IN THE SERVER

When dealing with consultants, just like technical staff, assume they're human. Most people respond to being appreciated. Like housework, much of what IT experts do is invisible unless it goes wrong. If someone comes to work on your computer system and it works better afterwards, consider thanking them.

At the same time, bear in mind that if something goes wrong it isn't necessarily their fault. If, for example, your managing director goes on holiday and insists that copies of all email be forwarded to his personal email address on a Freeserve account – and then doesn't check it often enough so the box fills up and the account gets suspended and your server collapses under the strain of 57,000 bounced messages – this is not the consultant's fault.

When you need to call in your consultant for technical help, do a cut-down version of the same process outlined on p. 198 for preparing to call technical support. If you have an existing relationship, you shouldn't have to tell your consultant what software versions you're running or what your hardware specification is – he probably knows that better than you do. But you should try to put together the same coherent explanation of what the problem is, including details of any error messages and so on. The more complete you can be in your explanation and the more precisely you can describe the problem, the more you help your consultant help you. This is doubly true, of course, if the consultant is someone new you're calling in because your system problems have reached a level you can't deal with.

TIP Do not have a configuration so eccentric that only one person in the country knows how to support it. Let your core business be the unique part of what you do.

In addition, you can help your IT consultant help you by telling them the truth. Consultants are not your parents; if you break something and say honestly, 'Oops, I did <fill in the blank> and the whole thing fell over, can you fix it?' in general they won't mind (unless, perhaps, you keep making the same mistake over and over again). What they will mind is if you insist you didn't do anything and the whole thing's their fault, especially if you try to cover up the mistake. Just assume that any cover-up attempt will be as noticeable as the cracks in a Royal marriage.

In addition, if something breaks, efforts you make to fix the problem will frequently add to the length of time and effort the consultant must spend to fix the problem. It is, of course, tempting to save on the consultant's bill if you can. But know your own limitations. If it's a system the consultant built for you, the chances are it's beyond your capacity to fix. It probably won't, however, be beyond your capacity to turn a simple problem into a major one.

On the other hand, if your system is working reliably, you keep good backups, and you are not in an emergency like a virus attack, and you are trying to complete a vastly important job and your consultant wants to make major changes before it's finished rather than waiting until it's complete, it is reasonable for you to object. Few major changes are easy or straightforward, and they should not be scheduled at times when they will conflict with core business needs unless it's absolutely necessary (and sometimes it is).

Just as many small businesses have been burned by incompetent consultants, consultants also get shafted by non-paying clients. If you are tempted to refuse payment to a consultant, even if you are dissatisfied with that person's work, you should bear in mind that this can be a truly dangerous area. When you enter into an outsourcing arrangement with a consultant to manage your network, you are perforce trusting that person with a great deal of sensitive and important information. Not only will he or she know the details of your system's configuration and how well it is (or isn't) backed up, but he or she is likely also to have sensitive information such as your passwords – both internal ones and those that are necessary to connect you to your ISP. An unscrupulous and disgruntled consultant with hands-on experience of your network can do a lot of damage: destroy data, take down your Internet connection, interfere with your email. There's no way around this, just as there's no way around trusting your doctor. A good consultant certainly won't behave this way, and would be in violation of the 1990 Computer Misuse Act if he did. Even so, it's wise to treat your consultant fairly, even if you no longer want to continue the relationship.

Also, one final tip: don't pour custard in the server. Or if you do, 'fess up.

THE UNIQUENESS PROBLEM, OR 'THE MAN UNDER THE CLAPHAM OMNIBUS'

When you rely on outside consultants (or, for that matter, internal experts), insist on – and pay for – proper documentation of your system. This is probably the area most businesses skimp on because it seems like a lot of money for nothing. But beware of the principle implied by 'the man under the Clapham omnibus'. If something untoward happens to your consultant you must be sure that you know – or can lay your hands on – enough information about how your system works so that another consultant can take over. The smaller the consultancy you use, the more important this principle is. In a larger firm, there may be more than one person who understands your configuration and the firm itself may have kept notes. In a smaller firm, this may not be true. (However, you may develop more of a relationship with a single consultant and get more personal service from a smaller firm.)

Ensure that all your passwords are written down and stored safely away from prying eyes (in a safe deposit box, if necessary), and that the details of the equipment you own and its configuration are all thoroughly documented. (This information will also be useful in case of a burglary or other disaster.) Information you may have forgotten to document includes: serial numbers for shareware and installation CDs for commercial software; the passwords for your email and Internet accounts; administrator account name and password on Windows NT/2000/XP Professional; IDs and passwords that unlock telephone or Internet access to bank (and other) accounts and supplier or client Web sites; and whatever updates have been made to your original software installation (service packs, upgrades, customized add-ons, and so on).

Similarly, you should regularly ask your consultant as to how standard or otherwise your system is. Do you run a set of software that no one else on the planet uses? Is your consultant the only person within 400 miles who knows how to support it? If so, you have a problem – a business problem, not an IT problem. The more dependent you are on a single consultant's knowledge, the more you are at risk if anything happens to that one person. Let your core business be unique. Let your IT be boringly standard. Let the principle of backups and redundancy apply to the IT knowledge you have available as well as to your data. This is one objection that some consultants have to Linux systems: there are simply too many variants of operating system versions and mail servers to be sure whether they can support a particular configuration.

TIP Techies are humans, too.

Of course there are times when parts of your system will be unique – and there may be reasons why you can't give up an old system that works for you (there may be nothing comparable available on the market). If that's your situation, ensure the system is thoroughly documented, even if that means paying a new consultant to do the documentation work. In most cases, it will work out cheaper to spend the money to change the system into something less unusual.

There is a side benefit to this, which is that you do not wind up locked into a bad situation. Ensuring that you are fully informed about your system and that it can be supported by more than just one or two people also ensures that you can walk away from a consultant if you need to.

BAD ADVICE: SOME FLAGS

You now have your consultant's initial report in hand. Maybe you even have two or three of them and they all disagree. How do you know they're not giving you bad, expensive advice?

The first point is that no matter how broken your current IT system is, the plan should give you a managed, affordable path out of it. It is almost never appropriate to rip everything out and start over. If someone is proposing a total rip-out-and-replace plan, get a couple more opinions and only go ahead with it if everyone agrees. Such a plan is typically very expensive and disruptive to your business. Certainly, if you have hardware that's less than two years old, it almost certainly doesn't need to be replaced, as it ought to be powerful enough for most current uses.

Anyone who is recommending major structural changes and says, 'We can do it all in one weekend,' is probably either lying or deluded. If it sounds too easy, it is too easy, and if it sounds painless it's probably wrong.

If they can't explain it to you, they're blinding you. Networking is difficult because it's composed of a huge mess of tiny details, but a consultant who's solving a business problem for you still ought to be able to explain the recommendations in terms you can understand.

Avoid anyone who's trying to sell you technology rather than a business solution.

Do not buy your hardware from the people you're buying your expertise from. From a supplier they recommend, certainly, especially if you've compared prices (remembering to compare like with like).

Never sign up for a total solution that isn't in clear phases. You should have a clear business plan, costed and phased, with written and understood acceptance criteria at each phase. Then ensure that phase one is complete before embarking on the next portion.

Finally, references, references, references: always follow them up.

TIP Tell your consultant the truth, whether it's that your business strategy is changing or that you've poured custard into the server. It will help him do his job better – and therefore save you money and aggravation.

11 Health and Safety

Even the smallest, most virtual businesses need to be aware of the health and safety regulations regarding computer use, as these apply to all employees using employer-supplied equipment, even if they work at home. Self-employed people are not required to abide by the regulations, but as these are largely commonsense advice to keep them from getting injured and being unable to work, even the self-employed would be wise to familiarize themselves with the basic principles involved. If someone who's self-employed works at home on equipment supplied by a client, the regulations do apply, in the sense that the client/employer is bound by them.

Whether it's your own health or that of your employees at stake, you should consider ergonomic principles when setting up a workstation. No one believes that anyone consciously sets out to design bad workplaces. Instead, bad workplaces happen through lack of thought because most people don't realize that devoting a little time and research to office purchases can make a big difference. Just remembering to imagine what the chair you sit in for a few seconds in the shop is going to feel like after you've been sitting in it for eight hours continuously is a step in the right direction. The difficulty is that human beings are so adaptable. Our eyes adjust to bad lighting conditions; our bodies adjust to hot or cold temperatures. It's only after prolonged periods that we realize how uncomfortable we are – and by then it may be too late.

TIP When's the last time you tested that your backups restored?

This is all particularly an issue for small businesses, which by their nature don't have personnel departments, experts on staff, or policies in place. And for small businesses ergonomic considerations are especially important because they don't have people or resources to spare. If a key staff member becomes incapacitated, it can have a severe impact.

Overall, designing a comfortable workspace is not so much a choice of specific products but a way of thinking about work and how we do it. The key point to bear in mind, whether you're buying hardware, software, or office furniture, is that people did not evolve specifically to do these jobs. It makes sense, therefore, to try to design the jobs so that people can do them – all classical management theory says that in any organization it's the quality of the people that's important. If you have good staff, you should look after them.

At the same time, an additional problem in bringing in anything new is that people are deeply resistant to change. Often, staff perceive something new as 'wrong' rather than 'different' – consider the last time you updated a familiar piece of software and found that the menu design had changed. It generally takes time for people to adapt to new equipment, even if it's designed to be more comfortable. In addition, you should make sure that staff understand how they can change their workstations to suit themselves. You can have the most adjustable chair in the world, but if the staff member doesn't know how to make the adjustments, it's wasted.

None of this has to be expensive, and you don't have to do everything at once. Instead, improve things gradually when you can. And remember to review the situation regularly, especially whenever there is a major change in software or hardware, workstation furniture, the requirements of the job, the workstation's location, or lighting.

HEALTH AND SAFETY LEGISLATION

The legislation in this area dates back to May 1990 and the EC ergonomics directive (87/391/EEC). The directive's primary supporting legislation, the Health and Safety (Display Screen Equipment) Regulations 1992, came into force in the UK at the beginning of 1993, although the 2002 package of updates to the health and safety regulations includes a couple of minor amendments. Two standards – the British BS 7179 and the European ISO 9241 – cover ergonomics requirements for office work with computers, often described in the legislation as 'video display terminals' or 'video display units'.

The Health and Safety Executive (HSE) publishes several leaflets related to this legislation that are intended to help people assess the risks and avoid health problems, particularly upper limb disorders. We're used to thinking only of heavy physical labour, such as mining, as dangerous, but the build-up of long hours at the keyboard with no breaks can cause permanent damage.

The EC directive lays down standards for VDU equipment, workstation furniture, and working conditions. Most of the regulations affecting computers merely reflect what the industry is doing anyway. Few manufacturers, for example, make monitors that don't have tilt-and-swivel bases or anti-glare screens. Other fairly standard requirements are that keyboards be separate and tiltable, that keys be legibly labelled and arranged so they're easy to use, the screen image should be stable, without flickering, and the on-screen characters should be clearly defined and adequately spaced.

However, it's easy to buy office furniture that doesn't conform, and many office environments are not as compliant as they should be. Chairs must have separately adjustable seats and backs and allow VDU operators some freedom of movement, and footrests must be supplied to anyone who wants one. Desks must have a low-reflectance surface, and be large enough to allow the operator some flexibility in arranging screen, keyboard, documents, and other equipment. Document holders also must be made available, if appropriate. These days, rather than a document holder you may want to take advantage of newer graphics cards that support multiple screens to provide twin or even triplet screens on a single desk, driven by a single computer. The productivity gain of not having to constantly shuffle papers and switch between windows holding work in progress and supporting material can be considerable.

The regulations also require employers to provide eye tests if necessary. Mostly, these should be ordinary tests by a qualified opthalmic optician, but there is software available designed to help a computer worker adjust screen settings for comfortable viewing under normal working conditions, something an opthalmic optician can't recreate.

Working with applications such as high-level word processing, DTP, and graphics is visually extremely demanding; people simply tend to stare at the screen. True, the screens have become larger over time – the standard fourteen-inch screen of 1992 was a standard seventeen-inch screen by 2002. But at the same time, the resolution – the number of dots (pixels) displayed on the screen – has increased, so that the picture is sharper and of much better quality, but everything in it is smaller. Again, frequent breaks to do other types of work are important. It's worth noting that research completed since the directive shows that extended computer use is not damaging to the eyes (as was feared in the early 1990s), although it is certainly possible to get headaches and the symptoms of eye strain if the lighting conditions are poor or the monitor fuzzy.

The directive includes environmental considerations. Workstations shall be sized and designed so that workers can change position. Lighting must be adequate and designed so that there is adequate contrast to make the screen readable and avoid glare and reflections. Noise, heating, radiation, and humidity levels all must be controlled to minimize discomfort.

Of that list, lighting is probably the most problematic, especially in small or home offices, where there may be fewer choices about where to place equipment. A computer placed next to a south-facing window can be almost impossible to read on sunny days, even with the brightness and contrast turned way up. If possible, place the screen turned away from the window. If you can't, make sure the window has adequate blinds or shades. You may also be able to shield the monitor somewhat with books or other equipment placed strategically on the desk.

TIP Colour-code the plugs for the UPSs (uninterrupted power supplies) so you can identify them at a glance and won't unplug them. Red, perhaps.

Otherwise, all these things are straightforward enough. However, like so many things related to computers, best practice in terms of health and safety is constantly being updated. The onus is on employers to ensure that they keep up to date with the latest research.

Fortunately, as time has gone on and people have become more accustomed to the technology, some of the fears of the early days have abated. One such fear was that pregnant women who worked with computers suffered more miscarriages; recent research does not show any such connection. Worries about the effect of radiation from monitors have died down now, just as no one now bothers about one of the other concerns of the early 1990s, ozone emissions from laser printers. Something similar will happen to today's mobile phone scares.

Even so, many of those scares had an impact. Alarm about the miscarriage stories led several countries to pass legislation specifying allowable levels of radiation, and the industry began designing better shielded monitors. Manufacturers also began reducing glare by applying anti-reflective coatings to screens, and these help immensely. In situations with extreme amounts of glare, mesh screens may help resolve the problem, although they have the unfortunate side effect of cutting down the brightness of the screen considerably.

One rather vague element of the directive deals with software, which must be 'easy to use' and 'conform to the principles of software ergonomics'. Little attention seems to have been paid to this (perhaps because the industry is always trying to make software easier to use anyway). However, one key provision specifies that employers may not engage in monitoring employees – for example, by installing software to capture keystrokes – without their knowledge.

The directive specifically exempts some equipment that could be classified as VDU equipment. This category includes drivers' cabs and vehicle control machinery; computer systems on board a means of transport; computer systems intended for public use (such as ATMs, for example); portable systems that are not in prolonged use at a workstation; calculators, cash registers, and similar equipment; and typewriters, even those with LCD (liquid crystal display) windows.

Laptops and PDAs fall into a middle ground; they were not widespread when the directive was written. Clearly, the average laptop's design must make compromises between ergonomics and considerations of size, space, and weight. Every element of a laptop is less flexible than those of a comparable desktop. Accordingly, the HSE advises that you should limit work with laptops wherever you can, for example by plugging the laptop into an ordinary monitor and keyboard when you're using it in a fixed location. However, this often isn't possible. Mobile workers need to keep the risks of overuse in mind.

There are a number of other health and safety regulations you should be aware of that don't relate to computer equipment, but basically are aimed at ensuring that employees work in a safe environment and get proper training. The best source of information is the Health and Safety Executive itself either through its main Web page (http://www.hse.gov.uk) or the section of its Web site that's specifically aimed at new small business start-ups (http://www.hse.gov.uk/startup/index.htm). Others updated in 2002 to comply with various European directives are the Workplace (Health, Safety and Welfare) Regulations 1992; Provision and Use of Work Equipment Regulations 1998; Personal Protective Equipment Regulations 1992; and Manual Handling Operations Regulations 1992. The HSE also publishes a series of leaflets (http://www.hse.gov.uk/pubns/index.htm) on subjects such as upper limb disorders and working with VDUs (its term for computers) to help small businesses.

HEALTH RISKS

Repetitive strain injury (RSI) is less in the news now, but it's no less real for those who are afflicted than when controversy raged over whether it was a genuine medical condition. In fact, RSI is not a single condition; rather it's a phrase used to describe a variety of conditions. Many ergonomists prefer the term work-related upper limb disorders, since it better describes the situation.

Upper limb disorders include several, such as carpal tunnel syndrome, that are well known from other professions that involve long hours of making the same repetitive hand movements over and over again. RSI has been controversial because doctors are often unable to find physical evidence of anything wrong. Nonetheless, it seems clear that it is indeed possible to severely damage hands and wrists with a combination of stress, long uninterrupted hours of typing, and poor workstation design.

Because there is no one physical problem, there is no one simple solution that applies to all cases. For some people, typing is the problem. For others, intensive mouse use causes cramping. For yet others, the problem is severe tension which manifests itself first in knotted muscles in the neck and shoulders and then transfers downwards. The variety of difficulties is why all the elements of a good workstation (desk, chair, etc.) should be separately adjustable. That way, employees can find optimal arrangements that specifically suit them.

Upper limb disorders are the best known computer workplace related risk, but they are not the only problem. Backaches, headaches, neckaches, and other muscular ills are common, too.

WORKSTATION DESIGN, PALLIATIVES AND PREVENTION

Many of the back problems and head and neck aches associated with computer work can be prevented by a little attention to the relative heights of the various pieces of a workstation. Most traditional desks designed for writing (and less formal desk substitutes such as dining-room tables) are actually too high for keyboards. Ideally, when you sit at a computer, the top of the screen should be positioned a little below eye level (more comfortable for the neck), and your forearms should tilt downwards slightly as you let your hands drop gently onto the keys. Your wrists should be straight, not bent backwards as they are if the keyboard is too high. You should not rest the palms of your hands on the desk or the edge of the keyboard when you type;

your hands and fingers should be relaxed. Wrist rests suit some people; they help keep the wrists straight and prevent damage by the edge of the desk (another reason to avoid using a desk that's too high). Desks designed specifically for computers usually have a pull-out keyboard shelf, and this is designed to be at the appropriate height for typing.

At the same time, feet should rest flat on the floor; dangling feet is one cause of lower back problems. It is often difficult to find an optimum chair height that accommodates both the right height for typing and the right height for keeping feet flat on the floor. This is why footrests are so important.

Other types of backaches may be postural problems due to any one of a number of causes. Monitors and lighting can play a part here, too: many postural problems are caused by workers trying to bend and twist to read their screens comfortably. In many workplaces, it's standard for the monitor to sit on top of the computer's system unit, and on a small desk that usually means the monitor is both too high and too close to be comfortable for the shoulders and neck. The advent of larger-sized LCD screens to replace smaller traditional CRT monitors is helping, as the larger, space-saving design encourages people to hide the system unit under the desk. As noted, shading the computer screen from reflections and glare from windows or overhead lighting is important in avoiding headaches and eyestrain. Here again a bit of education is helpful: make sure staff know how to adjust the brightness, contrast, and colour saturation on the monitors they use so they can find comfortable settings.

Standard advice for those with upper limb troubles or wishing to avoid them is to take frequent breaks, and get enough rest and exercise. Software is available that will monitor how much typing you're doing and essentially lock up the keyboard to force you to stop. The same effect can be achieved, however, by remembering to break up your work patterns. If you've been typing non-stop for an hour and your work patterns permit, take a break from typing and work on some other tasks, such as making phone calls or filing. There are also many technologies that can help reduce the amount of typing (see pp. 233–4).

These things are more easily fixed than another element that helps to make offices full of computer equipment tiring: high noise and heat levels. Every piece of computer equipment gives off heat, and many have fans to help dissipate it. Sometimes, newer equipment can help – a 2002 laser printer, for example, falls to near silence when it's not printing because of energy-saving designs, whereas a 1992 laser printer was just noisy pretty much all the time. Most newer computer equipment now automatically drops into a standby mode that consumes less power and emits less noise and heat after a user-configurable amount of idle time. Using these settings should help cut your electricity bills, too.

SUPPORTING TECHNOLOGIES

Bear in mind that the fact that a product is described as 'ergonomic' by its manufacturer doesn't necessarily mean it's the best choice in every circumstance. People vary widely in what they find comfortable.

It can be difficult to assess the success rate of a particular technology at fixing an ergonomic problem. For example, the makers of the (rather expensive) Maltron keyboard, an eccentric design that involves separating the keys into two wells that face outward, claim that it has been known to cure RSI. The difficulty is that when people are in great pain when they type, many changes are likely to be made at once, as part of an overall reassessment of their work habits: chair, keyboard height, table, intensity of work, and so on. It's difficult, under those circumstances, to attribute any improvement that takes place to any one single factor, even if the person concerned is convinced that they know what did it.

TIP If your insurance specifies that your server must be secured . . . secure the server.

Other 'ergonomic' keyboards, targeted more at the mass market, also have a divided design that's intended to help prevent upper limb troubles, but use a standard QWERTY layout. It is worth trying different keyboard designs if someone is having trouble. Keyboards vary substantially in feel, and some are softer on the fingers than others (Keytronics has an excellent line of comfortable keyboards). Certainly, if you feel tingling or numbness in your hands when you type you should change something.

An important alternative to typing is dictation software, which is much better and more accessible than many people think. Dictation software can actually speed up input once you get used to it by allowing you to store boilerplate paragraphs and recall them with a single word or short phrase. Speech recognition has come a long way, and today's software no longer requires the speaker to insert a pause after every word for the software to work. The two market leaders, Dragon Naturally Speaking and IBM's ViaVoice, both work on continuous speech. You do need to 'train' the software first by reading it a set text. This process takes about forty-five minutes. The more you use and correct it, the more accurate the speech recognition becomes.

It's also worth trying out several different types of mice – various shapes, plus trackballs, joysticks, and tablets – and choosing whatever's most comfortable. Newer designs such as optical mice can be less frustrating because they don't pick up dirt as easily, run across a wider variety of surfaces successfully, and are easier to clean. Wireless mice are also becoming increasingly available, using either proprietary standards or Bluetooth, and these can make navigation easier on a crowded desk because you don't have to worry about the cable. Most such designs are intended to operate at distances of ten feet or less, but a few double as remote controls for presentations and can work even further away, giving you the option of working on the computer while standing up and moving around. It can also help to swap the mouse to the other hand some or all of the time to help balance the load.

Pen-based computing may be appropriate in some situations where keyboard input is difficult. Aside from PDAs like the Palm and Pocket PC, which are really intended primarily as vehicles for mobile contact management, scheduling, and notes, the tablet PC, launched in late 2002, gives ordinary laptops pen-based input. This is a version of Windows XP with pen extensions supported by a number of hardware manufacturers that is intended to give people pen access to full-blown computing and familiar applications. However, handwriting is generally slower than typing, and the handwriting recognition in the tablet PC, unlike speech recognition, does not improve as you use it. Try before buying to see if it's adequate.

If noise levels are a problem, there are a few companies such as Quiet PC (http://www.quietpc.com) that are dedicated to supplying ultra-quiet power supply units, specially shielded cases, and other noise-proofing products that can help make the PCs in your office almost 'seen but not heard'. Try a Web search for these, as they are small specialist outfits.

People who do a lot of telephone work should put a little thought into the design of their phone; you can get real neck problems from trying to hold a tiny, poorly designed handset with your shoulder while you type notes. Large companies equip their telephone receptionists and telesales staff with headsets, and these are readily available from office supply catalogues and stores for under £50. You don't have to replace your phone; a little box plugs in between the handset and the phone, and that lets you switch between the existing handset and the headset. More expensive wireless headsets can further loosen the tether to desk and chair.

Those with problems operating their computers should take a look at their configuration options. Windows, for example, has accessibility options built in (Control Panel | Accessibility) that include turning the shift key into a toggle, to help users that can't hold down two keys at once, slowing down the keyboard and mouse response times, and other such aids. Additional help for people with disabilities is available from AbilityNet (http://www.abilitynet.org.uk), which keeps up-to-date lists of suppliers of alternatives to mice and keyboards, as well as other aids. Not all are aimed at people with disabilities, and some may be useful in specific situations where the usual input devices are inappropriate.

12 Onward

Obviously there is much more to know about networking than can fit in this single book. But hopefully by now the subject seems less foreign and intimidating. Whatever they tell you, what you do with computers is not about computers, but about your business and how best to take it forward.

As previously noted, there are very few links to resources such as products and companies mentioned or further information in the text itself, largely because books are slow and the Web is quick to change. You will find a complete collection of links on the book's Web page, at http://www.pelicancrossing.net/dtnw, and I hope to see you there. There will also be a forum for discussion and questions that I hope will be a useful resource, and readers are encouraged to direct comments and questions there rather than emailing me directly, on the grounds that a larger audience will be more likely to have useful answers.

Good luck!

Glossary

Active Directory Structure in Windows 2000 and later for centrally organizing and administering user accounts and groups.

ADSL Asymmetric Digital Subscriber Line. Form of high-speed, permanent Internet connection over ordinary telephone lines. Sold wholesale and retail by BT, and retail by a variety of **ISPs** such as Demon Internet, Freeserve (Wanadoo), Easynet, and many smaller companies. The connection is 'asymmetric' because the bandwidth going out is typically much lower than that coming in, on the assumption that most users receive more data than they send out. Configurations go from 512kbits/second downstream (about ten times the speed of the fastest modem) and 256kbps upstream to 2mbps/256kbps, and these speeds are available in both home and business versions, **NAT** and non-NAT.

APIPA Automatic Private IP Addressing. A feature of Windows 98/2000 and later that allows a **DHCP** client to automatically configure itself with an **IP address** and **subnet** mask when no DHCP server is available, assigning its machine an address in the range between 169.254.0.1 and 169.254.255.254, which is registered to Microsoft, and a subnet mask of 255.255.0.0. The client uses these settings until a DHCP server becomes available (it checks for one about every five minutes). It is useful for non-routed small (twenty-five clients or fewer) business environments.

ASCII American Standard Code for Information Interchange. Each character is seven **bits** long. Each character is typically stored in an 8-bit **byte**, however. This extra bit was at first used as a 'parity bit', used as an error correction scheme to verify that data has been transmitted accurately. These days, better error correction systems mean that all eight bits can be used to define additional characters such as non-English characters, graphics, and mathematical symbols. ASCII was originally designed for use with teletypes, and some of the control characters are therefore rarely used now. The term is often used interchangeably with 'plain text'.

ATM Asynchronous Transfer Mode. High-speed data transmission technology developed in Cambridge and used in wide-area networks. Typically used to supply ADSL to British subscribers.

Attached file Email technique for sending files such as graphics, audio, video, software programs which are not composed of plain text; these are referred to as 'binary files'. Attaching the file to an email message encodes it for transmission across the Internet; the recipient's email software decodes it on arrival. Word-processed files, although they look to the user like text, are binary files because they include coding to specify formatting.

Back door Opening (such as a hidden user account or an opened port) left through carelessness or malice that can allow access to a system without the owner's knowledge.

Backups Regularly updated copies of company data and system configurations so that in case of theft, fire, or computer failure the backups can be used to construct a copy of your system so that business can continue as normal. It is suicidal to operate a business computer system without keeping proper backups.

Bandwidth The amount of data a particular connection can carry at any one time. The greater the bandwidth, the greater the amount of data.

BIOS Basic Input/Output System. Code built into a computer that starts the services needed for basic operation before loading operating system software and applications.

Bit The most basic unit of computing, essentially a single 1 or 0 (representing an electrical signal, which can only be either on or off).

Measures such as kilobits and megabits (describing data throughput) mean 1,000 and 1,000,000 bits respectively, just like they do in metric measurement. In most modern computers, eight bits make a **byte**, which represents a single character. The 7-bit **ASCII** set is 127 characters (2^7 minus 1, since a string of all zeros doesn't transmit any information) because that is the number of possible permutations of seven bits where each has only two possible settings; by logical extension the 8-bit ASCII set is 255 (2^8 minus 1) characters. You will also see references to 8-bit, 16-bit, 32-bit, and 64-bit computing, and this terminology refers to the size of the largest chunk of data a processor can handle directly. Today's Pentiums are 64-bit processors. For the purposes of this book, a bit is abbreviated to a lower-case b.

Bluetooth Low-power wireless standard intended to allow devices from mobile phones to printers to communicate over short distances.

BNC Bayonet Nut Connector. Together with the word 'coax' or 'coaxial' it describes a type of **ethernet** cable that is becoming obsolete but can be found in many older small network installations.

Broadband High-speed permanent Internet connection, either fixed-line or wireless. Variants include **ADSL**, **cable**, **satellite**, and **UWB**.

Byte In computing, typically eight **bits**, or a single character. As in metric measurement, KB (kilo-byte) is 1,000 bytes, MB (mega-byte) is 1,000,000 bytes. For the purposes of this book, a byte is abbreviated to an upper-case B.

Cable (modem) High-speed permanent Internet connections available from cable companies such as ntl and Telewest. Like **ADSL**, cable service is asymmetric, with speeds from 512kbps/128kbps to 2mbps/128kbps, and is offered in both home and business versions, which (unlike ADSL) differ primarily in the level of technical support offered. A cable modem is in fact a bridge between HFC (Hybrid Fibre Coaxial, that is, the cable company's network) and **ethernet** (your network), and it may or may not contain a **DHCP** client. Non-**NAT** service is not available for cable Internet.

Cache Mechanism for storing copies of frequently used information to speed up access to that information. Used to speed up a single computer's memory and disk access. On the Internet, caches are used by ISPs and local area networks to speed up Web browsing. Used also by the search engine Google to make available copies of pages that have recently been deleted.

Cardbus The 32-bit version of **PC Card**, also formerly known as PCMCIA. It is a credit-card sized format for peripheral components such as modems, network interface cards, and even hard disks and is typically found in laptop computers and some other smaller devices. There are three physical form factors, known as Type I, Type II, and Type III in increasing order of thickness. Most modern laptops have one or two Type II slots; if there are two, together they form a single Type III slot.

Cat5 Also known as unshielded twisted-pair ethernet cable. The maximum distance any machine can be from a hub is one hundred metres. The higher the Cat number, the faster and more resilient the cable.

CD-R Compact Disc Recordable. CD drive that can write audio and data CDs as well as read them. Although CD-R drives use a technique called multi-session recording that lets you add data later to discs that are only partially full, each portion of the disk can only be written once.

CD-RW Compact Disc Read-Write. Rewritable CD-ROMs, so that you can rewrite the same disc many times. The disks are more expensive than those used by CD-Rs, and not all machines can read them.

Client/server architecture Computer network design such that one computer (the server) holds data and/or applications which can be accessed by other computers (the clients). It was originally designed for mainframes so many terminals could access them. The World Wide Web is the most obvious example of a client/server system; the Web site is in fact a series of files organized and sent for display by the Web server to the client software, your Web browser, and applications on the site may interact with Java programs running on your machine. Within a **LAN**, most often client/server simply means having a central data store, email, and database applications.

Coax (BNC) coaxial cable. An early method of wiring **LAN**s that is falling into disuse because it is less reliable and less flexible than **ethernet**. It is also known as 'thinnet' or 'thin ethernet'. The maximum segment length of BNC coax is 185 metres. Each end of the network segment connected by coax must be fitted with a BNC terminator.

Contention ratio Number of users vying – contending – for use of the same resource. It is included in the specification for **broadband**, as users must share the **bandwidth**. The greater the number of users, the slower the connection speed for each one. The contention ratio is one of the significant differences between home (typically 50:1 contention ratio) and business (20:1) ADSL services.

Crossover cable Cable wired so that the pins used for transmission are wired directly to the ones used to receive data; used to connect like devices, for example, to connect a hub to a router and to connect two PCs directly to each other.

Denial-of-service (DoS) attack Any attack that makes any service unusable by flooding it with junk. A **Distributed** DoS (DDoS) attack comes from multiple sources.

DHCP Dynamic Host Configuration Protocol. Built into routers and operating systems so that **IP addresses** can be allocated automatically and remotely within a network, making administration and addressing much easier, and also freeing up addresses for reuse when they are no longer needed by a given device.

DMZ Like the demilitarized zone that acts as a buffer between warring nations, in networks a DMZ acts as a buffer between the public Internet and a private network protected by a firewall. The DMZ may contain anything from a single machine to an entire network depending on your needs. Security experts recommend keeping the wireless part of your network, if any, in the DMZ because it is so much more difficult to secure wireless connections.

DNS Domain Name System. The system to assign human-friendly hierarchical names to **IP addresses**, which are what computers can read. The DNS is administered worldwide by the Internet Corporation for Assigned Names and Numbers (http://www.icann.org).

802.11 Wireless networking standard used in **LANs** to connect computers together. The first and most widespread version, 802.11b, runs at speeds of 11mbps, and is also known as Wi-Fi. Newer versions such as 802.11a and 802.11g run (or will run) at much higher speeds. It requires a wireless network interface card for each computer and an access point which is wired to the rest of the network (or the **broadband** connection). It uses the 2.4GHz radio frequency band and has a practical range of approximately fifty feet (depending on how many walls are in the way).

Ethernet Wireline networking standard (IEEE 802.3) used to connect computers and other network components such as routers into **LANs** at speeds of 10mbps (megabits per second) or 100mbps (fast ethernet). Each computer must have an ethernet **NIC**. Computers and routers using ethernet can be connected with a variety of cable types, including **BNC** coax, unshielded twisted-pair cable known as **Cat5** with an **RJ45** on each end, or **fibre optic**.

Fibre optic High-speed cabling that transmits data in the form of light. The most expensive and difficult to install, fibre optic cabling is typically used as a backbone rather than for hooking up individual computers.

Firewall A hardware or software barrier between a computer system and the outside world that acts as a central point for controlling access in both directions. A firewall may be used as much to prevent a system's internal users from accessing some Internet sites or services as to prevent access to the system by outsiders.

FTP File Transfer Protocol is a text-based service that provides a straightforward way of transferring files back and forth between two machines; it runs across the Internet as an application, much like the World Wide Web itself does. In a graphical form, FTP is built into

Web browsers, but a text version you can run from the command prompt is also built into Windows; many other standalone FTP clients are also available. The advantage to these is the built-in ability to resume a download that's already been partially completed, where a Web browser will start again from the beginning.

HTML HyperText Markup Language. The set of codes that are used to create Web pages.

HTTP HyperText Transfer Protocol. The standard protocol that defines the World Wide Web. Development of HTTP takes place under the aegis of the World Wide Web Consortium.

IMAP Internet Mail Access Protocol. A protocol that lets an email client access the server and read and manage the email without downloading it to the client. Web-based email services work this way. Within a small business, this system makes it easy to ensure that email archives are backed up correctly and allow users access to all their email archives from anywhere on the network. For more on IMAP, see http://www.imap.org.

IP address Internet protocol address, formed of four dotted clumps of up to three numbers each, such as 158.152.2.800. All computers in any network must have some type of address in order to receive and transmit data. Although computers in networks have names (because they're easier for humans to remember), each also has an IP number as these numbered addresses are what computers understand. IP addresses may be assigned to any intelligent device (computer, router, PDA). Typically, your ISP will assign you outward-facing IP addresses which are either dynamic (one of a pool of IP addresses the ISP has available when you make the connection, or that is changed periodically if you have broadband) or static (an IP address or series of addresses that is permanently yours). Most small networks have a single IP address on the wider Internet; several series of numbers (10.0.0.0 to 10.255.255.255, 172.16.0.0 to 172.31.0.0, and 192.168.0.0 to 192.168.255.0) are reserved for private use and your own network will use these for internal communication. See also **NAT**.

IPSec Internet security protocol. IPSec is a standard intended to provide privacy, integrity, and authentication for data traffic travelling across a network running on **TCP/IP** by encrypting traffic at the network layer. The standard is defined by **RFCs** 2401 through 2411, and is the product of work by the Internet Engineering Task Force (IETF). IPSec can be used with either IPv4 or **IPv6**.

IPv6 Internet Protocol version 6. The version of the Internet protocols that has run the Net since the mid-1970s is version 4. Version 6 was completed in 1994, and is slowly rolling out. Its most visible advantage for Net users: vastly more available **IP addresses**, enough to give every conceivable device its own permanent number. In addition, IPv6 is designed to bring with it improved security which will eliminate a significant number of network attacks.

IRC Internet Relay Chat. A system for exchanging typed messages in real time. There are many worldwide IRC networks, each of which has many channels that are usually named after the topics they cover. An IRC server is included in Exchange Server, and software to run IRC is readily available on the Net. On a local area network running on **TCP/IP**, you can run an internal private IRC server for use by staff and, if desired, by outside colleagues such as suppliers and customers. It can be a very effective and low-cost replacement for telephone and video conferencing, especially as logging discussions produces easily searchable text files.

ISDN Integrated Services Digital Network. A digital phone line that can handle up to 144kbps, usually divided into two 64kbps and one 16kbps channels. The two 64kbps channels are used for data and can be bonded together to form a single 128kbps channel. ISDN operates faster than an ordinary dial-up modem, not just because its raw speed is higher but also because its being digital throughout eliminates line noise and the handshaking that takes place at the beginning of each modem call. Like an ordinary phone line, users pay by the minute for all calls.

ISP Internet service provider. The company – cable, telephone, or specialist – that supplies your Internet connection.

LAN Local Area Network. That is, a computer network contained in a small geographical area (one building, for example). Bigger networks may be **MANs** (Metropolitan Area Networks), or, more commonly, **WANs** (Wide Area Networks). Occasionally, you run into **PANs** (Personal Area Networks).

Linux Free operating system software that is used on personal computers that provides an alternative to Windows. Correctly, Linux should be called **GNU/Linux**, as Linux itself is merely the kernel of the operating system. The GNU (for 'GNU's not UNIX') project existed for many years before Linus Torvalds wrote Linux, and much of what's commonly called Linux is utilities and routines written by the GNU project.

MAC address Media Access Control address. Each **NIC**, **router**, or other intelligent device on a network has a permanent physical address that is used as a unique identifier. An **IP address** or other network address is assigned to a specific **MAC** address. **Cable** broadband suppliers may require users to register the MAC addresses of the equipment using the Internet connection for security reasons. Until recently, MAC addresses were unique identifiers, but some routers have the ability to copy a MAC address from another device so they can be installed on these systems without configuration at the ISP's end.

Malware Contraction for 'malicious software'; used as an umbrella term to describe viruses, Trojans, worms, and any other type of software intended to damage a computer system.

MAPI Messaging Application Programming Interface. A standardized way for applications to handle messaging, so that as long as both applications are MAPI-compliant they can share mail with each other.

NAT Network address translation. Technique to assign a single **IP address** to a **LAN** so that every computer on the LAN may access the Internet without using up multiple IP addresses from the limited stock currently available in the wider world. **Broadband** suppliers (cable or ADSL) typically offer either a NAT service (in which the provider incorporates NAT as part of its security provisions) or a non-NAT service. The advantages of a non-NAT service are that it allows the small business to run its own Web and other Internet servers, and gives staff remote access to the network. However, the company must then supply its own security and NAT. See **firewall**.

NDS Novell Directory Services, also known as Novell eDirectory. The directory services for Novell NetWare networks and other platforms. It controls user security and access rights, and helps users find and access resources without necessarily having to know where they're physically located.

NIC Network interface card. Each computer on a network must have one. The card converts data into and from electrical signals and transmits the signals across the network.

Packet sniffer A piece of software that essentially eavesdrops on a connection, scooping up chunks of data ('packets') and storing them for future examination and use. Packet sniffers have a legitimate role as tools for system administrators, but they are also used by miscreants seeking to gain information about systems they want to crack into.

PC Card Formerly also known as PCMCIA. Credit-card sized format for peripheral components such as modems, network interface cards, and even hard disks. PC Card is the 16-bit version; **Cardbus** is the 32-bit version. PC cards are typically found in laptop computers and some other smaller devices. There are three form factors, known as Type I, Type II, and Type III in increasing order of thickness. Most modern laptops have one or two Type II slots; if there are two, together they form a single Type III slot.

PCI Peripheral Component Interconnect. The current (2003) standard for connecting peripherals to a PC via a slot on the motherboard. The PCI is supported by most manufacturers.

PDA Personal Digital Assistants; that is, handheld computers.

PDF Portable document format, a file format devised and promoted by Adobe. You need the free **Acrobat Reader**, a version of which is available for all the common computer platforms, in order to open and view these files. Recommended for use on the Web for files whose design and layout you need to preserve, because it does not carry viruses, it's readily available, and its files are relatively compact in size.

Peer-to-peer architecture Type of network on which all computers are equal, each running its own software and maintaining its own data store. The drawbacks compared to using a server are that beyond two or three computers it becomes very difficult to know where on the network the most recent version of a collaborative document or spreadsheet is, and **backups** become unmanageable. On the Internet, peer-to-peer architecture underlies popular file-sharing services, distributed computing efforts such as SETI@Home, and the new Web services beginning to launch.

PCMCIA See PC Card.

POP3 Post Office Protocol (version 3). The most commonly used standard for email stored at an **ISP** ready for retrieval by a customer. The address of the ISP's POP3 server is usually the one that needs to be entered in the email software configuration to receive email.

Port Logical endpoint for a communication. PCs may have up to 65,535 ports.

Port forwarding A technique to allow traffic of a specific type through a **firewall**. Essentially, you configure the router or firewall so that traffic intended for a particular port (that is for a specific application) is forwarded to the machine running that application.

POTS Plain Old Telephone Service. Used to describe a traditional copper-wire phone line.

PPTP Point-to-point tunnelling protocol. It is built into Windows 2000 and later versions and into other products and allows you to create a **VPN** – that is, a secure connection to your private network over the Internet.

Protocols Set of rules for communicating; the computers at both ends of a connection must use the same protocols in order to make it possible to exchange data ('talk' to each other).

Proxy A computer that literally stands in for another. In a network, a proxy server stores (**caches**) frequently accessed data (usually Web pages) to minimize network traffic. ISPs all run proxy servers to give their users faster service while decreasing the amount of onward bandwidth they have to buy; **LAN**s may use proxy servers for the same reason.

RAID Redundant Arrays of Inexpensive Disks. System of disk drives used to provide fault tolerance and better performance than a single disk drive for servers. Several different 'levels' describe how RAIDs are used. Level 0 is data striping, so the same files are split across multiple disks for better performance; Level 1 provides disk mirroring so that multiple disks all have up-to-the-minute copies of the same data, providing fault tolerance. Further levels up to 5 use various combinations of these techniques to offer both fault tolerance and better performance.

RFC Request for Comments. The standards that define key elements of how the Internet operates, everything from the design and formatting of email headers to standards for machine-readable data on the Web. These are called Request for Comments because the early engineers who wrote the first ones wanted to indicate that they regarded the process of developing the technical infrastructure of the Internet as collaborative.

RJ45 Plastic plug used in **ethernet** cabling.

Satellite In rural areas where **cable** and **ADSL** are not available, an option for partial broadband may be satellite services which require you to dial up to send data but offer high-speed downloads via a satellite dish.

SCSI Small Computer Systems Interconnection. A method for connecting certain types of both external and internal peripherals to PCs and Macs handling data at speeds between 5MB/s (the earliest version) and 160MB/s (the latest). It is used for external and internal hard drives and scanners; for example, SCSI allows devices to be daisy-chained so that a single SCSI port could accommodate up to eight devices. The big, clunky cables and multiplicity of plug sizes, plus the difficulty of configuration, has meant that SCSI has largely given way to **USB**.

SIM card Subscriber Identity Module. The tiny user-removable chip in a mobile phone that stores user settings, phone numbers, and other personal information.

SMTP Simple Mail Transfer Protocol. The most commonly used standard for sending email. The address of the ISP's SMTP server is usually the one that needs to be entered in the email software configuration to send/deliver email.

Spam Bulk postings to Usenet newsgroups, whether commercial or not. Sometimes also used to refer to junk email or **UCE**.

Subnet To make network administration and address assignment easier, it's common to break a network up into subnets. The mechanism for doing this is known as a 'subnet mask', which is part of a computer's or router's **TCP/IP** configuration.

TCP/IP Transport Control Protocol/Internet Protocol. The suite of protocols on which the Internet runs and that allows otherwise incompatible computers to exchange information. It is like a language that everyone has agreed to speak so they can understand each other.

Trojan An apparently innocent program that, like the Greeks hiding in the belly of the horse presented to the city of Troy, includes unexpected and undesirable extras, such as a bit of software that opens your system for exploitation by hackers.

UCE Unsolicited Commercial Email. Technical term for junk email. Also known as UBE, Unsolicited Bulk Email.

URL Uniform Resource Locator. That is, a Web address. Originally, Uniform Resource Identifier.

USB Universal Serial Bus. Widespread standard for attaching external peripherals to Macs and PCs, including printers, Webcams, mice, scanners, MIDI synthesizers, and even digital cameras that transmits data at speeds of 1.5mbps to 480mbps. USB has largely replaced earlier methods of connecting peripherals such as serial ports (115kbps) and **SCSI**. USB is favoured for its simplicity of configuration.

Usenet Short for 'users' network'. The blanket term for more than 10,000 worldwide bulletin boards ('newsgroups'), Usenet can be a valuable source of technical information. Access it either via a search engine or by subscribing to a newsgroup and reading it on a daily basis. Google maintains the largest single publicly accessible archive of Usenet going back to 1981; you can search individual newsgroups and postings via the Groups tab that appears at the top of its results listings.

UWB Ultra-WideBand wireless. Used as fixed broadband wireless links in some areas where **cable** and **ADSL** are not available.

VESA Video Electronics Standards Association. A standard for connecting peripherals to a PC via a slot on the motherboard. The design was based on the Intel 80486 processor, and it was never adapted to Pentiums. It is now found only in legacy systems.

Virtual Private Network See VPN.

Virus Program code designed to replicate itself which may or may not also be destructive to systems 'infected' with it. Originally, viruses were typically disseminated via infected floppy disks. Now, the most dangerous ones are generally disseminated by email hidden in **attached files** or **HTML** code, and infect computers when the files are executed or the HTML is rendered.

VoIP Voice over Internet Protocol. Technique for carrying telephone conversations over the Internet. You can buy VoIP services directly if you download the software and open an account (paid for by a credit card), but more commonly VoIP is used behind the scenes by companies offering discounted long distance and international rates.

VPN Virtual Private Network. A method for securely connecting a remote machine to the company network across the public Internet. The person sitting at the remote machine can use the network as if connected directly to it; but the connection is secured so that outsiders can't eavesdrop on the connection or use the connection to gain unauthorized access for themselves.

WAP Wireless Application Protocol. The standard for providing Internet services to mobile phones and other small, limited devices. The protocol is managed by the WAP Forum, a consortium of leading manufacturers of mobile phones, software companies, and mobile network operators.

Wi-Fi Marketing term for **802.11**b.

WINS Windows Internet Naming Service. Automatically updated database that determines the **IP** address associated with a particular network computer when those assigned addresses change dynamically because **DHCP** is in use.

Worm A type of malicious code that seeks to spread itself throughout a computer network by sending copies of itself to other computers. It is technically different from a **virus** in that a virus seeks to replicate itself on a single computer and must be hosted by a program file. Bugbear, Klez, and Yaha are worms.

XML eXtended Markup Language. A standard for customized extensions to **HTML** so that industry sectors can create specialized tags that enable them to exchange data without necessarily having to run the same application software.

Index

Acknowledgements

A lot of people helped with the technical aspects of this book. I'd particularly like to thank David Morton, a director of Open Consulting, whose idea it originally was and who answered a number of annoying questions and generously allowed me to crib (or allowed me to generously crib) from a series of columns he wrote on business computer networking for the California-based magazine *MicroTimes*. 'Custard in the server' and 'the man under the Clapham omnibus' are favourite phrases of David's, and I was heavily influenced by his ideas on a number of topics throughout the book. Thanks are also due to Jon Honeyball (especially on managing firewalls, backups, and background on future developments), Ian Murphy (security), Martin C. Brown (Apple computers), Olly Beaumont (dealing with suppliers and also making upgrading my own system painless), and Horus Communications' Mac Jordan (Web design). Special thanks are due also to Wizards Ltd's Chris Comley (who helped with the sections on Internet service provider economics and basic networking and who reviewed the manuscript at an early stage), and to Rachel Carthy, who helped with research and administration, and without whom doubtless I would have drowned in papers by now.

As always, thanks to my agent Diana Finch, along with Ben Mason and Bill Hamilton. Susannah Charlton helped ensure the book actually happened, and Charlie Mounter, Natasha Martin and Morven Knowles oversaw its passage from electrons to dead trees.